Rs. 1400; US$ 70

ISBN: 978-81-7541-805-9

First Published in India in 2015

Interest Rates in India: Towards Harmony

Published by:
SHIPRA PUBLICATIONS
LG 18-19, Pankaj Central Market, I.P. Ext.
Patparganj, Delhi-110092
Tel: 91-11-2223 5152, 2223 6152
E-mail: info@shiprapublication.com
www.shiprapublication.com

Interest Rates in India

Towards Harmony

G. Giridhar Prabhu

SHIPRA

Interest Rates in India

To My Loving Father and Mother

Preface

These writings came about after the great divide of 1991 when the liberalisation process in India acquired momentum. The economic environment was savouring freedom and the agenda for growth was widespread. The interest rates in India were "freed" and were declared as "market oriented".

The wide fluctuations in the call money market were observed and this phenomenon started a series of "papers" to the Reserve Bank of India, Government of India and policy makers. Over years the steady flow of opinion and ideas satisfied the needs of inputs in policy and practice.

Almost all of the papers were acknowledged at the RBI and presumably at the Government of India as well. I can presume that I would have been a dot in the giant gears and wheels of policy making at Reserve Bank and the Government. I also attribute the content to numerous discussions with Bankers, academicians and many others. A senior banker advised me that if I want my ideas to get across it would be better to write for newspapers or write a book. I am glad that this has materialised.

I would feel that I would have contributed if this be taken as a basis of research at Institutes and Universities, for discussion, debate and dialogue in the investment and banking community, as an input for policy and action at Government of India and also a basis for governance for Reserve Bank of India as a regulator.

My stint as a committee member, secretary for three years, Treasurer for a year and President of the Kanara Chamber of Commerce and Industry as a member of the Committee of the Cashew Export Promotion Council of India and as Secretary and President of the Karnataka Cashew Manufacturers Association gave me access and exposure to policy documents and a theatre for action on finance and interest rates. Most of the reflections in this book are from these interactions for which I am grateful to thousands of men and women with whom I could converse.

I am indebted to my Professors in College Prof. S. Udayashankar, who taught me Indian Economics and Economic Analysis and Prof. B.S. Raman who initiated me into Banking Theory and Accounting. Extensive reading in economics and management have influenced the writings.

My deep respects for the eternal love of my parents, the ever smiling mentor, guide and the wisest G. Sadananda Prabhu and My mother Rohini Prabhu who have made me what I am.

I am deeply indebted to My dearest Archana whose love, affection and companionship supported me all through these years in ever increasing activity, with my three adorable daughters Achala, Amitha and Anuja who make my life. I am grateful to Achala who went through my texts and improved on it.

I must make particular mention of Shri K.R. Shenoy Executive Director of Corporation Bank who went through most of the book and recommended improvements.

I must thank particularly Jacintha in my office who was instrumental in preparing of the papers all these years, Pankajavalli, who is unfortunately no more, Jane has been on this for the last six years and my affectionate daughter Amitha for assisting me and daughter Anuja for rooting for me.

I must also acknowledge the contribution of Amritha Srinath, whose transcription, corrections and editing have helped in the drafting and completion of the Book.

I need to mention that I am grateful to whoever associated with me that has helped me to write and complete it.

G. Giridhar Prabhu
04-10-2014

Contents

PART 2

Interest Rates 2011 - 2014
Towards Harmony

Annexures

Abbreviations

BPLR: Benchmark Prime Lending Rate
BRIC: Brazil, Russia, India and China
BTC: Bankers Training College
CAC: Capital Account Convertibility
CAR: Capital Adequacy Ratio
CASA: Current Account Savings Account
CD: Current Deposit
CORP DEB: Corporate Debentures
CP rate: Commercial Paper rate
CRR: Cash Reserve Ratio
DFHI: Discount and Finance House of India
DFI: Development Finance Institutions
DTL: Demand and Time Liabilities
DTL: Demand and Time Liability
Dy: Deputy
ECB: External Commercial Borrowing
ECGC premium: Export Credit Guarantee Corporation
EEFC: Exchange Earners Foreign Currency
FCNR rate: Foreign Currency Non-Resident Rate
FD rate: Fixed Deposit rate
FI BOND: Financial Institution Bond
GILT: Government Invested Long Term
GOI: Government of India
GRTS: Gross Real Time Settlement
GSEC: Government security
HZB: Hindustan Zaveri Bank
ICICI: Industrial Credit and Investment Corporation of India
ICRIER: Indian Council for Research and International Economic Relations
IDBI: Industrial Development Bank of India
IGIDR: Indira Gandhi Institute of Development Research
IRDA: Industrial and Rural Development Authority
ISDL: Indian Securities Depository Limited
ISEC: Institute for social and Economic Change
IVP: Indira Vikas Patra
KVP: Kisan Vikas Patra

KYC norms: Know Your Customer norms
LAB: Local Area Banks
LAF: Liquidity Adjustment Facility
LIBOR: London Inter Bank Offered Rate
LTPLR: Long Term Prime Lending Rate
LTPLR: Long Term Prime Lending Rate
MCA: Monetary Compensatory Account
MIBOR: Mumbai Inter Bank Offered Rate
MOF: Ministry of Finance
NABARD: National Bank for Agriculture and Rural Development
NBFC: Non-Banking Financial Companies
NCAER: National Council of Applied Economic Research
NDTL: Net Demand And Time Liabilities
NHB: National Housing Bank
NPA: Non Performing Assets
NRE Account: Non Resident External Account
NRNR: Non-resident (Non-Repatriable) Rupee Deposit
NSC: National Savings Certificates
NSS: National Savings Scheme
OECD: Organisation for Economic Co-operation and Development
OMO: Open Market Operations
PC: Packing Credit
PCFC: Packing Credit in Foreign Currency
PLR: Prime Lending Rate
PPF: Public Provident Fund
PSE/PUB NCD: Public Sector Enterprises/Public Utilities Board Non Convertible Debentures
PSE: Public Sector Enterprises
RBI: Reserve Bank of India
RRB: Regional Rural Banks
SBI: State Bank of India
SGL: Subsidiary General Ledger
SGs: State Governments
SHCIL: Stock Holding Corporation of India Limited
SIDBI: Small Industrial Development Bank of India
SLR: Statutory Liquidity Ratio
SME: Small and Medium Enterprises
SPOT: Today
SSI: Small Scale Industries
TBills: Treasury Bills
TOM: Tomorrow, i.e. next day
UT: Union Territory
UTI: Unit Trust of India
YTM: Yield to maturity

Introduction

My interest in interest rates began when I started to make interest payments. Running an SME agribusiness with a seasonal crop like raw cashew required large working capital. There was a passion for investment, innovation and long term capital and hence a never ending stream of payments.

India had inflationary times since the late 1950s and the growth phase from 1974 saw high inflation or high interest rates. In the 1980s, interest rates climbed to as high as 16 per cent for NRIs and 21.5 per cent on borrowings for working capitals. "Market" interest rates were as high as 24 to 28 per cent and the film industry and builders borrowed at 36 per cent.

The crisis of 1991 and the introduction of "market" economy brought "liberalisation" of segments of the economy. The freed sectors showed enormous growth and the expansion of the services sector and a diverse income stream in the growing working population. The spur in investment and the virtuous circle brought about a situation that since 2004 India' s momentum came from its own savings. FII and FDI investments, inflows of savings brought about the impetus that financed India's asset expansion as well as massive Government expenditure.

This book is not as much as an exposition on interest rate theory but the behaviour of interest rates in a context of a partially free and partially controlled economy. Even at the moment, India is yet to develop a deep and broad financial system and market. This may be for the good now. Our discovery for a better system is in process. This book provides an entrepreneurial view and complements what academicians, policy makers, regulators and practicians say on the financial system. It also measures the impacts on citizens who are the stakeholders as recipients or who make payouts of interest. It also provides for some out of the box ideas for developing institutions and better policy. The reader is guided on the development of the market economy. The structure of interest rates evolved since 16 years are decisively going towards harmony.

My writing started as "papers" to the Reserve Bank of India and Government of India. Chapters have a title, the year in which the paper was written and submitted is written at the end of the Chapters. Notes at the end of Chapters are contemporary. The book was intended to have a title, Interest Rates, Anomalies, Distortions and Aberrations. Each of the papers deal with an anomaly, distortion or an aberration. The attempt was to observe and describe interest rate behaviour contrary to established principles, theory or good practices elsewhere and that could be developed. The behaviour of interest and the conduct of the stakeholders is evident. This book brings in a lot of imagination in what could be done to achieve harmony. Hence the title *Interest Rates in India: Towards Harmony.*

The reader is guided through time in the evolution of the interest rate structure. The first such paper was written to the Reserve Bank of India on Call Money rates, (Chapter 1). This was acknowledged by the then Dy Governor. The action was evident as within nine months the gyrations in call money stopped. Except on one occasion, call money was brought under control in two or three days and has not stepped out of line since then. The Second Chapter covers views on the Small Savings Scheme of the Government of India and the divergence from market rates. Consequently, committees at Reserve Bank of India and Government of India guided the market oriented process.

Chapter Three covers the introduction on Open Market Operations. There is a difference in OMO conducted by the Federal Reserve and Reserve Bank of India. This is explained and the process is under evolution. Chapter Four, Interest Rates and NBFCs, covers the reasons why interest rates offered by NBFCs are higher and detrimental. This issue was addressed later by the Government. The definition, role and performance of NBFCs needs to get refined. Chapter Five outlines the opinion that the Government of India could effect savings in interest rates. The matter has worsened since then and is covered in further chapters. Chapter Six suggests the way towards primary debt issue by the Government. This matter is still evolving and needs a responsible Parliament and Government to look into. Chapter Seven describes an evolutionary interest rate structure. It has reached around ninety per cent of a truly manageable hierarchy.

Chapter Eight describes correlation between domestic interest rates and exchange rate premia. This has evolved to an extraordinary self-discipline over the years. Chapter Nine, Impact of multiple interest rates of Government securities on financial system, highlights the inheritances of the past and possible ways of dealing with the same. Chapter 10 highlights the Central Government's lending to State Governments and how market for State Government Bonds can develop.

Chapters 11, 12 and 13 give a review of interest rate policy management and actionable suggestions. Chapter 14 prescribes a debt issue calendar and since then it has been addressed. Chapter 15 revisits Open Market Operations and nudges for evolution. Chapter 16 promotes the idea of liberalism which requires self-discipline and regulation.

Chapter 17 highlights the need for looking at Bank Deposit Rates and need for regulation. Chapter 18 deals with the evolution of Prime Lending Rate and the meaning of sub-plr. Chapter 19 deals with imperatives in monetary and credit policy and its impact on borrowers and lenders. Chapter 20 deals with decontrol and regulation of the Savings Bank Rate.

Chapter 21 deals with the subject of a lesser used tool, the Bank Rate. Chapter 22 deals again with the regulation of interest rates on bank deposits and loans. Chapter 23 revisits the reduction in interest outgo of Government of India. Chapter 24 deals with interest rate subsidies and subventions and effects on the financial system. Chapter 25 concludes that management of interest rates policy requires institution building and radical proposals in the Indian context.

Like the waves in the Arabian Sea that are calm or agitated on the impact of winds, interest rates in India moved in waves. The regulation in interest rates has evolved. Interest rates from the beginning of economic history in India, the evolution of economics in the Western world and the state of financial markets currently beckons perennial study.

PART 1

Interest Rates
1992 - 2010
Anomalies, Aberrations and Distortions

One night Emperor Akbar was camping out under the starry North Indian skies. Sleepless, he woke up Birbal and asked him: "Birbal, what is happening in the world right now?" "Now, Interest is going on in the world, My Beloved Emperor," and went back to sleep.

—As told to me by my father, G. Sadananda Prabhu in my younger days.

One

Call Money

[1998]

There is considerable discussion and debate on the interest rate structure in the country. In Economics, interest is a price for money and the interest rate is normally based on the interaction of demand and supply. Present macro-economic management has considerable control over the interest rate and its structure.

In India, the interest rates were dictated by authority, either Government or the Reserve Bank of India. Some changes have taken place since 1991 which are very well known. It is necessary to analyse the distortions, anomalies, aberrations and movements in the interest rate structure. It should help policy makers and bankers to look at it from a different perspective.

Since 1991 the interest rates on call money were freed and mandated to be market oriented. The details of call money interest rates from the date of decontrol are a matter for study and research. A cursory glance at market movements have indicated that call money rates have been as low as 0.25 per cent and as high as 140 per cent in the last year. It is evident that call money rates fluctuate on an intra-day basis.

The daily movement of rates on a very wide basis is a distortion. The causes are a mismatch between an individual bank's supply and demand positions for the day. These could be attributed to inefficiency in treasury management, sudden withdrawals or credits which are not anticipated, deposits as CRR balances and happenings in the forex markets.

A policy and structure for stable call money markets and a well-defined interest rate mechanism needs to set in. The range in call money rates should be examined.

A study of call money rates in mature markets is made in the table below:

	Overnight	3 mth mm	Prime rate	Discount rate
AUS	5.00	4.75	8.75	
AUSTR	3.38	3.65	6.50	
BELG	3.37	3.69	7.25	
BRIT	7.25	7.44	8.25	
CAN	4.68	4.55	6.50	7.25
DEN	3.85	3.89	6.25	
FRA	3.38	3.57	6.55	
GER	3.53	3.63	4.95	2.50
ITA	5.81	4.76	8.25	
JAP	0.46	0.59	1.63	0.50
NET	3.38	3.47	5.25	
SPA	3.75	4.41	7.25	
SWE	4.25	4.49	5.08	
USA	5.63	5.49	8.50	5.00

In India call money is in fact overnight money. The table reveals that the variation between the call money rates is within 1 per cent of the three month money market rate.

INDIA	6.00	7.5	13.5	9.00
Deposit rate: 11 per cent for 3 years.				

Source: 1. *The Economist* dated April 18th.
2. *The Business Line* Daily.

In the case of US, Germany and UK, call money rates are higher than the discount rate and in the case of Japan it is slightly lower.

A certain distortion is also revealed when call money is compared to the rates at which Banks take money from public. In India, call money rates are lower than the long term deposit rates.

The average cost of funds for banks in India is in the region of 8-10 per cent. When call money rates dip below those levels, the banks lose. To avoid this situation there must be a minimum rate at which call money is employed at.

This should be decided at a reference rate of Bank rate plus or minus 1 per cent and in the present instance it should be 8-10 per cent.

When call money exceeds 30 to 40 per cent per annum, then the Banking community experiences an upheaval. Cash rich banks that play safe with their depositors' money utilise this opportunity to encash and harvest higher interest rates from the distress position of other banks who have a temporary cash crunch. This results in an unusual cost for the borrowing banks and a windfall to the lending bank. This distortion requires study and analysis.

At times, call money rates have gone out of range, not necessarily due to bankers' liquidity problems in the course of their operations but due to RBI policy when the CRR is increased suddenly. In other times, it has been due to a short term liquidity problem among banks which has been noticeably absent in the last 18 months.

Policy should be directed to meet the immediate requirements of Banks who have a temporary liquidity problem when CRR is increased suddenly or some banks are having problems during the Reporting Friday. The Reserve Bank of India must cognize contingencies when banks experience a short term liquidity problem in the market.

The recent credit and monetary policy has opened this avenue as the Reserve Bank has announced that it will resort to both REPO and Reverse REPO to maintain or absorb the liquidity in the market. This is a welcome move.

It is recommended that the concept of a reporting Friday should not be continued. At this time, every second Friday is a reporting Friday. The total DTL of the banks on that Friday determines the quantum on which the CRR has to be maintained.

Since CRR does not carry any interest, banks tend to keep the lowest possible amount as reserve during the period leading up to the reporting Friday. When there is a problem on the reporting Friday, then the treasury manager borrows at whatever rate in the call money market as it does not want to be a defaulter on CRR with RBI. It is also said in commentaries that paying higher rates on call money is better than paying penalties levied by RBI in the case of default.

CRR has been used as an instrument for mobilising excess liquidity in the market. The motive is apparently to control inflation. It would be better if Banks are required to keep the CRR on all DTL at all times than only on a reporting Friday. RBI could specify that a certain percentage of CRR should be maintained for the fortnight after reporting Friday.

CRR as an instrument for monetary control is now being gradually phased out. It is also proposed that the interest rate mechanism via discount rate and open market operations be more effectively used. Hence CRR is to be used only as Cash Reserve by

Banks. It is also proposed that this rate would gradually be reduced. It is also well known that CRR rate is 3 to 0 per cent in the advanced countries.

Research would reveal that call money markets have gone haywire when there was crisis management and not in normal circumstances. When sudden, extraordinary and unanticipated steps are taken by the Reserve Bank and the Government, distortions are bound to occur.

There is no dispute that an instrument like CRR is to be used occasionally to bring order into the banking system or prevent chaos or control short term excess liquidity. It is surprising that call money rates go haywire ranging from 35 to 50 per cent and sometimes higher with wild intra-day gyration.

The perfect solution would be to re-introduce a ceiling on call rates. This will curb the enthusiasm of cash surplus banks in exploiting temporary situations. The borrowing bank's cost will get reduced. The suggested ceiling is 25 or 30 per cent per annum. This will be a punishment for poor cash management. This requires a study by the Central Bank. This is not in favour of policy protagonists as they propose that no overt or covert controls should exist (*see* Tarapore Committee Report on CAC).

If the RBI wants more subtle management, then it has to conduct more subtle ways to manage the call money rates. It has to have a standing policy to guide call rates in a normal mode and a crisis mode.

In the normal day to day mode, the Reserve Bank of India has to take a near term view and a long term view. Since it is constantly thinking of managing the liquidity whether surplus or not, then it should not hesitate to have a support rate in the call market.

The support rate can be 100 or 200 basis points below/above the discount rate. Since the discount rate operates for the lending by the Bank the support rate would be for taking money from the market.

This again can be by three methods:

One, it can offer a rate for deposits in CRR above the amount which is mandatory. For instance, if the total DTL by the bank is Rs. 11,000 crores and the CRR rate is 10 per cent then the amount of CRR would be Rs. 1,100 crores. The Reserve Bank then can pay an interest of 7 per cent on all deposits over Rs. 1,100 crores for that fortnight. This will give the treasury manager to keep the amount in CRR balances always a little in excess of the actual requirement. This will also ensure that at any given time the call rate will not drop below 7 per cent. The Reserve Bank should not hesitate in trying that step because the excess liquidity in the system will stand deposited with itself. This sum can be utilised as it deems fit for the fortnight.

It also can use it as a tool for short term interest rate management along with the Bank Rate. In the discount rate mechanism, it is a lender and under the mechanism it can also be a receiver of funds. An individual bank will have different positions on each day. Just as it has recourse to borrowing from the RBI at times of temporary liquidity it has an option for keeping deposit with the Central Bank. Once this mechanism is announced and implemented in Indian conditions, it will be a tremendous boon and relief to Indian bankers.

Indian bankers can move in aggressively into short term low cost funds all over the country because they have no fear of losing in this proposition. This will improve the banking services in the entire economy. Bankers will not say no to heavy inflows for the day.

This method could give rise to operational or management issues at the Reserve Bank. Once they are addressed positively, then the Reserve Bank need not announce REPOs at all, as the resources it generates can be fine-tuned for other activities like buying Foreign Currency without the risk of generating excess liquidity.

It can also resort to purchase of securities at a price from the system which could help some banks. It could also sell some of its securities in the market. Overall it would add depth and ease in its open market operations.

If this method is a direct and gross method, one can resort to the second method that is more subtle:

Fine tuning of interest rates can be managed by Reserve Bank through intermediaries. One can think of only the DFHI Ltd. and SBI now, and more can be expanded later. The RBI should offer a one day REPO to DFHI and SBI at the close of Banking Hours or after close of Banking hours at a rate of 7.5 per cent. The RBI should absorb the entire surplus on a given day at that rate. In this even DFHI and SBI would act as the support mechanism. In the course of the day the demand and supply will take care of itself and the call rates will move upwards of 7 per cent on the basis of demand. It will not fall below 7 per cent. As the discount rate operates at

9 per cent, technically it should not go beyond 9 per cent. Therefore, the call rates will constantly hover between 7 per cent and 9 per cent as it should be.

The third method is where the Reserve Bank can have a daily three day REPO at a fixed rate instead of the variable rate REPO as at present. The fixed REPO rate can be again at 200 basis points below the Discount rate.

In the above process, as the market matures and integrates and has more depth, the whole system will operate and arbitrage between these two points and treasury managers will only have to operate and fine tune their systems.

The action on crisis mode can be examined in the context when call rates go out of range on the higher side. Call rates can zoom up when there is a sudden drop in the liquidity in the system, when a particular bank or bank is unable to meet its short term obligations to the system and also when a particular bank or bank is unable to meet its obligations on account of CRR.

In such a situation the remedy is to put a ceiling on interest rates on call money. The ceiling can be as high as 25 per cent or as low as 15 per cent. Hence, inject short term liquidity by purchase of Government securities selectively or generally and operate the Reverse Repo mechanism.

The RBI is always a lender of the last resort. Unfortunately, this has not been practised till recently. The discounting principle and the discount rate were introduced only recently; as earlier the only idea was of "mopping up" of excess liquidity and hence the Reserve Bank never had the necessity to manage short term liquidity.

The banks should have the option of exercising the discount facilities. Given the present structure where the banks have access to the extent of only 1 per cent of the total assets, the RBI should not have any conditions. At present discounting is *"frowned"* upon if it is used for arbitrage. This should not be the case.

The problem that arises then is - will the short term liquidity problems make all banks exhaust their discounting option? The Reserve Bank has to take note of this. If the call money rates do rise to 11 to 12 per cent or even up to fifteen per cent, then it is a symptom of a short term liquidity problem.

When we analyse this issue in depth, the Indian system exposes weaknesses and aberrations. In a strict sense call rates should not exceed the discount rate. If it does, it means that a portion of the banking system has a need for short term money which is in excess of the Bank's limit for discounting. The RBI has access to its own records as to which Bank has obtained discounting facilities. It is necessary that the operators in the market know to what extent each bank has accessed its discounting limit.

This will enable the RBI as well as the market operators to know which bank is straining at its limits. Such a signal would be vital both to RBI and the market as remedial measures can be targeted at the particular bank as against the whole system.

The problem in India is that call money rate can zoom up above the rate for Government securities. Research should be directed on likely causes. One of the reasons could be that banks individually and collectively do not have a temporary source of additional short term funds other than themselves. When the whole system is out of funds to meet the needs of the system then call rates rise disproportionately.

The aberration lies in the RBI not responding to such a situation. On such occasions the RBI should intervene not necessarily by lending cash, but by other means. They could be by purchase of securities from the open market or by purchase of securities only from DFHI and SBI at the beginning of the day at a cut off rate.

When the call money rate shoots up to, say 10 per cent in the course of the day, it indicates that the market is operating its discount mechanism and lending at 10 per cent. If it crosses 11 per cent then also some banks may deploy funds. When it exceeds 12 or 13 per cent then the bank which is short of funds should be able to sell securities in the market and then need not resort to call. Here at this time, if there is a systemic liquidity problem, then banks would find that there is no buyer.

It is at this point that the RBI could lend cash for one day at 14 per cent per annum on securities to DFHI or SBI. In such an event, the call money would then remain around 15 per cent till the banks individually or collectively are able to address the liquidity problems. The RBI can also intervene actively by direct purchase of 14 day or 91 day treasury bills directly from the market.

If RBI is liberal and generous to the market in the short term, then it should keep the cut-off at around 200 to 250 basis points above the Bank Rate till it is able to go into the causes of the liquidity problem and provide near-term and long-term measures to solve the same. A reverse repo at this juncture can also help the system.

Whenever there is a sudden drop in the liquidity in the system, it is a matter of grave concern. The RBI has to provide the liquidity to the Banking system temporarily till it is able to assess the causes of the liquidity problem and provide remedial measures. At any rate, the RBI and the Banking system should not allow call rates to go beyond PLR.

Liquidity problems arise due to the rigid structure in treasury management. It is also a system of lack of integration and communications. Each region of the bank may have a unique position of surplus or deficit on a given day.

In the instant case, liquidity problems arise due to the rigid structure in the treasury management in banks as also cross country problems. It could also arise due to decrease in flow of receivables or sudden outflow of payments in the system or with banks or with individuals. The aggregate position then determines the overall supply and demand of money in the short term and puts pressure on interest rates. The impact of gyrations in the call money market on the customers of banks and the public too needs to be examined.

There is no impact when call money rates drop low. The individual banks suffer in profitability which the managements and shareholders have to cognize. When call money rates go high, the smaller banks tend to take advantage of this situation and immediately hike their short term deposit rates.

The new banks as well as foreign banks that are nimble and flexible seem to resort to this tendency. This causes aberrations in the deposit rates which are used to attract customers. The bank which is short may also hike rates on CDs or NRNR deposits as a source of long term funds. Since the markets in India are not deep, the Banking system itself undergoes a temporary upheaval.

When the call money rates were extremely high two years ago, the nationalised banks maintained interest rates on commercial advances at 24 per cent. There were instances when foreign banks wanted to hike the rates to above 30 per cent but could not do the same.

There were also opinions voiced that lending rates could get linked with call rates. When the situation was more or less under control, the talk also subsided.

Wide fluctuations in call money rates are a systemic issue which the Government should be concerned about. There should be a core group or think tank which will act with alacrity and wisdom when such aberrations take place. Contingent plans must be drawn in advance to meet such situations. The decisions should not be hasty and ad hoc. If the Government and RBI demonstrate that they are responsive to the situation, then markets will not panic. This requires a pro-active approach.

The above suggestions will help both the Government and the RBI to develop a pro-active approach. Bankers should then view call money not as a source of arbitrage. It should be part of the financial system where short term liquidity is accessed and managed in mutual interest. They must also develop the right information systems and management initiatives, procedures and action plans to have a market-oriented system and at the same time in their own interest see that wild movements do not take place.

The Government, RBI and all the operators must agree that the call rate distortions in India must end. The Reserve Bank of India alone can provide the dumping ground for daily surplus money and therefore it should perform its role as developer and facilitator in not allowing call rates to fall below certain levels till markets on their own achieve the maturity and depth.

The market players must contribute towards creating, improving and maintaining a structure for call money operations in a way that the true function of call money, that is managing short term liquidity of a bank, is carried out efficiently and with good managerial skills. Preferably an on-line screen based system could be developed for bids and offers on call money that offers information and transparency and could also offer opportunities for wholesale bankers and market makers as well as the RBI to intervene at their convenience.

Though the call money market is free in terms of interest rates, it is only a small portion of the total banking systems assets or liabilities. The interest rate on call money should not vary more than 50 basis points in normal circumstances and 200 basis points under volatile circumstances during the day. This should be the objective of the banking system as a whole. In a mature market scenario, the banking system should endeavour to keep call money at about 50 basis points above discount rate. The Reserve Bank should not allow call rates to fall 50 basis points below discount rate. It will be a remarkable step forward for the financial markets in India.

NOTES

1. The call money rates were one of the first interest rates to be decontrolled by the Reserve Bank of India.
2. The contents of this Chapter were presented to the Reserve Bank of India in 1998.
3. It was acknowledged and definitely acted on as the distortions in call money disappeared in six months.
4. There is no legal provision to pay interest on CRR so we learn. Policy issue should be that we have CRR at 3% for economic efficiency
5. The Economic Survey of the Government of India makes commentaries on interest rates in the country from the previous year to date.
6. The wide fluctuation of interest rates from 0.25 per cent to 110 per cent was mentioned in the survey.
7. It is a surprise that economists, media, commentators or academicians in official circles and public did not point this out as an anomaly or distortion. The reasons for this wide fluctuation needed to be established.
8. The theory, policy and practices on call money are to be actively researched and regulated.
9. The evolution of banking from paper to technology, advancement of data and information from within and outside the bank, have all contributed to the development of the finance and interest markets.
10. Data reported to the Reserve Bank of India by banks is now regularly available in the Statistical Statements.
11. Banks could resort to lesser deployment with other banks as options in money markets have improved.
12. Call money between banks may be considered risky in a fragile economy or difficult and turbulent financial condition.
13. This may bring to fore that call money segment is a very nominal effect on the financial markets.
14. Whether it will be viewed so by Bankers or the Reserve Bank of India remains to be seen. The current practice of rapid turnover and investment in gilts reduces the requirement in the call money segment anyway.
15. In such an event call money and its interest rates will be relegated to the archives and economic history.
16. Banking technology, better practices and a well laid down procedure and practice at the Reserve Bank of India have made stability in call money rates possible today.

Two

Small Savings and Market Rates

[1998]

The interest rate structure in the country has to be examined in the context of avenues and comparative choices for savings by citizens. The discussion and debate centres around a metamorphosis towards a market determined rate of interest. The Government of India's policy on the interest rate offered on Small Savings demands scrutiny.

The Government of India does have a borrowing programme which comprises of loans, bonds and treasury bills. These are at market rates. In the earlier regime the Government resorted to artificially lower interest rates through the mechanism of compulsory maintenance of Statutory Liquidity Ratio (SLR) in Government securities. Currently, the Government raises loans and issues Treasury Bills at "market" determined rates. The subscribers to these loans are Provident Funds, Insurance Companies and of course Banks. Due to poor credit off take, the banks currently hold "excess" securities i.e. in excess of what is required to be held by them under SLR.

The Government also has another programme called the Small Savings programme. These are Post Office Savings Bank, Fixed Deposit, Recurring Deposit, Public Provident Fund, National Savings Certificates and the recently launched Indira Vikas Patra and Kisan Vikas Patra. They are issued nationally through the Post Offices. The Government of India also involves the State Governments in the funds raising exercise. It is towards this end that each State Government has its own Small Savings Directorate which helps the Central Government to market its small savings programme.

The Reserve Bank of India and the Government in various fora and in policy statements have professed that the interest rate regime is moving from rates decided and mandated by the Government or the Reserve Bank of India to a "market" determined rate. The Reserve Bank of India has gradually freed the rates of interest to be market determined. The commercial banks are now free to decide the rates of interest on various term deposits offered by them.

At present the interest rate on a Savings Bank account is fixed whereas no interest is offered on Current Accounts. While the Reserve Bank has moved to a flexible system from a controlled regime, the Central Government in the last five years has maintained the rates on various Savings Schemes on a steady basis.

The rates on term deposits are at 12 per cent. The rates on Indira Vikas Patra (IVP) and the Kisan Vikas Patra (KVP) are kept at 14 per cent. The rates on the Public Provident Fund are kept at 12 per cent free of income tax. At one stage the rates on term deposits in banks have been as low as 9 per cent. Recently Bank deposits bear a rate of interest of 11 to 12 per cent.

The interest rate on Public Provident Fund is 12 per cent per annum. The interest income is totally exempt from Income Tax. This is a major benefit to the investors. Even at a tax slab of 30 per cent, the net yield from investing in a bank will come to nine per cent. This is expensive for the Government of India. Like the high cost of interest on the IVP and KVP this also is an area where the Government cannot afford to have a high fixed interest rate. To retain the advantages of the scheme, the Government can fix a lower rate which can still be attractive considering the other advantages of the scheme.

The scheme can undergo a change. Instead of being a liability on the Government of India, the scheme can be managed by an independent trust or an organisation. The trust or an organisation can be governed by the same rules as in the case of the Provident Fund Organisation. This will reduce the fiscal deficit of the Government.

The scheme can be widened so that more accessibility is provided to investors. Presently it is only made available at the State Bank of India. It can be made available at the other major banks also. The maximum limit of Rs. 60,000 per year can be relaxed by a higher amount or by not having any limit at all.

PPF should be administered by an independent Trust or Organisation and the proceeds invested in permitted securities as in the case of the Provident Fund. The rate of interest can be lowered considering the total tax exemption.

It can also be a variable rate depending on the general movement in the rate of interest. The scheme should be more widely accessible. The maximum limit can be relaxed to a higher amount or totally removed.

The Government borrowing programme is now at around 11.5 to 12 per cent from the market. Yet the Government continues to give interest at 14 per cent per annum on IVP and KVP. The Central Government incurs expenditure by way of administrative costs as also the commission payable on canvassing of National Savings scheme. The State Governments also incur considerable cost in repeating this exercise for the promotion of small savings and deploying their employees in additional efforts for the same activity.

The Government of India makes available a major portion of the small savings mobilised at each State level into a loan to the respective State Governments. The overall costs to the State Government as well as Central Government are high. The Government cannot afford to have an open ended borrowing scheme under its Savings Scheme at 14 per cent per annum in today's context. It is more cost effective for the Government to raise money by Treasury Bills (T. Bills) from the money market than directly from the public. This aberration in the interest rate structure has to be corrected.

This is not to suggest that Small Savings Schemes should be stopped or discouraged altogether. It is merely to point out an ambivalent situation where in one sector of the economy, a concerted effort is made by the RBI, Government and economists for a "market" determined rate of interest and while on the other hand, the Government continues to have a fixed rate and open ended scheme like the Indira Vikas Patra and the Kisan Vikas Patra at 14 per cent per annum.

Recently, the rate of inflation was down to 4.5 per cent when the Government continued to borrow from the public at 14 per cent the incentive moved to the saver rather than the borrower. The major reason for slowdown of growth in the last 18 months was that the real interest rates were high.

Any attempt to bring down interest rates by banks on Term Deposits would result in customers shifting to NSC, IVP and KVP or to other instruments offered by NBFC, DFIs and the private sector. The obvious solution is for the Central Government to declare variable rates for its savings schemes. This should not be difficult as the rates can be announced periodically. The Government should take into account the rates announced by banks on their savings schemes, the discount rate, the rate prevailing for government securities for the same tenor, etc. The possible objection could be from State Governments who could then claim that they would be losers if the collections under Small Savings dropped.

The practice of providing loans to State Governments on the basis of their mobilisation of small savings should be discontinued. The Central Government should not involve the State Governments in its Small Savings drive. At present State Governments use the official machinery to coerce people into savings. Targets are given to various departments and officials down the line. In this process officers of State Governments harass the people to put their money into these investments.

It is a form of corruption. People who are in contact with various departments of the government are in turn pressed for small savings. This is also a waste of the time of State Government officials and unnecessary effort on their part. This process causes a spurt in the fiscal deficit. The National Savings Schemes is open ended. Proactive management by State Governments leads to larger collections than budgeted and thereby contributes to the increase in the fiscal deficit.

The current borrowing programme of the Government of India as and when savings are done, are automatically lent to State Governments which encourages them to profligacy as they take into account the loans from the Central Government in their budgetary provisions. Usually State Governments end up in revenue deficits and these types of borrowings add to the overall interest burden.

The necessity of the Central Government to involve the State Government in promotion of savings among the people is a subject for debate. It started when the National Savings drive was launched and a participative process was generated. Indians have a natural propensity to save. If you provide enough avenues for deployment, a reasonable return, assurance on the safety of the money and good service by the financial sector, there will not be any problem in mobilising savings.

The financial sector has the potential to extend its reach to a larger section of the population as also the Government of India through its current network of financial entities to mobilize the savings of the people. The State Governments and for that matter the Central Government do not give a perfect example to the people of India in the matter of thrift and savings.

Time and again in the last two decades it is written on the wall that the savings in India is positive in as much as the people of India have a very high saving rate and there is dis-saving or negative saving in the Government and public sector. In this sector profligacy and waste is both visible as well as insidious. It is debatable whether the State Government should do both functions: promote savings on one hand and borrow and spend on another.

The issue has to be addressed squarely and not hide hypocrisy. The State Government can continue to overtly profess the need for savings by the people and also can offer directly savings instruments in the form of bonds. It would be wise to end the expenditure and effort that is now incurred by State Government in promoting Small savings with the sole intention of getting back loans from the Government of India. The Central Government can apply a test and announce a policy to withdraw the loan facility. It would be interesting to see the reaction. In all likelihood the State Governments will protest.

It is best to discontinue the facility. In a pragmatic way the Central Government can take over the staff engaged in the Small savings scheme in each state and engage them in the activity of mobilising and promoting the concept of savings.

State Governments can be permitted to borrow directly from the market. The economy in terms of time and effort and money could be enormous for State Governments without loss to the centre or the public as savings will be resorted to by the people if they are attracted to it whether the State Government promotes it or not.

Karnataka has a Minister for Small Savings. One former Minister in Karnataka remarked that "force" is necessary for generating savings. The State Government sets targets for all Government departments to promote National Savings among the public. This in turn translates to individual targets to district officials and offices down the line. These officers are then made to approach the saving public. More often than not it results in a "suggestive" investment by people in contact with the officials.

More often than not businessmen and industrialists oblige by investing even though they are net borrowers at higher rates of interest. In some cases, like the Regional Transport Office it has become a system where an IVP is demanded at each registration or transaction from all citizens.

The Chief Minister of Maharashtra announced a target of Rs. 10,000 crores for Small Savings in 1997-98 and all sections of society were addressed by officials from all departments. It was relaxed when there were problems in the State on the compulsive element. Various State Governments offer incentives including lotteries and prizes to entice savers.

The Government of Karnataka has a dual policy when it comes to interest rate. The Chief Minister is on record requesting the Central Government not to reduce the interest rates on Small Savings Instruments. In the State Budgets, State Finance Minister said, "The Union Government has also reduced the interest rate on small savings which may hamper the collections resulting in harming one of the State's important resources. I urge the Government of India to restore the interest rates on small savings".

It is well known that states promote National Savings for increasing their level of borrowings from the Central Government for budgetary purposes. As states also incur revenue deficits, it is well known that the borrowed money is used for revenue expenditure.

It is surprising that the State Government is asking for increasing the rate of interest to be paid to capitalists. Anyone who accumulates the capital is a capitalist. The intention of the State Government seems to incur higher expenditure on interest which is paid by all the states that will benefit some of the people who are savers. It was again surprising to note that the State Government had requested the Eleventh Finance Commission that the rate of interest charged to State Government should be reduced to 5 per cent.

This defies logic. The State Government wants National Savings rate to be increased to financial investors. In the same breath a reduction in the rate of interest to be charged to itself is asked for. The statement implies that the Central Government should pay 14 per cent to the citizens who had invested in National Savings and in turn provide the same funds at an interest rate of 5 per cent.

If the State Governments suggestions are to be followed, the net burden on the people of India would be Rs. 18,000 crores, this being the simple arithmetical calculation between 14 per cent and 5 per cent on the entire outstanding amount of Rs. 2,00,000 crores which is owed by the State Government to the Centre. If this suggestion had been made by ignorant politicians the same can be forgiven as they are the representatives of the ignorant people. Our bureaucracy comprises of educated, enlightened and intelligent people. That they should have agreed on and prepared this policy reflects the quality of our administration, which is in a state of drift.

It baffles the citizens that the State Government should request that higher rate of interest be paid to the saver who forms a section of the population and the burden is passed on to the entire nation. The sad part is that the very same bureaucracy is forcing small savings down people's throats.

The state administration has issued diktat to all Government employees to use their offices to promote "Small Savings". When any citizen come to a Government office, for any service by the state and the National Savings Certificates and Indira Vikas Patras are thrusted on the citizens, whether he likes it or not. This is based on hard evidence. The state also spends public money, in announcing prizes and incentives. This money is taken from state finances. This money has been deprived of its use in the other functions of the state.

It is also an alternative form of corruption, as people who enforce laws are obliged to procure these investments from people on whom they have enforced law. This obligation may interfere with their duties. Apart from this, it is a categorical waste of time and money and energy on the part of the state government, as it can very well raise money from Bonds, directly from the markets at a cheaper cost.

It is also the case that various State Governments woo banks, financial institutions and large finance companies to invest in small savings in their State. There have been instances when UTI has invested in chunks of National Savings instruments in particular states.

The savings drive in the country should be a philosophy and a mass movement. It is the responsibility of the financial sector inasmuch as the Government of India which provides the ultimate safe investment opportunity to create conditions in which people tend to save.

There is an enormous amount of transaction money and liquid assets which people are holding across the country. Lack of education, absence of confidence in the system and diffidence make the savers keep the money with them. The financial system has not created the atmosphere where all people have access to them. Information and education have not penetrated across the population and procedural and bureaucratic barriers exist which prevent a smooth flow of transaction money into the system.

RBI could consider a prohibition of the financial sector investing in National Savings instruments. This could be resorted to if the Government of India continues to adopt a fixed high rate policy on IVP and KVP or any other instrument. The Government could consider discontinuing of IVP and KVP.

These popular instruments could be designated to DFIs. For instance NABARD could issue the KVP and have a continuous stream of fund flow which can be utilised, for instance in the State of collection. The IDBI or ICICI could issue the IVP and channelise it for industrial or infrastructural investment in respective states.

The Government has not launched any innovative schemes to attract small savings from a wider spectrum in recent years. The competition for savings though higher interest rates and incentives is a self-defeating exercise as the cost is passed on to the borrower.

The Government and RBI have not been able to attract the general public to government securities. Steps should be taken to do so aggressively. At present the banks have been allowed to market government securities to the public by having a sub-subsidiary to the SGL account. The government should go a step further and de-materialise a portion of the government securities or bonds and create a channel to reach the public.

Today bank-managers would be reluctant to market Government Securities to the general public as they would lose deposits. It is still a practice in India, that a bank-manager is rated on his performance to bring in deposits. This practice should be discontinued and a bank-manager should be rated on different parameters of service and profitability.

The Government should decide on a trade-off between promoting aggressively national savings and increasing fiscal deficit. It should have a policy that if the National Savings collections are in excess of budgeted figures, then the market borrowings be reduced accordingly.

Meeting the genuine requirements of State Government should not pose a problem. The Central Government and the Reserve Bank of India can devise a formula whereby a State Government can raise loans directly from the market. This could result in lower coupon rates than the current financing rate from the Central Government. The State Government could save in interest cost if they resort to market borrowings. The borrowing from the Central Government under the National Savings Programme is proving expensive.

This will directly result in disintermediation as the Central Government need not borrow, to again lend to the State Governments. If the Central Government could allow State Governments to tap the market directly then its fiscal deficit can be controlled considerably.

The State Governments borrowings should be rated by a national agency. When State Governments are rated and their performance monitored then, their ability to borrow in markets is judged impartially. They will be forced to perform to market expectations. When State Government loans are auctioned the best rated State Government will probably be able to clinch loans at cost effective rates.

The programme could be:

- the Government must follow a variable rate of interest policy offered on its Small Savings Schemes;
- the Government should dispense with the system of providing loans to the State Governments on the basis of their "net collections";
- the Government and Reserve Bank should allow State Governments to raise directly from the markets to the extent desired or to the extent of the "net" Small Savings raised in the previous year or as deemed fit;
- the RBI and Central Government should set certain criteria in determining the borrowing powers and eligibility of different State Governments. End use and conditionality can be part of the criteria.

- the State Governments' budgetary and fiscal performance should be rated by a rating Agency, both national as well as international.

Gradually the current outstanding loans by State Governments to the Centre could be securitised and offered. This in turn could reduce the fiscal deficit.

NOTES

1. The National Savings Scheme has been an important part of the economic history of the Nation and has played a significant role in mobilizing savings across the Nation.
2. Any deposit in the National Savings Scheme is automatically a liability of the Government of India.
3. The option for Government of India at that time was to take it as a borrowing for budgetary purpose.
4. The Central Government decided to involve State Governments and in the matter of Public Finance it decided that State Government can borrow simultaneously.
5. This resulted in borrowing and lending by Government of India and borrowing and spending by State Governments.
6. The paper addressed the issue of interest rate distortion and did not challenge the scheme per se.
7. This was addressed to Government of India as well and later a committee was formed to address the issue
8. The intelligent savers in the nation took advantage of high interest rates when the market rates went down rapidly while NSS rates were stagnant at higher levels. This cost the Central Government dearly without its knowing!
9. The Public Provident Fund also had tax free interest rates.
10. Currently National Savings Schemes interest rates are aligned to market rates as Government of India has recognised the need to be market oriented.
11. The lending to State Governments has been in the form of investing in State Government securities. The borrowings and investment in securities are now reflected in the budget. (This will be addressed in India's Unbalanced Sheet, forthcoming).
12. National Savings Accounts are now reflected in the Assets and Liabilities of Government of India.

Three

Open Market Operation in Government Securities

[1998]

The current scenario on interest rate management is an interesting and exciting situation. It is slowly evolving from the earlier fixed, authoritative and arbitrary regime.

What is now witnessed is a period of flux. There was exhilaration on the control of inflation. It is doubtful as to whether it was controlled. It was just a happening. The too low a rate of inflation has had its impact. Most of it was negative. This will be discussed separately.

What is now emerging in recent weeks is that there appear to be "contradictory", "confused", "mixed", "directionless" and other adjectives applied to the "signals" that were given or ought to have been given by the Reserve Bank of India.

It is a fact. The Reserve Bank of India by itself does not give the signals. It is the respected people at the helm of affairs who convey their impression in their talks, speeches, statements or directives. But it is mostly the action or the lack of it that is more effective in conveyance. This is where there needs to be some discussion.

The Reserve Bank of India has now professed that it will rely more on Open Market Operations. This is a welcome step forward. This is where the interest rate as a function of demand and supply of money can be managed with finesse. The Dy. Governor has gone on record saying that there is sufficient quantity of securities in the RBI to effectively engage in Open Market Operations.

It is important to go into the theory of Open Market Operations in the most advanced and integrated economy in the world, United

States of America. The Federal Reserve is the Central Bank of the United States of America and also called as the Fed. The following is taken from an Economics text book written by a Nobel Prize winning Economist.

> The Fed's most useful tool is "open-market operations"
>
> By selling or buying government securities in the open market, the Fed can lower or raise bank reserves. These so called open-market operations are a central bank's most important stabilizing instrument.
>
> Samuelson and Nordhaus,
> *Economics*, 15th ed., pp. 508-9.

It is found that the RBI has a one sided approach. It announces sales of securities. On certain occasions, purchases were announced but not of any significance. This area needs to be addressed. The Reserve Bank of India must have its own assessment of the structure of interest rates in different segments and the desirability of reducing or increasing the supply of capital in the market.

The Statement of objectives of the Fed reads as follows:

> The Federal Open Market Committee seeks to foster monetary and financial conditions that will help to reduce inflation, promote a resumption of growth in output on a sustainable basis, and contribute to a sustainable pattern of international transactions.
>
> The most important part of the procedure is instructing the front-line troops at the New York Fed about how to manage financial markets on a day-to-day basis. Ibid., *p. 509*

Three important factors emerge from the statement. What needs to be managed by the Reserve Bank of India is that it should have front-line troops of its own at Mumbai and other centres, that it should "manage" the operations and that the activity cannot be one-time or reactive but has to be on a day-to-day basis. The desired objective can be attained only with active management and this requires both purchase and sale of securities. The RBI is required to assess the market situation, the state of the banking industry, liquidity flows, effect of foreign exchange transactions, macro-economic situation and then decide what the interest rate band should be.

Time and again there has been a lament that the Indian market lacks depth and turnover. A beginning has to be made at the Reserve Bank of India. In the process the RBI cannot have a mercantile approach. It is said and confirmed that the Central Bank has to have an altruistic approach. And this should be carried out in practice. The RBI should be active in the secondary market to the extent that it gives liquidity, stability and a sense of direction to the market. Certain pointers towards practices should be implemented. It is hoped that the Reserve Bank gives the foundation or substratum to a sound and active Gilt Market in India.

The Reserve Bank of India has to decide what the interest rate should be for the market: for the day, for a period. The discount rate which has of late become one of the significant indicators has been pegged at 9.5 per cent. It was set at the above rate so as to maintain the rate of interest on the lower side as also to check the inflation below 4.5 per cent. Recently, however, inflation has been showing an upward journey currently hovering around 7 – 8 per cent mark.

One of the anomalies in the Indian market is that, the rate offered to the public or the depositor is higher than the discount rate. Ordinarily, it should not be so. This will be discussed separately. The gilt yield rate therefore should be hovering around the discount rate.

In an open market operation, the Reserve Bank can have any rate it chooses to simply by exercising the decision to buy or sell securities on the given day. Again the gilt yield is measured in two terms—the current yield and the yield-to-maturity. Since the Indian gilt market has coupon rates ranging from five per cent to 14 per cent, the yield-to-maturity is the chosen way to determine the gilt yield.

The gilt yield curve has to be determined by the market. The market looks always for two aspects: maximising its yield and the value of its security. Since all the securities are marked to market each market operator will look at the market from his point of view and act accordingly. The interest rate being a function of supply and demand of money at a particular point of time, the gilt yield curve will be determined by the market.

The gilt yield curve represents the market rate on a given day across all maturities. The Reserve Bank has to look at the gilts market from its point of view. Interest rate is just one of them. Another is the effect it can make on the reserves by its open market operations and the most important the level of interest rates which would prevail for the economy.

It is well known that high rates of interest though necessary to curb inflationary tendencies could also result in affecting economic growth. Low interest rates are said to be a stimulant for economic growth. If India is truly going towards a market economy, then interest rates should have reflected economic conditions. Interest rates should have dropped to single digits for investors as well as for borrowers when the inflation rate had dropped to four per cent. It would have then stimulated the economy and would not have led to the situation which is now prevalent.

Another situation is that in particular times, the rates can drop for investors reflecting the excess savings in the economy whereas the borrowers are charged higher rates. This higher spread could give enormous profits to banks because they are precisely in a position to do so. In a competitive market economy this would not happen because competition could result in borrowers switching lenders to have better rates. Whether in a rigid structure like India this could happen, is doubtful, because mobility among borrowers is confined to very few persons or corporate.

Whenever there is a surge in savings or higher inflows into the banking system it could result in a situation in which it cannot deploy funds in commercial lending. At least, initially, this will end up in purchase of Government securities which constitutes the safest investment for banks. Whenever there is an opportunity to lend at higher rates, the bank has a choice to lend it out of fresh resources or by resorting to sale of securities.

At any rate the bank cannot go below the amount it is required to maintain under the Statutory Liquidity ratio with approved securities. At one point of time SLR was as high as 37.5 per cent. Currently it is 25 per cent for incremental deposits. Today, banks hold investments far in excess of their requirements. Whenever the banks are required to cover for their SLR requirements, they resort to purchase of securities either by participating in the Government issue or by buying in the secondary market.

The RBI should resort both to purchase and sale of securities. At present it is presenting the sale list regularly. In the sale list it mentions the name of the security and the rate it intends to sell. The resulting YTM is also arrived at by the market. Any operator who finds it attractive to buy that security from the RBI instead of the market will do so. The RBI must also publish and operate a purchase list. The purchase list will also determine the market for interest for a particular period as the market operator has an option to sell to RBI when the market is not purchasing that particular security or any other security.

This would be particularly so when the RBI wants the interest rate to go down. The quantum of total securities the RBI holds is always available to the market. Whether it would be mandatory or ideal for the RBI to reveal the extent of its purchases and sale of securities on daily or regular basis is now not known to the author. The RBI should not hesitate to purchase securities in the market and inject cash into the system should the situation warrant. It can sell the securities in the market to mop up cash if need be on the following day. An infusion of cash for one day into the banking system would hardly cause inflation. What is more important is stability in the near term.

As the economy in India grows so will the financial system. The market may experience large flows into and outside the banks both within the country and from outside the country. One particular bank may face a huge inflow of funds on a particular day which could be the outflow of another bank. There are limitations for banks to accept funds larger than their ability to handle it. Banks cannot exceed their capital adequacy ratios by taking deposits more than the Capital Adequacy Ratio prescribed by the Central Government.

Given a stable inflation and macroeconomic scenario, the Governor decides that the interest rates could be stable over the next period. Then the RBI list should be as follows.

Indicative List of OMO – RBI on a Given Day

Years to Maturity Data: Years	Interest	Security	Purchase	Sale
1998	13.62			100.45
1998	13.65		100.10	
1999	13.70			102.70
1999	12.00		100.85	

(Contd.)

Years to Maturity Data: Years	Interest	Security	Purchase	Sale
2000	12.14			101.60
2000	11.64		100.40	
2001	11.75			100.55
2001	13.55		104.75	
2002	11.00			98.00
2002	13.80		105.75	
2003	11.10			97.80
2003	11.10		97.30	
2004	12.50			102.40
2004	11.50		98.00	
2005	14.00			109.80
2005	14.00		109.30	
2006	11.75			98.60
2006	11.75		98.10	
2007	13.05			105.30
2007	13.05		104.80	
2008	12.10			99.90
2008	12.00		99.10	

It is suggested that the RBI has its own perception of interest rates on gilts. Its own internal gilt yield curve should look as below:

Year	Sale YTM	Purchase YTM
1	9.75	9.25
2	10.05	9.55
3	10.45	9.95
4	10.75	10.25
5	10.95	10.45
6	11.15	10.65
7	11.35	10.85
8	11.55	11.05
9	11.75	11.25
10	11.95	11.45
11	12.05	11.55
12	12.25	11.75
13	12.35	11.85
14	12.45	11.95
15	12.55	12.05

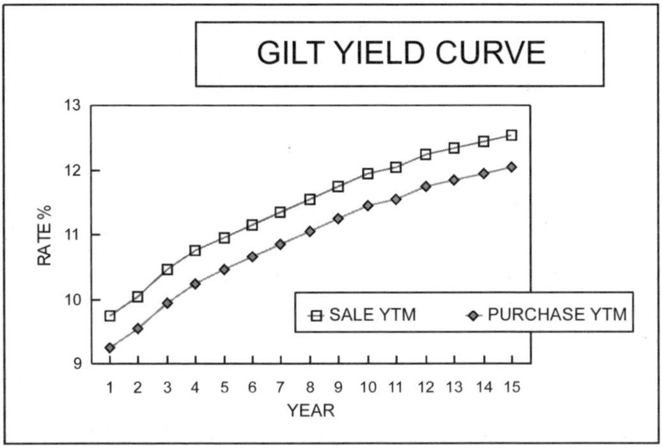

Month	Sale YTM	Purchase YTM
3	9.00	8.5
6	9.25	8.75
9	9.45	8.95
12	9.65	9.15

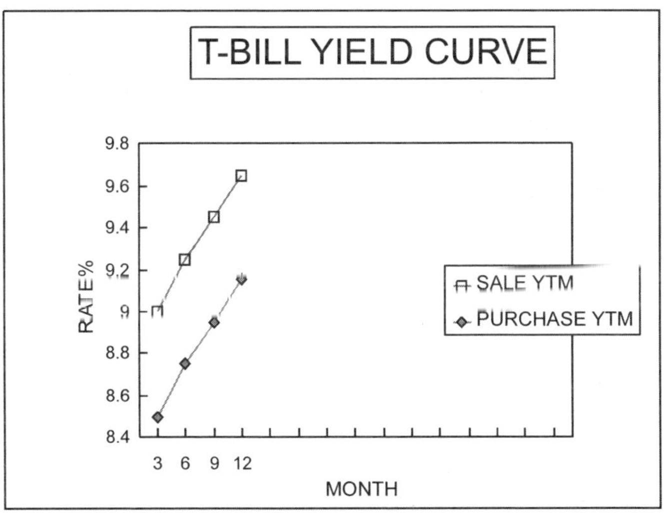

Since the RBI is both selling and purchasing, it is not necessary that it should be the same YTM. There has to be a difference initially between its purchases and sales. How narrow it should be will depend on RBI's decision in this regard and the extent of fine tuning it can do. Initially the difference can be half to one percentage point between the Purchase YTM and the Sale YTM.

The security of purchase for a particular year need not be the security offered on sale for that year. It should necessarily be different. The RBI should shuffle the list every day and put as many securities on the approved list as possible on different days. This will enable treasury managers to shuffle their portfolios. It will also enable the RBI to fine tune interest rates.

When the RBI wants to introduce more liquidity into the economy it can put on purchase a less traded security on a slightly attractive price which will enable the operator to cash in on this opportunity and this will in turn put pressure on the high yielding security and reduce yields.

Initially, the RBI can help out some banks that have a heavy share of low coupon rate securities on their books. This will enable the weaker banks to shuffle their portfolios and move to higher yields. The RBI will not be a loser as it will merely be shuffling between YTMs. If the RBI chooses to, it can help out Provident Funds by selectively offering higher yield paper when it is not available in the primary market. This will be beneficial for the PF operations.

Effective Open Market operations could pave the way for taking off interest rate controls. At the moment India is ranked 46 in matter of Interest Rate controls in world competitiveness ranking. The recent downgrading by Moody's fundamentally addresses the issue of macro-economic stability. The management of interest rates and the increase and decrease in bank reserves are crucial in ensuring it. Competence and effectiveness in Open Market Operations are therefore a must for ensuring continuous market economic stability. This importance is already recognised by the Reserve Bank of India. A decision is already taken by RBI in principle. Action should emanate from this decision.

Prof Peter F. Drucker says:

> Converting the decision into action is the fourth major element in the decision process.
>
> Yet a decision will not become effective unless the action commitments have been built into the decision from the start.

> In fact, no decision has been made unless carrying it out in specific steps has become someone's work assignment and responsibility. Until then, there are only good intentions.
>
> Converting a decision into action require answering several distinct questions: Who has to know of this decision? What action has been taken? Who is to take it? And what does the action have to be so that the people who have to do it can do it? The first and the last of these are too often overlooked with direct results.
>
> Excerpts from Chapter 6,
> The Elements of Decision Making,
> Peter F. Drucker, *The Effective Executive*

RBI is far from incompetent or ineffective. RBI has some of the best brains in the country. There is no common knowledge of the working of RBI or the workings of macroeconomic theory. There is scope for harmony and synthesis.

The assessment of the total quantum of securities to be held by the RBI or the System, the total issues of Government Debt are to be taken into account by experts and subject matter specialists. The elements in managing interest rates as well as satisfying the demand and supply of money at a given time require attention to operational details and their impact on the markets and minds of market operators.

The fundamental issue that crops up at any given time is that purchase by the Reserve Bank results in money supply to the system and could be inflationary. The result is also an increase Reserve Bank's credit to the Central Government. It can be argued that purchase is not a one way situation. The sales during the day also could occur as another market operator buys securities. The managerial option would be that purchases and sales can take place simultaneously so that the net holding of the Reserve Bank remains the same at the end of the day. If done intelligently the interest rate will be held at equilibrium.

It would be a mistaken notion that if the RBI purchases securities worth Rs. 5,000 crores today, the same will be lent by banks to vegetable vendors or grain merchants who will then corner stocks and force up the prices which results in inflation! The experts or economists should decide that interest rates need to come down so. This obviously would result in a growth in the economy.

Similarly, at the time of action to be taken during a foreign exchange management crisis or a bout of high inflation then interest rates have to be raised. Money supply has to be controlled or sterilised. Possibly, securities have to be sold by the RBI.

The parallel economy in the country is today is so vast and having such a tremendous impact that all the official verbiage and action have little impact on the workings of that market.

We should give up the fear of inflation!

Quotation from Swami Vivekananda:

> Fire and enthusiasm must be in our blood.
> Already everything is opening out before us. Be bold and fear not. It is only in our scriptures that this adjective is given unto the Lord—Abhih, Abhih.
> We have to become Abhih, fearless, and our task will be done.
> Be not afraid of anything. You will do marvellous work. The moment you fear, you are nobody. It is fear that is the great cause of misery in the world. It is fear that is the greatest of all superstitions. It is fear that is the cause of our woes, and it is fearlessness that brings heaven even in a moment.
>
> Page No. CW3.318 & CW3.321

When the RBI works out an efficient open market operation the greatest achievement would be stability and equilibrium in the interest rates. Interest rates are arrived at the intersection of demand and supply of money. When the RBI becomes the purchaser of last resort in the securities market and a lender of last resort in the banking system, it meets the demand and supply of securities at all times and an effective system remains in place for fulfilling its role. The entire market develops activity and a new vibrancy is in place. The market operators will digest the information in the market and the players in the market at the same time will try to maximise their returns by shifting from a lower to a higher yield.

The working of a smooth open market operation in Government securities increases the efficiencies of the financial markets. At present, when there is a flush in the system the call money rates turn to low levels. Sometimes, they are as low as 1 to 2 pc per annum. The treasury operators cannot be faulted for this state of affairs as call money is available or given only for the day and cannot be employed in long term investments or loans.

When there is an efficient open market operation, it gives a support level to the interest rates. The treasury operator has an option to invest it in government securities or various tenors as he is confident of realising money at will by selling it to the RBI at any given time. The opportunity for profit from this to banks can be as high as 3 to 4 percentage points per annum at this point of time. Considering that now around Rs. 25,000 crores is employed in the call money system it could translate to profits of Rs. 700 to Rs. 800 crores to the banking system without any loss to RBI. This is too big an amount to overlook.

Once there is an opportunity to deploy short term funds efficiently and at a good margin, the banking sector will move in aggressively towards attracting short-term and transaction money. This will facilitate checking transactions instead of the widely prevailing cash system. Cash in the economy which is dead money and does not yield anything could be converted into revenue yielding accounts to the general public. This can be a source of finance to the economy as a whole.

There is also a risk element. If the real interest rates are high they could attract arbitrage, especially by foreign banks. They could bring in funds which yield them rates of 10 to 12 per cent for short term as against a cost of funds of 3 to 4 per cent abroad. This could mean heavy inflows of foreign exchange as well as outflows. Temporary heavy inflow could mean that the RBI has to purchase foreign exchange and make it available when there are temporary heavy outflows. There could be volatility. This situation could be managed.

If well managed such sources of funds could be an important stabilising factor for the financial sector and make domestic fund managers to concentrate on deployment of funds for the near term and long term.

More important is the crucial decision on the rates of interest that will govern on the purchase and sale. The Governor will have to be ably assisted and the decision of the Governor will have to be near perfect. It is here that Central Bank independence has to be acquired and practised.

The Reserve Bank and the Governor always have the macroeconomic view in mind. It should be independent of the thinking and the requirements of the Government. The Government's cost or impact of the RBI decision on Government borrowing should not come in the way of proper decision making insofar as open market operations are concerned.

In fact, the primary issue of Government debt should be transferred by the Government from the RBI to its own Public Debt Office. This has been recommended to the RBI by expert committees. The RBI could do well by initiating internal exercises on segregating the primary debt issue from the top management of RBI. The cell can be very well looked after by a competent management team. The mandate to the team should be to develop its own talent and expertise on primary debt issue without referral to the top management. In this process, when it is finally decided that primary debt issue and management of debt moves away from the RBI, then the team can move away with the decision leaving the RBI with the Open market operations and monetary management.

The transition is now from control to management, direction to leadership, imposition to responsibility. The bureaucracy in the country is more prone to react to issues than to be proactive in policy and action.

> The action must also be appropriate to the capacities of the people who have to carry it out.
>
> All this becomes doubly important when people have to change behaviour, habits, or attitudes if a decision is to become effective action.
>
> But everyone can think what action commitments a specific decision requires, what work assignments follow from it, and what people are available to carry it out.

Therefore, RBI would develop the human resources, technological and physical to meet the requirement of effective open market operations in India.

> All power is within you; you can do anything and everything. Believe in that do not believe that you are weak; do not believe that you are half-crazy lunatics, as most of us do nowadays. You can do anything and everything without even the guidance of any one. All power is there. Stand up and express the divinity within you.
>
> Swami Vivekananda, p. 284

Market operations in Indian context cannot be construed as leaving them in the open for vagaries or aberrations. It is useful to recall.

> Nevertheless, we cannot just disrupt and hope for something better without having some vision of the future we are working for, however vague that vision may be. We cannot just create a vacuum, or else that vacuum will fill itself up in a way that we may have to deplore. In the constructive schemes that we may make, we have to pay attention to the human material we have to deal with, to the background of its thought and urges, and to the environment in which we have to function. To ignore all this and to fashion some idealistic scheme in the air, or merely to think in terms of imitating what others have done elsewhere, would be folly.
>
> Jawaharlal Nehru, *Discovery of India*, p. 243

Efficient open market operations will not leave any room for devolvement on the RBI. The primary market yield hinges on the rates and depth prevailing in the secondary market. A vibrant secondary market will always ensure that the Government borrowing programme proceeds without any hitch. Efficient open market operations will obviate the need for Ways and Means advances. The Government can always raise money in the T. Bill market. The depth provided by the market will always enable the Government to access cash. The Government has to decide on its own its requirements and the effect of borrowing on markets. The crowding out theory is very much valid in Indian conditions and should be analysed for negative impacts.

The REPO will continue to be an interest rate instrument. But, open market operations will make treasury managers more efficient. The efficient open market operations will have no political impact. In fact, it will depoliticise the true functioning of market insofar as interest rates are concerned. The net result will be economic efficiency which will result in tremendous advantages to the system as a whole, the financial sector and to the people of the country.

NOTES

1. This analysis was a suggestion to bring in uniformity in interest rates and elimination of duality by the Reserve Bank of India. Unfortunately, Reserve Bank of India has not moved towards this final step. It has created a "corridor" by having two rates for buying and selling.
2. There should be considerable depth in the study of this mode in the Indian context, internally within RBI and externally within Parliament, the Ministry of Finance and the academia.
3. The model to have a single OMO rate will be the ultimate step in the stabilization of the interest rate within the financial markets and also increase the integration of Indian economy with the rest of the world's economies.
4. Reserve Bank of India has done massive unloading of securities called as Open Market Operations since 2004 when Indian savings turned positive and outpaced investment. Recently, it had to resort to purchases of securities from the market in the light of exit of capital from markets as well as indirectly supporting higher Government borrowing without lifting interest rates significantly.
5. The Reserve Bank of India will then have a greater responsibility in arriving at the right middle rate at which Open Market Operations are conducted on a daily basis.

Four

Interest Rates and NBFCs

[1998]

Non-Banking Financial Companies (NBFCs) evolved and exist in the Indian financial scene. NBFCs confine themselves to the function of raising deposits from the public and are primarily engaged in utilising the resources for the purpose of hire-purchase and leasing activities. Some also indulge in investment and trading activities. They are also permitted to some extent lend money to borrowers.

Interest rate behaviour in the country is highly influenced by NBFCs activities. The interest rate offered by NBFCs is higher than that of banks. In addition they pay brokerage or fees on deposits collected. The interest rates charged by NBFCs to the borrowers are also correspondingly higher and therefore translates as costs to the economy.

The NBFCs are allowed only to raise term deposits. The rates offered by them have generally varied between 14 to 15 per cent. These rates have been offered when comparable rates were between 9 to 13 per cent by banks for the same period during the last five years.

There is need to examine whether it is a desirable state of affairs. While interest is a function of demand and supply of money or the price of money, why should a portion of the financial sector pay a higher rate of interest? Is offering a higher rate of interest the only reason for their existence? The reasons for the necessity or otherwise of the existence of NBFCs will be discussed separately. The impact of the interest rate variation is subject to analysis and debate.

The difference in the form of higher rates of interest offered to a depositor should be explainable. It is essentially a matter of compensation for risk. Higher the risk, higher the reward is the principle of market operations. But the risk of non-receipt of principal due to bad management or system failure is carried by the depositor. Safety in NBFCs is a separate issue and a comparison of interest rates with other instruments is a matter for study.

The depositor is enticed by a higher rate of return and better service by the NBFCs. It is debatable whether it is good for the economy to have a system where a substantially higher rate is offered by one part of the financial sector. Interest paid is a cost for a finance company. In addition, it incurs expenditure normal to its business. The difference between total cost and interest and other charges collected constitutes its profit.

Any higher interest paid, therefore, is naturally passed on to the customer. As a corollary, if the business is able to generate asset that yield higher returns, an element of competition enables the company to pay higher interest to depositors or incur higher costs. It is debatable whether Non-Banking Financial Companies (NBFCs), as financial entities, should have an enabling environment which enables them to offer overly high rates of interest on deposits from the public.

This has a foundation that

(a) the deposit with NBFCs should be as least risky as in instruments other than offered by the Government,
(b) there is a consequential harmful effect on the economy due to the higher interest rate cost to consumers of the financial services offered by the NBFCs.

NBFCs carry out two activities which are not allowed to commercial banks i.e. hire purchase and leasing. Lending to citizens for the purpose of purchase of transport equipment whether for own, professional or business use is not done by banks. Leasing activity is prohibited. Hire-purchase is now solely confined to NBFCs and other financial entities who can be partnerships or sole-proprietors.

The existence of NBFCs is justified on the grounds that hire purchase and leasing are necessary for the economy and useful financial instruments for the people of the country. However, there is no justification for their being allowed to pay higher interest rates to depositors.

In the above scenario, the interest rate offered by NBFCs cannot go much higher than those offered by the banks. The system of offering brokerage and incentive should be done away with. Although, controls are not envisaged, it would be possible for NBFCs to raise deposits at the rates offered by banks or marginally higher rates, say, 0.5 to 1 per cent. The deposits can be attracted on the basis of high safety and a better element of service.

The consequence would be that the rates of hire purchase and leasing would be more reasonable than they are now. In the earlier period, the rates of interest would work out from 24 to 30 per cent in the case of lease and hire charges to customers.

They can come down to more reasonable levels of 18 to 21 per cent. At these rates the services offered by these financial intermediaries would be very attractive for businesses and individuals. As consumers they would have a wider range of comparable choices. This will also stimulate the economy.

Higher profitability will ensure that the net profits of NBFCs are reasonably good. They will generate higher income tax revenue to the government. Good profitability will mean good returns to shareholders and higher shareholder value. This will in turn attract more capital to the NBFCs which is more advantageous than attraction for deposits in the long run.

NBFCs was not a creation or innovation by the Government or born out of authority or mandate. It was a nomenclature given to companies founded by citizens to engage in purely financial activity. These companies primarily evolved as there was a demand from the commercial sector, primarily the auto sector, for finance against hypothecation of motor vehicles whether commercial or for own use. The earlier concept of priority sector for finance excluded vehicle ownership for the purpose of credit. Hence this sector was driven to the finance companies for their finance needs. These finance companies seemingly thrived on this niche as the rates were attractive and they developed the competence in making loans and recovery of loans specialising in this sector.

As these finance companies needed funds, they attracted public deposits. These public deposits needed to be enticed from discerning savers. The savers obviously had to be attracted by higher rate of interest and other incentives. By this saving public also necessarily undertook the risk of investment. The attractiveness was proximity of the companies to the public, good personal contact, reputation of promoters, confidence built up over a period of time by prompt payment of interest and principal. NBFCs grew in numbers and size over a period of time.

A higher growth rate for NBFCs came about three years ago. The commercial and nationalised banks had a period of healthy inflow of funds without utilisation and they dropped their deposit interest rates to 9 or 10 per cent. The NBFCs moved in for the kill and offered interest rates on deposits up to 14 per cent and incentive of two per cent. This created a shift of deposits into finance companies. Finance companies were then perceived as a vehicle for manufacturing and trading companies to "diversify" and climbed on the bandwagon.

The growth in regional savings then spawned an incredible number of NBFCs that a staggering 22,000 number of companies were in operation. These were companies registered under the Act. The amount of partnership and proprietorship finance companies engaged in deposit taking and lending activity number were in hundreds of thousands.

Surprisingly, the financial sector took this development lightly. The RBI even as evident from recent pronouncements considered and even now considers NBFCs as an important financial sector segment. Truly, as businesses, NBFCs justified their existence. One, they satisfied the needs of people at large both depositors and borrowers. Two, they were profitable.

Profitability in the financial sector is governed by the concept of "spread". This is the difference between the rate of interest earned and the interest expended expressed as a percentage. The spread calculated on employable assets is the gross profit. After deducting other operating expenses the net profit is earned. The finance company also earns on fees. These are paid by borrowers upfront. These help in recovery of costs to some extent. The advantage that NBFCs offers to both depositor and borrower is obviously service. Given the cold and bureaucratic responses given by other parts of the financial sector NBFCs scored with the people on service.

The question now is whether it is justifiable for NBFCs to offer higher rates to depositors and whether it is also right for RBI to allow NBFCs to pay commission on deposits. The answer to the second part is negative. NBFCs should not be allowed to pay commission on deposit. The amusing part of the rule is that the commission is to be paid to a third party i.e., other than the depositor. NBFCs, who marketed directly, paid it to depositors indirectly by requesting depositors to nominate the recipients of incentive. Hence, the system evolved around paying depositors the incentive indirectly. There was no stipulation that it should have been paid to a registered or regulated broker who would be an intermediary.

The banking system has been denied this facility. Banks are prohibited from offering any incentive to the depositor directly or to offer brokerage on the deposits claimed by them. There is no reason why the same should not be applied to NBFCs. NBFCs operate through their own offices. NBFCs cannot be equated with companies and their fixed deposit schemes. NBFCs should have their own staff and cadre to reach depositors rather than through third persons.

If at all NBFCs contrive to pay back the depositors this incentive, it can as well be loaded on the interest rate. Indian consumers are always enticed by inducements. Anything offered free or apparently without cost or as a difference over a competitor is salivating to an average Indian. If this concept is to be extended as a marketing tool, it has to be viewed differently.

But if the NBFCs are permitted to give brokerage, the principle should very well extend to banks too. Unhealthy practices also come into play. For instance, persons close to NBFCs sometimes induce deposits from non-individuals or institutions. Since these cannot be recorded in the institution, these persons are prone to pocket incentives. It would be better if RBI withdraw this permitting clause with a view to provide transparency to the depositors. As highlighted in the main paper, interest being the interplay between demand and supply of money, it should not be on the higher side. Any high cost of operation is passed on to the customer. Hence, a rate which is naturally higher is naturally passed.

This could hit some productive sectors of the economy. These persons who incur high financing cost necessarily work harder to pay interest and the loans and incur high transaction costs. These are in turn passed on to customers and to the economy as a whole. High transaction cost could inhibit spending on productive sectors and could have cascading effects. For example a competitive rate could attract more operators and create competition which would help the users.

High costs in interest could mean that the operator could exploit other areas. For instance, truck operators are prone to encourage overloading; they could pay less to their employees, and cut short on proper maintenance. All these have hidden costs on the economy. As long as an NBFCs or a finance company earns it spread, the rate of interest borrowed at does not matter. Now the Finance companies incur a cost of 17 per cent and lend at 25 or 26 per cent. They are earning a spread of about 8 per cent. If their cost of funds is at 13.5 per cent, would it mean that they would continue to charge 25? They would do so if the market would bear it! But competition will not allow it for long as more players will get into it. It is therefore safe to assume that their lending rate could come down to 21 per cent or thereabouts.

In a market economy the interest rate has to be by dynamic i.e. reflecting the conditions of demand and supply. If there is a huge demand from this sector for funds for deployment of a gross return of 21 per cent then it deserves to be allocated the funds. The market will do so, as funds will shift from a lower yield to a higher yield. If profitability is high, it will naturally attract more capital.

The Nationalised banks earn an average spread of about 2 per cent. When the scenario highlighted in the paper i.e. a CRR of 3 per cent (non-interest bearing), a SLR of 25 per cent (average yield today 11.5 per cent) is imposed on NBFCs then they would not be in a position to offer more than 1 to 2 per cent spreads over banks. This should be incentive enough for people to deposit their money with NBFCs as a reasonable higher security is offered.

In this event the cost of lendable funds will be around 14 to 15 per cent for NBFCs. This should permit them to have a lending rate of 20 to 22 per cent which is what the market is bearing today. If interest rates float lower, then the dynamic activity in a free interest rate regime will force both the deposit and lending rates lower.

When an NBFCs is credit worthy, it should be eligible for refinance at PLR. This would be cheaper than raising deposits from the Public. The moot question would then be—what would be the eligibility of the NBFCs for borrowing from banks. At present it could be anywhere between 60 to 75 per cent of the "asset" value. In all, an NBFCs should not have an advantage which it can offer a more than ordinary rate by way of interest. The sector requires conditionalities which need to be governed, prescription of prudential norms as well as a code for self-discipline.

In the regime of free interest rates what could the equilibrium be? The demand for funds from NBFCs from operators and businessmen cannot be under rated. If the demand is unsatisfied then the interest rate will move up. If the amount available for disbursal for that sector is limited then that pressure will cause the lending rates to go up. If the interest rates should be market oriented then it should be a corollary that supply of funds to that sector must also flow according to demand.

This is not the case in India as supply and demand of funds for each sector is compartmentalised. The funds do not flow, as a rule naturally towards a higher return. The demand and supply curve for each segment will operate. If the norms set out in the main paper were applied then the interest rates should not go above 1 per cent of term deposits offered by banks. This also is true only if there are alternate sources of funding at PLR which would be equivalent of the rate of interest + cost of taking deposits from the public.

Therefore, if interest rate stability is to be achieved where the deposit rates are not in wide variance and so also the lending rates to creditworthy borrowers, the NBFCs sector must have a source of finance like rediscounting or other institutional means of borrowing. This the RBI alone can decide. Given this scenario the rates of interest on Deposits should be not more than 1.5 per cent over that offered by banks. The question of spread should be left to the market as a long as stringent safety and business code norms are mandated, implements and observed.

The question that is before the Government is what should be its policy on NBFCs. The Government and RBI are not wanting in expertise in dealing with the subject. The only submission that can be made is that what is to be done with the past and what is to be the policy for the future. The dealing with the past is to be a separate issue. The concentration should be on the future.

> No other principle of effectiveness if violated as constantly today as the basic principle of concentration. This, of course, is true not only of businesses. Governments try to do a little of everything.
>
> The future is not going to be made tomorrow; it is being made today, and largely by the decisions and actions taken with respect to the tasks of today. Conversely, what is being

> done to bring about the future directly affects the present. The tasks overlap. They require one unified strategy. Otherwise, they cannot be done at all.
>
> Peter F. Drucker, *Managing for Results.*

Once a policy for the future is decided, then it is easier to deal with the past.

> Pick the future as against the past;
>
> Focus on opportunity rather than on problem;
>
> Choose your own direction—rather than climb on the bandwagon; and Aim high, aim for something that will make a difference, rather than for something that is "safe" and easy to do. p. 111
>
> Today is always the result of actions and decisions taken yesterday. Yesterday's actions and decisions, no matter how courageous or wise they may have been, inevitably become today's problems, crises and stupidities. Yet it is the executive's specific job—whether he works in the government, in a business, or in any other institution—to commit today's resources to the future. p. 104
>
> Peter F. Drucker, *The Effective Executive*

It is therefore very important that the analysis of events in the NBFCs sector that have taken place and the needs and contingencies of the present have to be matched with the future. The Government has to deal with an aspect of the economy which does not have a direct bearing on the Government in terms of finances and attention.

Therefore, in dealing with the past the Government or RBI should deal with it not inasmuch in respect of the effect of right or wrong of a policy but whether there has been a violation of rules, acts procedures and regulations of the Government or RBI. In this eventuality the Government has only a role of enforcing a law especially that which deals with the problem between a citizen and another citizen.

If a person does not return the money he has borrowed from the members of the public, then those members should file for recovery of the money. The person, if he is liable under civil law can only repay to the extent of assets encashable by him. If the person is bankrupt and not able to pay the citizen, who lent the money, loses. It therefore becomes a loss to the lender for which the Central Government or the RBI cannot be held responsible or accountable. If the borrower has violated any central law, then the Government should proceed expeditiously against the offences. If the borrower has violated any criminal law, then the law should proceed against him.

In all above respects Government failure looms very large as the Government has not created an atmosphere where judicial remedies are expeditiously and efficiently decided. Such matters cannot be decided administratively or by state action.

The Government, the bureaucrats, the RBI, the judiciary and the bar should imbibe from the words of India's Philosopher President:

> So we must make our courts and institutions proper arbiters of the relations between man and man, between the citizen and the State. If there is to be an end, a goal for law, the end has been beautifully described in the preamble to our Constitution: Justice, Liberty, Equality and Fraternity. Justice not to be purchased, not to be got by hook or crook, but impartial justice given to us by people who are wedded to justice and who will interpret the law so that justice may be there.
>
> Justice should be there in every kind of law, otherwise it is not true justice.
>
> A kind of law which voices the will of the strong prevailed long ago. That is not law.
>
> Justice must cater to the needs of all the individuals, of the citizens and it must be able to give proper judgment on controversies between citizen and citizen, between citizen and State, the States and the Union itself. That is the kind of justice we have to bring about.
>
> Dr. S. Radhakrishnan, *Search for Truth*, p. 128

If the judicial system backed by an efficient administration could evolve to meet the needs of our people most of our present day problems would not surface at all. It is therefore, suggested that the Government and RBI look to the future and specifies the norms for NBFCs as mentioned in the paper.

With regard to the past, a compassionate and considerate view has to be taken. Those companies which are doing a good job and interested in the right conduct of business should be given time to meet the requirements.

Wherever, fraud or misconduct has been discovered then the due process of law must take place. With regard to safety of depositors, though the Government and the RBI are in no way directly responsible, the Government and the RBI must not take steps which affect the citizens adversely. The resources available with the Government and the RBI should be utilised to mitigate the wrongs done. This can be done patiently and over a period of time so that all the pros and cons of effects of action and salvage can be examined and actions taken which will be fair and just to all citizens.

NBFCs is a terminology difficult to comprehend (though not as bad as Indian Made Foreign Liquor). Banks can never be called as finance companies and one wonders why finance companies need to be called as non-banking.

All finance companies can be segregated based on their activities, e.g.

- FC (HPLC) (Hire Purchase and Leasing Co.)
- FC (Investment)
- FC (Securities)
- FC (Brokerages) etc.

Each should be prohibited from the other activities which will make them focused and easier to monitor. The RBI and the Government should then work out the code and practices, rules and regulations governing all aspects of functioning and relationship with the public in respect of all such companies. The principle need not extend only to taking of deposits from public but the entire possible gamut of activities a financial company can undertake and the aspects of relationship with the public.

There has been a newspaper report that one of the proposals before the Ministry could be that the State Governments could be involved in regulating NBFCs. There are no resources nor is there competence within State Governments to do so. As it is most of their institutions are mismanaged and in a financial mess.

The least State Governments could do is proceed firmly and swiftly on violation of civil and criminal law. It would be a wise decision not to pursue the idea of State Government involvement in regulation of NBFCs.

The RBI or a separate Board of Financial Supervision alone can be there to regulate, monitor and inspect NBFCs as it requires a national institution. The RBI may have a problem of sheer number of personnel required for this purpose. There is no option but to deal with it effectively and efficiently both in the interest of monetary and financial sector management and in the interest of the nation and the public.

What RBI should do is to regulate, monitor and inspect NBFCs. The first two functions it can do within its resources. The inspection function can be delegated to two agencies —

1. The Banks
2. Retired Bank/RBI Personnel.

NBFCs have to deal with banks to perform their transactions. Therefore, banks are the best agency for achieving certification on various objective parameters. These can be in specific areas like capital adequacy, compliance of reserve requirements and cash flow, etc. Inspection functions as designated by RBI can be conducted by approved bank personnel retired from banks or RBI. These are a valuable resource now available in society. They can be empanelled on the basis of competence and prior experience. As they are generally available in each area, the cost will be minimal but remunerative enough for them to perform their specified duty. This will save the RBI from administrative expenses and field work. They can rely on the inspection reports from these competent inspectors and if there is anything adverse that warrants an investigation it should do so.

There would be no political impact from above steps. In fact, future embarrassments and political intervention could be saved if proper regulatory and preventive steps can be taken. Improvement in functioning of NBFCs could be recognised as a major achievement for the State especially if interest rate is reasonable to both depositor and borrower and service is improved. The positive contribution of NBFCs to local economy and the employment potential could well be popular with the people at large.

Ensuring Safety of Depositors in NBFCs

The following steps are necessary for safety of depositors:

- More than adequate capitalisation
- Adequate reserve ratios
- Good management and structure.
- Prudence in asset management
- Adequate profitability to meet risks in losses arising from default by borrowers.

Capital Adequacy: Capital provides the buffer for safety of public money deposited with NBFCs. Capital is employed in NBFCs in fixed assets necessary for business. Beyond that capital employed in business generates revenue in the form of return on assets where the capital is employed. The business can ensure a return on capital employed which would be adequate to meet servicing shareholders. Therefore, there should not be any problem for NBFCs to be highly capitalised. The capital adequacy ratio can be as high as a minimum of 12 per cent. Fifteen per cent can be taken as prudent and 20 per cent can be taken as an NBFCs with high safety.

Reserve Ratios: As NBFCs are a part of the financial system they must be brought under the system of cash reserve ratio and the statutory liquidity ratio. As NBFCs resort to only term deposits and the fund flow is measurable the CRR can be restricted to 3 per cent. This can be either in Current account with nationalised banks or in 14, 90 and 364 day T-bills which are highly liquid. The SLR should be the same as that of the banking system i.e. 25 per cent.

This system will ensure a higher degree of security as nearly 40 per cent of the deposits (Capital 12, CRR 3 and SLR 25) can be accessed to meet the liabilities to depositors.

Good Management and Structure: A consolidation of NBFCs industry structure is necessary to ensure its productive use for the economy. Therefore, it is necessary that a good management exists in NBFCs which conveys strength, resourcefulness and confidence. The management structure should also be professional.

Prudence in Asset Management: Prudence in asset management will ensure that the borrowers or lessees are selected and evaluated on the basis of credit, character and capability. This will ensure the prompt repayment of loans, collection of lease rentals or hire purchase receipts. The system will also take care of dealing with defaults and asset recovery in the event of delinquency.

Adequate Profitability: As in all businesses the NBFCs should ensure itself adequate profitability so that it will provide for the costs of business as well as an adequate return for the stake holders.

Currently, many subtle changes are taking place in this sector. Interest rates to depositors have come down. Aggressive marketing by car companies has brought down lending rates. The recessionary trends in the auto market have made players cognisant of the fact that high real rates will not work for long. An educating experience for the public about the good and the bad is evident. These factors are conducive for effective and forward looking public policy.

The Reserve Bank of India should consider the proposals from the point of interest rate stability, health of the financial sector, concerns for both depositors and borrowers from the NBFCs and growth of the economy.

- The incentive/brokerage fee at 2 per cent which is now allowed to NBFCs should be cancelled.
- The interest rate offered by NBFCs should not be more than 1 per cent difference over comparable bank deposits not by diktat but by market forces.
- NBFCs promoted by industrial houses, manufacturing companies should be persuaded to be independent professional companies
- NBFCs activity should be confined to hire-purchase and leasing only. Any other form of investment or lending should be prohibited or should be carried out by other companies.
- A CRR at 3 per cent and SLR at 25 per cent should be specified. SLR should be in permitted securities only and not in bank deposits and Indira Vikas Patra as specified earlier.
- Capital adequacy ratio should be 12 per cent. Rating companies must be advised that high safety can be awarded only to NBFCs with a minimum CAR of 20 per cent.
- Supervision over NBFCs should be by a different structure. This should be arrived after by a detailed examination of

issues involved. This should cover aspects in statutory audit, Company law and angles in financial supervision.

It is hoped that the Reserve Bank of India and the Government of India take cognisance of the above discussion as inputs in policy making on dealing with the issue of NBFCs.

NOTES

1. This submission on NBFCs was made to the Finance Ministry and also the Reserve Bank of India in 1998. There were a large number of NBFCs who were Limited companies, Private Limited companies as well as partnerships.
2. The financial sector was dominated by Nationalised banks and a handful of private banks. There were huge restrictions on them in the form of SLR, CRR and stipulated lending that it gave very little room for commercial loans.
3. The NBFCs filled that gap by being aggressive in lending at higher rates and correspondingly taking as much low cost deposit as follows. However, most of the time they paid higher interest rates for want of credibility and strength.
4. NBFCs enticed deposits by giving commission to agents which was not permitted practice in Nationalised banks. Hence there were thousands of companies and firms in India whose only way in competition was to take deposits at higher rates of interest.
5. The result was that NBFCs had to compete only by higher rates for deposits and inevitable charge higher rates of interest to their borrowers.
6. There were registration requirements with authorities like RBI but there was no regulation of interest and the practices were different.
7. The Government and RBI recognised over period of time that regulation was essential.
8. There was a change in practices in Nationalised banks that they aggressively started to lend to segments which they ignored earlier thus undermining viability of NBFCs.
9. In just two or three years there was a massive change in industry sector when thousands of firms and companies engaged in finance activity closed shop. The firms that could compete continued.
10. Subsequently major growth in this area made direct lending more feasible and has resulted in fewer NBFCs who are now competitors in a limited strength.

Five

Effecting Savings on Interest Payments of the Government of India

[1998]

The Government of India has a major item of expenditure on its hands, that is, interest. The following table reveals the growth of interest payments over a period of time.

Year	Interest Receipts (Rs. in crores)	Interest payments	NETT
1980-81	1795	2604	–809
1993-94	15062	36695	–21633
1994-95	16234	44000	–27766
1995-96	18419	50031	–31612
1996-97	21945	58500	–36555
1997-98	24092	68000	–43908

Source: Statistical Outline of India.

Time and again expressions of "concern" over this growth are expressed both in official, bureaucratic, political and academic circles. The overwhelming aspect is the effect of interest payments on revenue expenditure and consequent increase in the revenue deficit and not to mention, ultimately, the fiscal deficit.

There has been mention from moderates and a set of thinkers, but reflected only occasionally, that the receipt of interest is also a factor. When an amount of Rs. 68,000 crores is mentioned as outgo, interest receipts amounting to Rs. 24,092 crores is ignored.

A policy for examining interest outgo by itself and dealing with it has to converge on a decision in principle, viz., that interest outgo must be reduced in the near term, medium term or the long term.

Two factors could contribute for a reduction in interest outgo. One, the borrowings should get reduced and two, the rate of interest that is paid must be lower than it is now.

The nominal interest payments have galloped after the liberalisation process. A conscious decision was taken that the Government should borrow at "market" rates. Hence the nominal rates of interest incurred by the Government which was in the range of 6 to 8 per cent in the era of directed interest rates jumped to as high as 14 per cent in the year 1996. Currently the Government security yield curve is ranging from 9.5 per cent to 12.25 per cent depending on the maturity of the loan or security.

Excessive Government borrowing from the available capital in the market results in a phenomenon called "crowding out". Available capital in a nation or internationally tends to go into Government securities as it is implicitly more secure than an instrument by any other entity. Hence, if the yield on Government securities is high, the financial sector could continuously invest in this safe investment than to venture into giving loans to private entities. As cost of funds keeps on increasing, higher Government borrowing crowds out private investment.

The move to market is by itself a desirable and pragmatic step. In an artificially controlled interest rate regime, the saver or the intermediary tends to be punished as he is denied of the benefits of the market rate in terms of interest. Second, the necessity to borrow at market rates makes the Government to think about its borrowing programme and its effect on the budgetary position. The Government also has to be efficient in the use of its resources.

While examining the choice mentioned, it is the business of the Government to decide whether to increase or reduce its borrowing. It makes its choice every year at the time of the budget. If the borrowing increases due to the expenditure of the Government, whether revenue or capital, then it should be very well prepared to accept the increase in interest outgo in that or every subsequent year.

Exercising the choice to reduce borrowing can be done only if there is "buoyancy" in revenue or a reduction in the "outlay" of the budget. Increase in revenue has always had its demands as there are a lot of unfinished agendas and dire needs in Government which always takes care of additional revenue generated. Economic and political compulsions make it very difficult to do the latter. It requires to make "hard choices" in decision making.

A "balanced budget" where revenue and expenditure match exactly can be done only by an agreement among all parties. But the average politician's and layman's definition of what the Government should do for the country is varied and unfocused. The programmes for "development" and "poverty alleviation" are mind boggling and have unsustainable budgets. Each party's and politician's pet ideas of their means to achieve the same ends and goals are untested and untried but still forced on the public, not to mention the philosophy of "take the money from the rich and give to the poor" which is extremely ingrained. Today, the bureaucrats' capacity to expand his own expenditure with or without results is also entrenched. Sadly the people's and voters' perception of what the Government should do and not do does not figure in any debate.

The next choice that is available is reduction in interest rates. This agenda has its conflicts. The current buoyancy in savings and bank deposits has greatly helped the Government borrowing programme. The RBI which is managing the Government's primary debt programme has "managed" to meet the Government's requirements and at the same time, interest rates have declined.

The potential for reducing the Governments interest costs in a market economy in the current situation requires study and analysis.

(a) Today's Government paper ranges from 14 days to 20 years.
(b) It comprises of Treasury Bills for duration less than 364 days and Loans, securities and bonds for 1 year to 20 years.
(c) Such securities issued earlier are outstanding now for various maturities.
(d) What is more important is that the coupon rate for these securities outstanding ranges from 6 per cent to 14 per cent.

It is without doubt that an interest rate fixed for a period is an outgo over the entire period. Therefore, a six per cent loan which is outstanding has an outgo of six per cent only today as much as the fourteen per cent loan having an outgo of fourteen per cent.

Innovative solutions require a deeper understanding of the market and its mechanisms. Innovation is a specific task of the entrepreneur. According to Prof. Peter F. Drucker, entrepreneurship and innovation are no longer confined to business but are more needed in Government and non-profit organisations.

Abundant material is available to prove that the yield of resources deployed by Government is below par. This reveals scope for improvement in the management of public finances. An exploration in avenues for exercising efficiency and competence is worthwhile. Even as it is beyond doubt that past actions have resulted in today's predicament it is imperative that we act today for a better tomorrow. This paper discusses options for policy-makers and managers of the economy.

Five innovative steps can be adopted by the Central Government for an immediate reduction in its interest outgo:

1. Swap its loan/bond of longer maturity which is in RBI's portfolio with shorter maturities.
2. Recall loans issued by it to public enterprises and retire its securities.
3. Recall loans issued by it to State Governments and retire its debts and allow them to go to market directly.
4. Reduce the interest rates on its National Savings instruments.
5. Realise the economic assets it holds and retire debt.

These steps are elaborated below:

1. A Government/RBI Swap: The RBI holds a large volume of Government securities. These were due to earlier developments, subscription to issues and meeting the Government's requirements from time to time. The holdings are mostly of long dated securities and loans.

The market now wants more of short term securities. There is no adequate supply of the same and this has grave consequences for the market. It loses considerable revenue as it is not able to find assets for its matching short term liabilities and secondly it does not have the incentive to chase transaction money which gives them low cost sources of funds[1].

---

1. The argument could be that the Government cannot have a large chunk of short term debt. This conventional thinking can be challenged. The market will chose short term securities as long as the SLR regime favours it and an efficient open market operation guarantee the liquidity in the secondary market.

The current net borrowing of the Government is almost at its end and the market has a feeling that there are no instruments available for short term deployment. It also hesitates to go for long term paper on the basis that there will be no liquidity in the event of a crisis and they would have to take a loss on valuation if interest rates go up.

The current yield to maturity of long term securities is around 12.25 per cent. Considering the opinion of the Reserve Bank that the interest rates ought to be stable over the near term, the Reserve Bank and the Government can take a massive swap. All securities of a coupon rate of above 12 per cent can be swapped for treasury bills of 14, 28, 42, 182 and 364 days at an average coupon rate of 9.5 per cent.

The proposal could be that Rs. 50,000 crores worth of long-dated securities which are held by the Reserve Bank of India could be swapped by Rs. 50,000 crores worth of T. Bills. Suppose the average interest outgo is 13 per cent in the case of all of these securities then the current interest outgo from that group would be Rs. 6,500 crores. If they are converted into Treasury Bills and the average coupon is 9.5 per cent, then the saving would be 3.5 per cent per annum which is amounting to Rs. 1,750 crores per year. This would be the perpetual saving of the Government of India for the next seven to eight years. This is incumbent on the interest rate on treasury bills remaining constant at 9.5 per cent in a stable economic scenario. If the financial system gets vigorous enough to chase the low cost funds in the short term market there is absolutely no fear of increase in rates.[1]

In the Mid Term Credit Policy review a mention was made of interest rate swaps for the market. A beginning can be made by the Government and RBI of engineering an interest rate swap among themselves.

1. There would be an argument that the Government's gain would be RBI's loss. It need not be the case. The RBI can sell t bills in the market for which there will be ample demand and buy back long dated securities which are running at 12 to 12.5 per cent. Then it will create an environment for more efficient management of interest rates as well as lend strength to its open market operations. The RBI cannot operate on the basis of generating revenue for itself. It has to first provide for stability of the financial sector and meet the objective of lowering cost to the Government in a market oriented scenario.

A revenue saving of Rs. 1,750 crores is a considerable saving not to mention the opportunity of utilising the same for the social sector, especially education, administration of the judiciary and other collective assets. A swap of this magnitude requires a change in mind-set. It calls for shaking up established thinking and working processes. A truly entrepreneurial organisation or person indulges in a process called by Prof. Schumpeter as "creative destruction".

2. Recall of State Government Loans: The state Government Loans are priced higher than Central Government loans. The banks are happy to subscribe as they are secure instruments and their returns are higher.

The Government has lent money to State Governments. The coupon rates are varied. The Government can recall a portion of the loans and allocate more for their borrowing from the market. This reduces the fiscal deficit of the Government, if the Government retires national or international debt. This is a win-win situation for the Central Government, State Government and the banks as the disintermediation process gives benefits to everybody. The Government need not pay high rates for national savings instruments, the state governments get the benefit of direct borrowing at lower cost and banks get higher spreads on secure investments. The gains to the economy may be in the region of Rs. 3,000 crores to Rs. 5,000 crores.

3. Recall the Loans Given by Government of India to Public Enterprises: The Government of India used to give loans to various public sector enterprises (PSEs). These loans were given for long periods at different interest rates.

The Government must recall all the loans given to all public sector enterprises and retire its debts. This will result in a reduction of fiscal deficit. The Commercial banks must be able to subscribe to bonds issued by these enterprises. The bonds can be guaranteed for repayment and interest. As the fiscal position of GOI improves due to this scenario, there will be no problem for the enterprises to repay the loans nor for Government to ensure its safety.

The Government will gain from the fact that the present interest income from these loans is lower than its payment to the market. Some of the loans would be from as low as 8 per cent to 12 per cent. When it retires its high cost debt from the market it makes a net saving.

This will also prevent the cost of intermediation. The market will directly cater to the requirement of the PSEs. They will do so gladly if the coupon rate is above 13 per cent. They will have the opportunity of deploying their funds speedily and efficiently. The Commercial banks earning will improve. Their net profitability will improve the health of the banks and thereby their ratings. The Government will earn by way of tax on their net earnings which will boost direct tax revenue. Overall outstanding amount being Rs. 20,000 crores the Government can stand to gain at least Rs. 400 crores to Rs. 500 crores not to mention the saving in administrative costs.

4. Reduction of Rate on National Savings Intstruments and Administrative Costs: When the Government can raise short term papers at 10 per cent there is no point in having high rates for National Savings instruments. The Government can reduce interest costs and administrative costs by focusing on borrowing from the market and leaving the job of retail savings to the various intermediaries in the market.

5. Realisation from Economic Assets: The Government has a disinvestment programme. The market conditions for a disinvestment programme are not exactly favourable. The Government has not thought of other innovative areas where it can realise its economic assets.

Recently Government decided to establish an independent broadcasting authority, Prasar Bharathi. The assets are huge and came progressively out of public money, from taxation and borrowings. The revenues run to Rs. 600 crores per year.

The Government could have realised some amount for its assets. Similarly, the corporatisation of the operations of the Department of Telecom can easily realise Rs. 20,000 crores if structured well. These options should be looked at seriously as the potential from looking at other sources is severely restricted at present.

Conclusion

The first four will reduce both the gross outgo of interest and reduce the net interest cost to some extent. Exercising the fifth option reduces the net interest outgo in Government.

The above steps call for not only meeting criteria for policy and objectives but also to quote a phrase from Dr. E.F. Schumacher, for "education, discipline and organisation". This is a continuous process and not a one-time declaration of intention.

The sooner we understand and implement innovative and entrepreneurial practices of which Prof. Drucker is a very good proponent, the faster we will get out of the "muddle" we are in today.

NOTES

1. There is not much change in Government's approach on spending. The fiscal situation in absolute terms is much worse than in this paper.
2. The recent figures show Government of India's interest outgo from the Budget Estimates for 2014 – 2015 at Rs.4,27,011 crores.
3. The figures for borrowings also are at extraordinary high levels from the Budget 2014 – 2015 at Rs.38,81,106.34 crores.
4. The suggestions given above still merit attention as there has not been enough focus from within and outside Government on innovative solutions to fiscal problems.
5. The Reserve Bank of India and Government of India still have long term debts on the issue calendar.
6. This will be highlighted in "India's Unbalanced Sheet", forthcoming.

Six

Transition of Primary Debt Issue from RBI to Government

[1998]

The structure of the primary market in gilts was developed over a period of time. Considerable improvements have been put in place since the decision to move from dictated to market oriented interest rates.

The management of primary issues rests with the RBI. A decision needs to be taken that the primary issues will henceforth rest with the Government. The RBI will then concentrate on the secondary market through the instrument of "open market operations". This paper examines the impact on interest rates in the process of transition.

At present there is a concern about excessive Government debt and the interest rate outgo from the budget. Everyone is "worried" that interest outgoes are too excessive and are a prime cause of the fiscal deficit and related tensions.

Since interest rate is a function of demand and supply who will be the final arbiter of interest rates? It has to be the Reserve Bank of India. In a market economy, interest rates cannot be set by talk, feeling or conveyance. It has to be met by the interaction of supply and demand of capital. Interest is also a function in time and is expressed in terms of per annum the interest rate will always be determined by the demand and supply of funds for the relative stated period of time.

If interest rate is expressed for keeping it overnight with another bank, then the demand and supply of funds in the overnight market alone will influence the rate for the day. If the contracted period is a month then interest rates are valid for that period.

The interest rate announced by the Reserve Bank of India can be basically in four categories:

1. The Bank rate or discount rate where banks can access funds for a period of four weeks from the RBI - now the rate is 9.5.
2. The repo rate where the rate is offered by the Reserve Bank for selling securities to the bank and entering into a buy back after one or three days at a certain notified interest rate - today the Repo rate is 8 per cent.
3. The funds rate, or the OMO (open market operations); a rate at which the Reserve Bank could offer to purchase and sell securities by which it absorbs all the liquidity in the system at a fixed interest rate or makes available cash by purchasing the quantities of securities offered at a fixed rate. This is not practised in India, though the RBI has the practice of offering for sale, it seldom offers to purchase.
4. The reverse repo, the rate at which the Reserve Bank lends cash against securities for a fixed period; the RBI has accepted this in principle but has neither implemented it, nor offered a price.

Given such an array of instruments the RBI can theoretically maintain equilibrium on the interest rate for the day and over a period.

Why is it then that interest rates in India are skewed? On a typical day, the interest rates on call money could be 4 per cent, discount rate 9.5 per cent, repo rate 5 per cent, bank deposit rate from public at 12 per cent, CP rate at 9.8 per cent, T-Bill rate at 9 per cent and Government loans at 11.3 to 12 per cent.

It is conclusive that our markets are fragmented. We are not an active, disciplined and organized market. There is a deficiency in our management. There are gaps in information. Furthermore, the lender of last resort, which is usually the Central Bank of the nation, has not been acting a lender of last resort.

The questions then arise are:

Who sets the interest rates for the primary market? How does the Government arrive at its decisions on matters which require daily attention and concentration?

Interest rates for consumers will be based on the secondary market. Who determines the secondary market? The operators, the individuals or the RBI?

In advanced countries the secondary market is determined by the market which is a sum total of the demand and supply of individual operations.

But again the, substratum, the foundation of the structure for interest rate is determined by the Central Bank. The ultimate money supply to the Market is controlled by this institution.

One can visualise the scenario when the Government of India has its own agency to raise debt from the primary market. The current system was structured in the control and command economy. Will it now be structured to "Manage" interest rates and "respond" to market conditions?

In this sort of scenario, how would the Government decide the cut off interest on its loans? How will it ensure that the sum required on the day will be raised? How will it decide its quantum of borrowing? Will it borrow at any cost if its requirement is excessive? Who will support the borrowing programme? Public, Banks or RBI? What will happen to devolvement? Since RBI will not issue Government paper there would be no question of devolvement on RBI; then how would the RBI support the primary issue when it commits itself not to lend to the Government over certain levels? How will the Government manage its daily cash flow? How will the treasury management take place? What will happen to the ways and means advance?

These and other questions—relevant and irrelevant—will no doubt be asked and will need to be answered effectively. If not, then there are bound to be anomalies, aberrations, distortions and gyrations. Markets will no doubt be always guessing and acting on uncertainties.

The management of the primary issue, particularly in this year and the immediate previous year has been characterised by an extraordinary interest by the Government and the RBI to "take advantage" of the lower interest rates and "trying to complete" the borrowing programme.

One would be under the presumption that the Government and RBI should not look to their sole interest but be pragmatic and far sighted in their approach.

The Government cannot take a position that it needs to borrow urgently or more than necessary to take "advantage". If so, it will have to face the economic consequences when things are not so favourable and it makes the effort of borrowing when the funds position is tight.

The market today reads the Government programme from different perspectives. The short term and medium term papers are viewed differently from long term papers (more than five years).

At present the primary issue of securities is handled by the Reserve Bank of India on behalf of the Government. The Reserve Bank decides the amount, type of security, tenor, the coupon rate and more important the timing of the issue.

It has been widely debated and discussed in the Government, at RBI and at various committees that the primary issues should move away from the RBI and be taken over by the Government. This is a positive step that must be taken up and implemented forthwith. It would be incumbent on the Government of India to organise the requisite competence and expertise in this matter which now resides with the RBI.

Once a decision in principle has been taken, a smooth and efficient transfer is a must. Otherwise the financial markets would be in a state of turmoil. The next important step is to manage the transition. Both these can be achieved without much of a strain when a carefully articulated programme is envisaged and launched. Assuming that an efficient transition and transfer process is underway a minimum and maximum time frame is the first step that has to be undertaken.

It therefore evolves that a proper plan has to be in place when Government takes over the debt programme. It would be prudent if it takes into account every known contingency. Later it could develop its own stance and master the techniques of primary debt management.

It has therefore necessarily submitted to central bank independence. And once it is subservient, its plan of action has to take into account all factors in the market. The paramount importance will be to meet its own demands from the market. Whenever its own borrowing is excessive, then it will cause a rise in interest rates and thereby increase its own cost and the theory of crowding out will occur denying the other productive sectors of the economy.

The influence of Government Borrowing on interest rates, monetary policy and foreign exchange movement should be separately analysed by RBI management. The interest rate should be solely concentrated as for its own sake and as a corner stone of future Central Bank's policy.

The Government's MOF should now have its focus on Government Borrowing and exercise its options purely on the current monetary stand of the RBI.

The fundamental philosophy in a modern Central Bank is its independence. By independence, it does not mean physical independence or presence of authority. Presumably, it would mean independence from the influence of the Government and its thinking on the minds of persons who have control on monetary and credit policies. As a policy, when it delinks itself from the Government's borrowing programme, the RBI will be singularly concentrating on the secondary market and will determine the market's direction on money supply and interest rates.

The Reserve Bank of India will have an even tougher job on its hands in the future. As it is, it is under deeper scrutiny than ever before, not only by the Indian financial institutions but also the world markets, the international institutions and international financial operators. As the nominal size of the economy grows, the policies and practices of yesterday get outworn and obsolete even on a daily basis. It has to confront the market on an hourly basis rather than over a period of time. Its action or lack of it will have impacts which will be measurable in minutes.

This again is a question of management than that of policy; a question of practices, tasks and responsibilities. This equally applies to the managers of the public debt as well as the "mandarins" at the Ministry of Finance. The immediate task before the RBI and more so in the Ministry of Finance, not to speak of the market operators, is to get prepared for this event. Details must not be spared.

At first, the RBI must develop a dichotomy. The top management must divest itself from the management of primary debt and concentrate on developing and deploying tools to moderate the Interest Rate structure to for the days to come. The top management should first fine tune the open market operations and its effect on the secondary markets. The mechanics of transparency should be first discussed and then disseminated. Its interaction and participation in the open market should broaden and deepen at the institutional and personal level. No doubt, the physical infrastructure of dealing in the securities in secondary market should be taken care of.

The second tier should be left to manage the primary market. The cut off limits, the management and timing should be structured for a smooth transition to the Government. The practices and procedures should be laid down so that they will be understood easily by future operators. The thinking process should develop now to enable the Government to take current and future decisions based on the interest rate structure of the bank as decided by top management.

At present, it is learnt that a calendar has been done. The RBI has the calendar and gives notice to the market only a few days in advance. Sometimes, it resorts to borrowing depending on market liquidity conditions rather than the need to borrow. A calendar should be made considering the Government's actual cash flow requirements and treasury management.

A tentative calendar is tabled below for consideration. This can be modified or improved upon. This calendar takes into account an ideal mix which will help the Government to have a systematic programme and the market to plan its mix, shuffling and realisation of Government securities.

The market appetite for short term funds is going to grow in the future. The asset-liability matching programme which is launched should also note that the market already has excess long term securities in hand.

There is, on the other hand huge demand for short term paper which is not satisfied. This has partly resulted in skewing of interest rates. A larger issue of short term treasury bills not only reduces the interest cost for Government, but also satisfies the demand for such paper.

This is precisely where fine tuning in the management of Government borrowings is called for. If the United States can borrow US Dollar 6.6 Trillion in the market keeping both interest rates and inflation under control, there is a good case for building up the financial institutions to take care of India's requirements too.

The ways and means advance can be done away with, as market conditions will always permit the Government to access the funds in the markets for its weekly requirements.

The following table gives an indication how a calendar can be formulated for primary issue of Government securities:

Issuing Calendar for Securities

	Issue	Redemption
1. a) 14 days T. Bill	Friday	Thursday
b) 14 days T. Bill convertible	Wednesday	Tuesday
2. 42 days T. Bill	Thursday	Wednesday
3. 91 days T. Bill	Tuesday	Monday
4. 364 days T. Bill	Wednesday	Tuesday
5. 1½ to 3 years Tenor Security, Loan Bonds **Every Tuesday**	Tuesday	
6. 3 to 5 years (FOUR TIMES A MONTH) Security Loan Bonds **Every Wednesday**		Wednesday
7. 3 to 5 years maturity (TWICE A MONTH) Security Loan Bonds **Every 2nd and 4th Wednesday**	Wednesday	
8. 5 to 8 years (ONCE IN A MONTH) Security Loan Bonds **Every 3rd Friday of the Month**	Friday	
9. 8 to 15 years (ONCE IN 3 MONTHS) **of Every 3rd Week of February, May, August and Nov.)**	Thursday	

- In the above calendar the operator can always move from short term to long term easily.
- There is no need for 28 days and 182 days as issues in fixed Calendar will give scope in the secondary market.
- The calendar for long term has to be fixed in advance. This gives the long term investor time to plan his commitment.
- On sudden requirements the Government can keep more money for itself when offered on the day auctions.
- The Government can always raise fresh money to repay previous loans or Bills.
- Reserve Bank can participate in secondary market in a way that can absorb liquidity or support the market by buying

and selling such securities in the market that will keep the interest rates range-bound.
- In the era of rapid inflows and outflows and the potential for greater volume of transactions in the domestic market, the RBI should effectively participate in secondary market to ensure that interest rates do not go below a certain level and rise above a certain level for a given period.
- The Banking and Financial Sector will then concentrate on maximising yields for each segment of their resources.
- This would result in economic efficiency as the sector would not have resources idle at any point of time.
- It would be beneficial if RBI/Government resorts to "benchmark issues" of bonds.
- As Banker to Government, RBI can offer a flexible operating account where it can deposit money for short period and even interest.

Conclusion

It is imperative that the Reserve Bank announces a "predictable issuing calendar" for raising debts on behalf of the Government. This programme should be carried forward by the Government.

It should develop the dichotomy in itself on determination of the interest rate for the secondary market and make the primary subservient to it.

The process of transfer of primary issue and its later management from RBI to the Government must be harmonious and not lead to anomalies, distortions and aberrations.

The above objective can be obtained within the ambit of the macroeconomic parameters that any central bank looks for without losing sight of the micro economic factor, i.e. skewing of interest rates.

NOTES

1. The main issue raised in this is that Government has to decide about having a dedicated agency in the Primary Issue of debt.
2. This is not merely a budgetary process on how it can economically raise debt but also ensuring that the financial system subscribes to its debt so that it can keep itself liquid.

3. Debt is raised to clear previous debt as well as to meet the capital and revenue expenditure of the Government in that year.
4. This requires a thorough internal review and can be supported by the polity in India.
5. Any risk factors associated with Government raising debt on its own need to be evaluated internally within the Government of India and the Ministry of Finance.
6. This requires a mastery on the interest rate situation and very careful assessments on financial flows within India and externally.
7. It is made out that this process has to be extremely cautious and needs a systematic approach.
8. Sufficient material is available from expert committees on this subject.
9. Parliament oversight on the Sovereign debt of India as well as the debt markets is more than ever needed and the required inputs to Parliamentary committees must get enhanced.

Seven

Evolution of an Interest Rate Structure for India

[1999]

The interest rates in the economy have exhibited a skewed behaviour since the liberalisation process started in 1991. Information contained in documents, including, the successive Economic Surveys of the Government of India, various reports from the financial dailies and periodicals, and own experience, reveal that interest rates for each category of transaction between a lender and a borrower have not been harmonious and symmetrical.

Interest rate is expressed as the price paid for borrowing money for a period of time.

In developing or least developed economies, interest rates are determined either by the Government or the Central Bank of a nation. All other institutions, operators and individuals are then subordinate and subservient to the Central Bank and its policies. The more advanced and mature the financial system, more refined becomes the role and intervention of the Central Bank.

In advanced economies, the market is considered supreme and Central Banks have to take cognisance of the sum total of demand and supply, not only within their borders but across all economies where capital is freely convertible and no controls on capital flow exist.

The importance of a study of the interest rate structure is to understand the impact of interest rates in a market economy on all stakeholders within the market ecosystem. In a market economy, no single person can determine the rate, but the operators in the market as a whole determines the interest rates. When we say the market determines the rate, it would be the aggregate supply and aggregate demand that would influence the interest rate in particular segments. Systematic research would then reveal how interest rates act in practice vis-à-vis theory.

The hypothesis is that the interest rate structure for the economy has to evolve around the interest rates set by the Reserve Bank of India, as it is the ultimate controller or manager of supply and demand of money.

A close examination of various interest rates set by the Reserve Bank of India, for deposits and lending by the operators, and interest rates for money market and capital market instruments over a period from 1991 to date reveals a variety of rates. Rates have also fluctuated narrowly and widely over years, over months, over weeks, over days and also within a day.

The market operations seem to have integrated over the last 10 months. Any variations, anomalies, aberrations and distortions could have taken place due to gaps in information, sudden shortages or surpluses, gradual impact of key macro economic and micro economic components, externalities, Government policy or absence thereof and of course, RBI policy, procedures and action.

It is more important to conduct independent research on the structure prior to 1991. Interest rates were directed in that era, when the operation of the market forces was limited. The allocations of investments or credit by the financial institutions and banks were made on a mandated basis. The avenues for investment by private sector was varied and rich enough for satisfying demand for investible resources and rates, though directed, were in line with economic fundamentals.

It would be an area of tremendous scope for research in interest rate behaviour and its causes in the Indian economy from 1991 to now. The study would reveal not just the inadequacies of data, information, knowledge, management, skills and equipment within the financial sector, but also it would be able to unravel the very process of formulation of policy during transition from a command economy to a market economy.

The conclusion would be that the individuals and operators in the market were ahead of the policy makers and the central bankers in the absorption of the concept of market. At the same time, it would conclude that the gradual process was far better than the faster process advocated by many commentators.

A policy framework alone will not be enough to manage a market economy very well. While operators have good measures, in the form of results, by which performance is measured, the Government and the Central Bank do not have such measures. The success of any programme managed by these institutions should be measured by only one parameter: Economic efficiency.

> Markets rest on a foundation of institutions. Like the air we breathe, some of the public goods these institutions provide are so basic to daily economic life as to go unnoticed. Only when these goods are absent, as in many developing countries today, do we see their importance for development. Without the rudiments of social order, underpinned by institutions, markets cannot function.
>
> *World Development Report 1997*, Chapter 3, p. 41

Unfortunately, the scenario reveals that sectarian and narrow views have prevailed. Whenever, any policy is decided, its impact on the Government, its fiscal management and its finances are dominating the issue and not necessarily that of the public.

The TABLE attached gives the picture of interest rates on the widest spectrum. It has been classified into four areas: 1) Rates determined by the Reserve Bank of India; 2) Rates meant for the funds of the public across all possible choices; 3) Rates for instruments where both the financial sector and the individuals among public have access to; and 4) The inter bank market.

The true principle of the market that is the operation of fundamentals is not spread evenly on the economy as a whole. This is primarily due to the fragmentation of financial markets and arbitrary allocations of the investment, credit and lending portfolios. Even here, there is no reason why interest rates to the market should vary.

The markets also function in a situation where the individual operators function in an atomic environment and even though integration exists between other players in the financial markets and the Reserve Bank of India, it is not thoroughly organic.

The rates from 1991 to 1998 reveal a wide variation across the board in individual components for some items. For others, particularly, the Government National Savings instruments, it has remained remarkably static. This reveals the combination of static and dynamic activity in the financial sector.

Rates are indicative and based on secondary sources. They may be off the mark in some respects. It is left to economic research assistants in the financial sector to pick up exact rates for the entire period.

If the Ministry of Finance or Reserve Bank of India chooses to do so, they can direct banks to furnish precise rates from the Pre-1991 and Post-1991 periods. Each element of interest rates is required to be analysed for the operators to reflect on.

Interest Rate Structure for India

Interest rate structure for India needs to be examined for each of the established and popular financial segments. An attempt is made to give shape to the interest rates in each segment to arrive at a structure.

Discount Rate (Bank Rate): Discount rate is set by the Reserve Bank of India. This rate of interest has to be determined by considerable deliberation and the decision has to be taken weighing all aspects, macro-economic and micro-economic, the financial parameters of the banking system, and the effects of changes of rates on the entire economy.

The effectiveness of the discount rate depends on the amount accessible to the Commercial Bank and the nature of the use of funds. Competence in the administration of this mechanism will make the financial system competitive. This mechanism was frozen for a long period and revived only recently. The author does not have access to the periodicity and the outstanding amount under this window to individual banks or the whole system.

In the situation given today, the discount rate or the bank rate has been ineffective on the interest structure as a whole in comparison with mature markets.

In the mature markets, no citizen can get interest from the banks on deposits made by them at a rate higher than the discount rate. In India it is not so. The explanation for it may be available with both banks and the Reserve Bank of India. But then what should the discount rate be?

If one takes the bank's deposit rate and applies the position of the mature markets in reverse, then the discount rate should be

12.5 to 13 per cent, which is higher than all the rates offered in the market today.

If the current rate of nine per cent is right and if the operators are in a mature market, then no deposit rate should be more than 8.5 per cent for deposits for any tenure.

The author's opinion is that the discount rate should be between 10.5 and 11 per cent and the access to the funds should be three per cent of the bank's assets. These should make it attractive enough for banks to keep all deposit rates below the discount level.

Subject to the situation that the discount rate has been correctly determined, all interest rates in the country have to be aligned towards the same. In a scenario where markets behave unexpectedly, the changes are due to an underlying phenomenon beyond the immediate comprehension of the Reserve Bank of India and the operators, indicating an unexpected source of demand for funds or an unexpected supply of funds. This gives scope for providing a correction or a tremendous opportunity for innovation and entrepreneurship.

REPO Rate: The current repo rate is eight per cent. A discussion is necessary as to what the repo rate should be and how it is to be constantly operated. Obviously, the repo rate acts as an indicator for the Banks to keep their short term money with the Central Bank. It is worthwhile to study, for instance, how Germany operates the repo rate.

The REPO rate has worked admirably well since it was raised to eight per cent. It has prevented the gyrations in the call money market. It provides a choice for a safe overnight investment for banks. The call money market will remain in a narrow range instead of wide fluctuations on the lower side.

The efficiency of the banking system and return on assets will be optimum. Otherwise, banks with sudden short term inflows will not have a safe avenue for their funds.

As the market has to read a clear signal on interest rates, the RBI has to target REPO rates lower than the discount rate. How close is the question to be answered next? As the choice of the individual banks at any one point of time is either the REPO or the discount depending on whether it has surplus funds or need for funds, the choice rests with either the market or the central bank. In the market it can either resort to call money, or sell securities. Both are feasible, but again to what extent?

If the Reserve Bank of India targets REPO at one per cent below the Discount rate then, in an active and mature market the call money will necessarily fluctuate between a band of that one per cent.

This answers the question on what the market should read as the call money rate is required to be.

It will always have to be between the REPO rate and the Discount rate.

In today's scenario the call money is bang on target, i.e. between eight and nine per cent. Though, occasionally it does drop below eight, recently it has not gone above the discount rate.

Reverse REPO: A reverse-repo is source for temporary funds for the banking sector. This practice has been considered in principle but not put into practice. The Reverse Repo is an important instrument to be used in the run towards perfect market conditions.

It offers a safety valve when a particular bank needs to shift resources from lower yield to higher yield for a particular period or needs funds after exhausting the options of discount window, the call money market, open market operations or selling securities in the market without loss.

More interesting would be the use of this tool as a benchmark for an upper limit for the inter-bank and securities markets.

Even though, at present the call-money markets are stable and Government securities yield perfectly aligned, previous experience during periods of volatility on account of policy measures, externalities, and movement in the foreign exchange market indicate that short term rates can get out of hand. The operators need an effective tool to maintain the short term liquidity in the entire market.

The Reverse Repo rate can therefore be set at about 150 to 200 basis points above the highest Government security rate for the past four weeks.

The importance of the above indicators should not be underrated. These can be the most powerful signals that the Reserve Bank of India can provide today to the Indian and global markets. As emphasised the rate itself has to be right. Once the rates are announced they have to be maintained by action to ensure that all demand and supply for that particular tool is met.

Another factor is that the market must be subservient to the Central Bank's direction in these three parameters. Supply and demand of funds in individual markets could make it possible for banks to move out of these ranges. The operators should do their utmost to maintain equilibrium within these parameters. Opportunities would be available to maximise their profit opportunities by managing their activity efficiently by determining their cost and realisation. Banks need to ensure that they will have a regular and profitable spread.

Funds Rate or the OMO Rate

There are no active open market operation in India of the type and size prevailing in the US. The open market operations of the FED are highly efficient. This rate is the benchmark interest rate of the world's largest economy and global financial markets. It also absorbs and provides the demand and supply of funds in such a way that the market is always at equilibrium. This has already been emphasised in Chapter 2.

Without an effective purchase, open market operations do not have the wholesomeness and fullness of character and will hence fail in their objectives and purposes at the times needed most by the market.

Just as the discount rate is the key rate in Japan, Germany, and UK the funds rate is key in the US. It will entirely depend on the Reserve Bank of India, whether the discount rate or Bank rate will be the key or the Funds/OMO rate will be the guide to the market. It could be a combination of both as the Reserve Bank currently is not giving full throttle to the supply of funds under the discount umbrella and it is a very restrictive and procedure oriented function. The Open Market Operations, being the selling and buying of Government securities, will provide a better window for deploying funds and ensuring liquidity in one window of operations will be a more valuable tool for giving direction to the interest rates. This rate itself depends on the overall rates for Government securities.

There should be no confusion between the coupon rates or rates decided for different tenor of Government securities and the open market operation rate. The OMO rate will become effective rate for the financial market for parking of "temporary" funds in the event of liquidity and a cut-off point for selling securities in the event of need for funds. Hence, it is more of a homogenisation process for harmonising interest rates without losing the opportunity of earning on one's funds.

This OMO rate has naturally to have a correlation with the Government securities rate which in turn depends on the general interest rates. The OMO rate has to be necessarily higher than the discount rate. The extent can be 1 to 1.5 per cent higher than the discount rate depending on the level of liquidity and interest direction the Reserve Bank has to provide here.

At this point in time, it is necessary to point out that the nature of operations in the OMO demand that there should be a large volume of identifiable and benchmark securities for the convenience of the Reserve Bank of India as well as the operators.

Since OMO could result in large volumes from the entire sector, there must be sufficient volume and depth in the securities market. Another point to bear is that such securities should not have Loan, or Security components which have interest pay-outs. This will make the pricing and trading difficult. For instance, if one security is bought this Friday and sold next Thursday, the trader must realise the interest as a difference between the buy and sell price.

It is, therefore, advisable that RBI should offer OMO only in Treasury Bills of 14, 42, 180 and 364 Days. All such T. Bills should have a denomination of not less than Rs. 10,000 or even Rs. 100,000. Trading should be up to two decimal points. In this eventuality, the realisation will be perfect. Similarly, in the medium and long term segments, the OMO should be in ZERO coupon bonds.

For ensuring that the supply of sufficient short term securities are available. A proposal has already been made in Chapter 5.

Current Account: The current rate is 0 and can continue to be so.

Bankers have to be cautious that in an era of efficiency, there will be a lesser tendency to keep large amounts in current account. Competition will create conditions where large corporations or current account holders will be offered options by competing banks to invest in securities. There would also be opportunity for clients to earn money for temporary periods by resorting to buying/ selling of specific T. Bills or securities.

Savings Bank: This rate is still under regulation. The author has pleaded for deregulation since the last few years with RBI. The time is ripe now for deregulation. The band can be set at 0 to

8 per cent to begin with. Each bank can offer tailor made SB accounts. These accounts would factor separately cost of services, i.e. pricing of cheque books and credit entries, service charges, etc. and offer a higher level of interest. Another choice could be excluding interest up to a certain amount to bring down costs of transaction.

There could be some confusion among customers to begin with as many banks; especially the smaller and newer ones loose no opportunity in one-upmanship to improve their profile. They choose to do it by competing in interest rates. Given the time for clients to understand this move can wait for sometime but at the same time, banks can be given a broad guideline on the possibilities of the future so that all banks have opportunities for evaluating products for consumers.

Fixed Deposit: The fixed deposit is the major component of the banks in its service area and in attracting and keeping of customers. The current FD rates are enclosed in Annexure I.

The present scenario reveals a certain maturity. All operators have aligned within themselves within a range of two per cent. It is an Indian phenomenon that can be confirmed by research that FD rates also go up during an economic or political upheaval. This is during times of volatility in the financial markets or during a foreign exchange management crisis.

As outlined earlier in the part on discount rate, technically all fixed deposit rates should be below the discount rate.

It is an unfortunate phenomenon today that all bank business at the branch level and the apex level in any Bank is that the performance of a branch, a region, a state or the country is measured in terms of deposits raised. This approach needs a correction. It is well understood that deposits raised must find a destination. The destination will be the CRR, the SLR, the securities market, and the loans and advances to customers.

Chasing deposits for the sake of deposits is the source of all irritants within the banking sector. The managers and advisers should work out a better set of parameters for measuring branch and national performance.

The deposit rates have been manipulated with in order to attract business to the bank. Now, FD rates are determined at the national level for all the branches. Certain discretion has been given to banks to attract high volume deposits.

It is argued that interest rates on deposits should not be an avenue of competition. This is especially so if the Government and RBI desire that economic efficiency of the whole system is to be taken into account.

Whenever there is any attempt made by banks to equalise deposit rates overtly or covertly, it gets a backlash of criticism of cartelisation and accusations of effects of monopoly. When it is left to the market, individual operators i.e. the banks, vary the interest rates frequently and the customer is confused and deflated. For instance, if a customer has just renewed a deposit for three years at the rate of 11.5 per cent in one bank and suddenly the next day another bank announces 12.25 per cent for the same tenure, the customers feel a level of frustration.

Take for instance; in any developed country the banks have almost the same rates for deposits. The variation could be sometimes less than 0.10 or 0.15 per cent. The natural question would be—have the banks colluded with each other to keep those rates at the same level. The author has no specific answer, but it is alluded that the answer is no, because the law on anti-trust and monopoly is much stricter in those countries than in other countries.

Then how do the rates operate in such a narrow range? The answer is the market. The financial market has developed into such a level of maturity, that the citizen or the financial sector can move massive amounts of funds within a matter of seconds for a fraction of a percentage point difference in yield. The sheer impact of demand and supply on such transaction forces operators not to price their products at too high a difference from equilibrium.

To make it more specific, if Bank A declares an interest rate of 7.6 per cent against the rate of 7.5 per cent by Bank B, then immediately about 3 to 4 billion Sterling or US dollar will shift from Bank B to Bank A. This will force either bank B to raise the interest rate and match it to his competitor or the bank A will find more funds than he can use or hit his capital adequacy ceiling and will be forced to roll back his interest rate. Therefore, any conversation with a bank executive working in London will tell you, that they do not go out to seek deposits but continuously look out for good borrowers. If one finds a good borrower and earmark funds, then they can easily raise the required deposits or match it with a borrowing from the inter-bank market.

In India, we have a compartmentalised segment in the market. The surest sign in an advanced economy is maturity, which results in an organic market. There has to be a tremendous effort in integrating the financial system within the banks and also geographically, in India. On this event, the markets will get the required information and the physical matching of demand and supply and the prices will get narrower.

In today's context and structure of the banking system, it is advisable that the bank boards take their own decisions. In the process, they should look to the financial system as a whole. No doubt that there may be occasions to give higher rates to depositors on account of good positions in their credit portfolio or their profitability is higher than that of manufacture or services industry. This does not call for disturbing the FD rate structure unusually. In the same way, banks with low profitability should not look to lowering rates unusually just to exploit their position with a geographical market or with particular class of depositors. This game of offering higher rates has been especially followed by smaller private banks and the newly started banks. With better technology and marketing, they have used FD rates as a tool to bring in new customers from the entrenched banks. Some banks have not followed social obligations imposed in terms of priority sector and export credit. Having an advantage of a higher yield on their assets they seek to pass them on to their depositors.

Keeping this in view, the FD rates need not be less than 150 basis points to the discount rate. The spread between different maturities should be the same as that in the money market. In today's structure, if the discount rate is nine per cent then the rate would be 7.5 to 9 per cent. Again, under any circumstance the FD rate should not be more than the discount rate. In the event it does so, it should be considered an aberration worthy of enquiry and investigation by all operators and the Reserve Bank as to whether there has been a fundamental shift in the demand and supply of funds in the whole economy.

CD: CD rate should be higher than FD rates by 50 to 200 basis points depending on need for funds and matching use.

FCNR Rates: The FCNR rates are priced correctly now.

NRE Account: This account should be priced slightly lower than domestic deposits. The Reserve Bank can stipulate that 25 per cent of NRE deposits have to be backed by foreign balances.

This will reduce the load of the Reserve Bank in maintaining of foreign reserves.

NRNR Account: During a certain period, NRNR Accounts were freed from interest rate controls and also exempt from statutory reserve requirements. The rates shot up to 18 per cent. Now these rates are stable. There is no reason why these deposits should be priced higher than domestic rates. The Reserve Bank can stipulate that 20% of NRNR deposits should be backed by foreign Balances. This will cover Interest repatriation in forex.

PPF: Should be priced 100 basis points below FD rate as it is tax free.

NSC: KVP/IVP: Should be priced at FD rate or OMO rate.

T-BILL: T-BILL should be marginally below discount rate.

GILT: Gilt should be equal to the funds rate or OMO rate. + / - 25 basis points.

T-Bill Convertible: Should be priced by auction. Cut off at 200-300 basis points below domestic T-Bill Rate.

NBFC Deposit Rate: The NBFC deposit rates should not be more than one per cent over the FD rate for that period. The NBFC deposit rates are enclosed in Annexure-II.

Company FD: Company FD System should be abolished. Companies should resort to market only and not canvas retail FDs.

Corp DEB: Corp Debentures may become redundant if Corporate Bonds are popular.

Corporate Bond: The Corporate Bond market in India is undeveloped. There is a need to develop homogenous corporate bond as an instrument. Initially, it should be targeted at the financial sector, which can be later retailed to the individual customers. The Corporate Bond rates are enclosed in Annexure-III.

The rate of interest on the Corporate Bond can be 14.25 to 18 per cent depending on the risk perception. Corporate bonds can be issued for different tenors from 1 yr. to 5 yr. to begin with.

The strategy for development of a corporate bond will be outlined in a separate chapter.

PSE/PUB NCD: PSE Bonds may be more attractively priced.

FI Bond: FI Bond being one issued by an institution cannot be priced more than the FD rate. Otherwise FI should borrow in the Inter Bank Market.

Call Money: Call money should hover between the REPO rate and the discount rate.

MIBOR: Mibor should be priced above the discount rate

PCFC US $ and PC Rupee: The PCFC rates are priced correctly now.

PLR: The PLR has now become a board decided and well-structured interest rate. There is no aberration in the pricing of the PLR at present. It is dynamic enough to respond to market conditions governed by discernment and competitive conditions.

LTPLR: LTPLR should reflect the difference in the yield curve as well as the risk premium.

Commercial Paper: Rate on Commercial Paper today is less than PLR. It is an anomalous situation. It should be equal to PLR.

Loan 1, Loan 2, Loan 3, Loan Unsecured: These are now priced at difference of 100 basis points. This should be decided by board.

Bill Discounting: All Bills Discounting should be priced at PLR + risk premia.

Term Loan SSI: Same as PLR.

Auto Financing Banks: Priced at top of loan slabs.

NBFC Lending Rate: The lending rates also should not exceed two per cent points over the banks highest lending rate.

Lease Cost: Lease Cost pricing should operate on a low interest cost scenario.

Small Savings Rate: The small savings rate should be in total alignment with the bank structure. Small savings should compete in service and security offered and not in rates. A review of Small Savings Rate has been made in Chapter 2.

This completes the review of interest rate for the public from the banking sector.

Government Securities: The Government Securities market is a key pointer towards the deployment of funds in any economy. What would be the interest rates for Government securities in a market oriented economy? The answer is provided here in an analysis of the nine major markets.

It is noticeable that the interest differential between the overnight market and the Government Securities is ranging from as low as 16 basis points. The Corporate Bond is higher by 60-70 basis points but also lower in some cases. The prices reflect true market conditions as some Corporate Bonds reveal lower yield compared to Government securities. There is also a differential between spot rates and forward rates depending on the economic outlook of respective countries.

Interest rates % p.a. (Feb. 3rd 1999)

Country	Over night	3-mth money market latest	3-mth money market year	Banks prime	2-year govt. bonds	10-year govt. latest	10-year govt. year ago	Corporate Bonds
Australia	4.75	4.77	5.01	8.75	4.83	5.24	5.92	5.80
Britain	6.25	5.66	7.50	7.00	4.87	4.24	6.10	5.14
Canada	4.90	4.75	4.56	6.75	4.86	5.02	5.42	6.07
Denmark	3.75	3.61	3.84	6.50	3.44	4.08	5.38	7.10
Japan	0.20	0.49	0.78	1.50	0.86	2.45	2.00	1.71
Sweden	3.40	3.20	4.39	3.64	3.36	4.08	5.61	3.97
Switzerland	1.17	1.24	1.19	3.00	1.59	2.42	2.96	3.07
United States	4.56	4.76	5.40	7.75	4.69	4.83	5.56	6.56
Euro-11	3.19	3.09	4.24	4.50	2.94	3.63	na	3.58

Source: The Economist, Feb. 6-12, 1999.

In India, it is doubtful whether the Government securities market will remain so fine tuned. In the directed market, the rates were fixed. Now the rates are variable and the auction system has been introduced. Given today's market conditions, the rates have remained remarkably within range, both in the primary markets and the secondary markets.

It is a noticeable phenomenon that the rates of some securities have fluctuated in the past beyond range. The Treasury bill market (secondary) went as high as 18 to 20 per cent during exchange rate volatility. Recently, the market has developed a reasonably established gilt yield curve. Compared to a few months ago, the market has exhibited considerably improved maturity.

Recently, newspaper reports and the daily financial presentations by leading business newspapers are a valuable source of information. These are given with vivid graphics on the securities market. This is a positive development and the sign of a maturing market. More accurate information on the inflow and outflow of funds from and to the banking system on account of the securities is now provided.

State Government and Municipal bonds should be developed along the above lines and can be priced higher than the Central Government bonds.

The mechanism for improving the gilts market is explained in Chapter 3.

Other Advances: Other advances can operate in a band of four per cent over PLR. Individual banks follow their own policies on pricing interest rate based on credit criteria. This structure is adequate.

Export Credit: Export credit rates are now priced at nine and will be restored to 11 per cent. At 11 per cent, it is priced correctly. But there is scope for improving this rate to PLR as the option is always there for the exporter to access cheaper finance through PCFC.

The pricing for SSI Term Loans, Auto Financing Banks, LTPLR and NBFC Lending should be priced on differential in costs and risk perceptions.

Each segment is an "individual market" in economic terms. Variations in interest rates constitute effect of change in fundamentals. The "vision" or "indicative" rates are provided not from the point of view of idealism but from a rational, economic and management point of view.

What is provided is an "outside" view. Any variation in pricing is an entrepreneurial opportunity. An attempt has been made to present scope for harmony. It is required of policy makers and bankers to deliberate on this issue.

Conclusion

a) It is necessary for all players in the market to integrate. Integration should imply that economic fundamentals should play a more dominant part than individual or sectional views.

b) The Government of India and Reserve Bank of India should play a truly institutional role. After due deliberation and appreciation of thought by political, executive, academia and in the view of general public, economic efficiency should be declared as the end goal and the means to achieve it must be deliberated on.

c) The Reserve Bank of India should be able to both absorb and provide short term liquidity without the least effect on interest rates. Monetary and macro policy for the long term and management of fund-flow for the short term must be integrated without disturbing equilibrium on an hourly, daily or weekly basis. This has been a declared intention but interest rates do not reflect it carried out in practice, especially in unusual and unanticipated situations.

d) The Indian market is not short of ideas or entrepreneurial abilities. What it is lacking at times is education, organisation and discipline. Lack of all these or any one element at a particular time can distort markets and prices.

e) The maximum benefit to the Indian population would take place when market operators take their profits from honest earnings and not by manipulation or deceit. Institutions work efficiently when they provide the necessary requirements at all times for common good.

f) Interest being a price for money, it is best that it is not reduced or increased or used for a benefit or detriment of a particular section of the population. Whenever any section deserves attention, other means can be thought of.

g) Conditions should be prescribed for operators of the market to function efficiently. What is more important is that the human element should take precedence. People should matter in Indian conditions given a set of principles, codes and practices. Interest rates can operate in harmony even with infra-structural constraints. To make a statement that harmony will have to wait for technology, and anomalies, aberrations and distortions will persist till such time, reveals lack of authority, direction and leadership.

NOTES

1. This paper was written in 1999. Within a period of just five years, a revolution had taken place in the financial markets in India.
2. A reasonably good structure has evolved with an active role played by all market functionaries.
3. There is definitely scope for building the interest rate structure more seriously by Parliament, Government of India, State Governments, Reserve Bank of India, Universities and Institutes, and the public.
4. Detailed study and research can evolve improvements in institutions as well as introduce education, organisation and self-discipline amongst operators in the financial market as well as within Government of India, State Governments and RBI.

Eight

Interest Rates and Exchange Rate Premia

[1999]

The Indian economy after 1991 has undergone a change for the better after a series of measures that created the conditions for movement from a managed to a market economy.

This controlled or plodding change has proved to be an exercise borne out of intellectual ability blended with pragmatism. This process which has been named as "gradualism" has proved to be on hindsight, far better than the rapid change that has happened in East Asia and the traumatic conditions prevailing in Russia.

This chapter discusses the correlation between interest rates and the exchange rate premium that prevails in India and its effects on the decisions and behavioural aspect of the Indian financial system and the exporters and importers.

Exchange Rate Movements

The players in the Indian financial system and the exporters and importers in India had very limited choices in the system of cover for their forex exposures.

The exporters and importers had choices to cover their forward exposures up to six months. The system allowed for exposures for merchant transactions only. Economic liberalisation has made available more choices to exporters, importers, investors, NRIs and individuals.

The exchange rate is expressed now both for spot and forward. Forward exposures are standard for six months and available up to one year. This service is provided by Authorised Dealers (AD), primarily Banks.

In the forward market the exchange rate quoted is at a premium or discount. A premium is the additional amount expressed that the seller will get or the buyer has to pay in selling or buying the currency of trading.

This premium is expressed in the unit of currency as well as in percentage terms. Since the premium is usually for periods ranging from days, weeks or months, the financial system measures the premium also on the basis of a percentage called the annualised premium.

The spot rate of a currency against another currency undergoes changes every day if it is a floating currency. This is a result of the supply interacting with demand.

The demand and supply on a particular day, of a particular currency determines the spot rate not only for the day but for every minute of trading that takes place during the day. It naturally follows that the demand and supply of the particular currency determines the forward rates for the particular currency.

In India, the policy of "Managed float" is adopted. The Table 8.1 shows the forward rates for the US Dollars (for purchase by AD) on 27.5.99 and the annualised premium.

Table 8.1

US$

SPOT Rs. 42.80	Rate Rs.	Premium in Paise	Annualised Premium %
1 month	42.96	16	4.49
2 month	43.14	34	4.77
3 month	43.34	54	5.05
4 month	43.54	74	5.19
5 month	43.73	93	5.21
6 month	43.95	115	5.37

Source: Canara Bank, F.D. Mangalore.

This is the reproduction of a chart on the forward premium in annualised percentage terms.

Variations in Premia, Criteria and Causes

The issue for discussion is that of distorted structures in the annualised premium 4 to 5 times in the last seven years. It also projects exchange rate premium during stable times. By distortion, it is meant that the premia went beyond the interest rate difference. The Table 8.2 reveals exchange rate premium prevailing at different times.

In economic or commercial terms, the exchange rate premium should be the difference between the interest rates of the two currencies. This could happen when capital flows between the two countries are sufficiently large and the institutions trading are sufficiently strong and the markets have sufficient depth with adequate number of players.

In India the sources of supply and demand are from merchant transactions, coupled with inflows and outflows of capital. Exchange rate fluctuations take place on intra-day basis as well as for the forward based on the demand and supply for the particular month.

Future demand and supply is based not on physical availability but on the basis of perceptions, notions, projections, feelings and a host of subjective issues backed by the needs and decisions of the players. The supply and demand for futures is therefore on the basis of "agreement to sell (or buy)".

The financial system takes the cue from the providers of supply and demand and the market determines the future rate also. It also follows that the buyers and sellers of foreign exchange depend on the financial system for service as well as information and opinion based on which they take their decisions. In India, till recently all foreign exchange had to be sold to RBI at the end of the day.

What exactly is therefore the role of interest rates in the future market? None, if it is purely a paper market but substantial if the financial system uses the current supply to satisfy future demand.

Current demand has to be satisfied with current supply. But how is future demand to be met with future supply and vice versa? This could happen only if every merchant or capital transaction is exactly matched by another merchant or capital transaction for that delivery period.

The financial system has developed the system where Authorised Dealers are able to satisfy the future demand and supply of the currency not only to the merchant community, the providers of capital in the world and investors, but also to themselves.

Table 8.2

Date & Year	Annualised %	Date & Year	Annualised %	Date & Year	Annualised %
2 Jan 1997	3.86	29 May 1998	8.64	27 Nov 1998	7.49
17 Jan 1997	2.81	1 June 1998	9.99	30 Nov 1998	7.60
29 Jan 1997	5.84	12 June 1998	10.76	1 Dec 1998	7.43
19 Feb.1997	5.88	18 June 1998	10.52	2 Dec 1998	7.24
25 Feb 1997	3.61	16 June 1998	10.26	3 Dec 1998	6.92
6 Mar 1997	5.02	23 June 1998	9.28	18 Dec 1998	7.20
14 Mar 1997	5.53	24 June 1998	9.99	23 Dec 1998	6.50
18 Nov 1997	5.01	25 June 1998	9.23	24 Dec 1998	6.78
1 Dec 1997	7 12	26 June 1998	8.91	30 Dec 1998	6.59
11 Dec 1997	8.20	3 July 1998	9.34	1 Jan 1999	6.77
31 Dec 1997	8.30	6 July 1998	8.68	8 Jan 1999	5.88
1 Jan 1998	6.63	10 July 1998	9.32	19 Jan 1999	5.97
15 Jan 1998	12.29	15 July 1998	7.01	25 Jan 1999	6.26
20 Jan 1998	14.24	29 July 1998	5.65	30 Jan 1999	6.41
22 Jan 1998	18.56	7 Aug 1998	6.45	2 Feb 1999	6.50
23 Jan 1998	15.55	12 Aug 1998	7.57	5 Feb 1999	6.13
28 Jan 1998	11.92	20 Aug 1998	8.05	15 Feb 1999	6.80
2 Feb 1998	12.92	28 Aug 1998	8.43	24 Feb 1999	6.89
18 Feb 1998	12.22	1 Sept 1998	10.27	3 Mar 1999	6.31

(Contd.)

Date & Year	Annualised %	Date & Year	Annualised %	Date & Year	Annualised %
27 Feb 1998	7.80	4 Sept 1998	8.47	4 Mar 1999	6.64
2 Mar 1998	10.69	11 Sept 1998	7.31	15 Mar 1999	6.41
5 Mar 1998	9.13	18 Sept 1998	6.97	24 Mar 1999	6.71
20 Mar 1998	6.89	21 Sept 1998	6.31	26 Mar 1999	6.91
23 Mar 1998	6.44	24 Sept 1998	6.78	5 April 1999	6.19
30 Mar1998	7.10	25 Sept 1998	6.36	22 April 1999	5.91
31 Mar 1998	5.38	28 Sept 1998	7.30	29 April 1999	5.75
2 April 1998	6.60	29 Sept 1998	6.88	4 May 1999	5.58
13 April 1998	5.83	5 Oct. 1998	6.80	6 May 1999	5.35
23 April 1998	5.55	6 Oct. 1998	7.52	10 May 1999	5.25
30 April 1998	4.94	10 Oct. 1998	7.19	14 May 1999	4.87
5 May 1998	5.74	20 Oct. 1998	6.77	20 May 1999	4.64
12 May 1998	6.54	30 Oct. 1998	7.57	27 May 1999	5.37
14 May 1998	9.40	2 Nov. 1998	6.77	31 May 1999	5.14
15 May 1998	9.00	11 Nov. 1998	6.17	2 June 1999	5.14

Source: Own compilation.

Interest rates come into play because the players in the system have comparable choices to park their resources in the respective countries of operation. Whenever future demand has to be met from a current resource of supply, the interest rate factor comes into play. The player has to deposit his money in that currency to prevent his future risk and the forward premium operates on the notion that the player has to keep the particular currency at a particular rate of interest, as he is providing the cover for the risk for the client who pays him the cost or "premium" for the same.

Whenever he has an opportunity to cover his risk at a profit, the need for keeping the money vanishes and he uses that for another opportunity to provide another client a cover for risk. This continuous process needs a foundation or a substratum to operate and that is why the interest rates of respective countries are crucial in stabilising the forward premium.

The most advanced countries provide the most stability in terms of premium or discount. The emerging markets or other backward countries suffer from inadequacy of institutions and markets. The questions that are to be determined are:

1. Is India moving towards maturity in the financial and forex markets?
2. Is India's narrow market a hindrance towards providing stability in the forex markets?
3. Is there sufficient expertise and resource to manage forex stability?
4. What should be the basis for determination of the Indian interest rate as a benchmark towards a point of comparison for foreign exchange premium?
5. What are the means for ensuring that forward exchange premium is stable on the basis of interest rate differential when there is a change in the fundamentals in the spot as well as future markets?
6. What should be done in terms of providing the resources — financial, material and human for meeting the desired objectives?
7. What are the benefits that are available to individuals, to the buyers and sellers of foreign exchange, the intermediaries, the operators, the RBI and the country when forward premia reflect interest rate differentials?

The answers to the above are there in the system and require careful study and elaboration.

The Indian Situation

In India, banks are not allowed to hold positions abroad more than a certain extent. All demand and supply factors, even on a particular day, depend on the physical and future purchases or sales by the Reserve Bank of India.

Therefore, for true reflection of the market forces, banks must be allowed to have adequate facilities for keeping balances abroad in the currencies of trading or borrowing overnight from abroad to a larger extent to provide the necessary depth to the foreign exchange markets. This makes the Reserve Bank's intervention occasional rather than on an hourly or intra-day basis. This has been one of the recommendations of the Tarapore Committee awaiting due consideration and action.

Another factor that has to be borne in mind is that RBI keeps the Rupee stable by preventing it from appreciation. It does intervene when there is a sudden and unexpected depreciation. It is on these occasions that the current practices need to be reviewed.

The exchange rate has to depreciate to the extent of the inflation differentials of two countries. Unfortunately, due to capital inflows actively encouraged by the Government and RBI, a depreciation even though warranted, gets prevented.

Exporters suffer in the process as they cannot account easily for the inflationary pressures on their costs and at the same time they have no possibility of increasing their prices at will. There have been four to five phases where the rupee was rock steady for as much as 18 months and the inflation rate was around 6 to 8 per cent.

When the fundamentals really catch up, the rupee depreciates suddenly. These situations have to be managed. Unfortunately, the Government, RBI, Media and an assorted medley of correspondents, editors and commentators let loose a volley of unconnected and extreme statements which unnerves everybody but the exporter and importer. The economic reason for the depreciation in the rupee is higher inflation rate for which neither the exporter nor importer are responsible. However, in India, depreciation of the rupee is considered as a sign of sickness while it is actually a symptom of the effects of inflation.

Is holding the rupee "stable" or "steady" a virtue in itself? Or is it a demonstration of "strength" or "virility" that a hue and cry is raised on the sudden depreciation of the rupee? This will be warranted only when it goes beyond the REER! The Government and the RBI along with independent economists, educationists and columnists should take effort to educate and explain to the people the real cause of depreciation.

It is important that one assumes control in such a situation, but disparate and contradictory actions hardly remedy the situation let alone "talk". The market, including the international agencies too gets involved in the process. Every word of the key influential's i.e. the Reserve Bank of India and the Finance Ministry is read, heard and interpreted for clues.

This can be avoided if the exchange rate is managed and information flow under any circumstances is accurate and trustworthy. A better strategy is to depreciate slowly in line with the inflation rate differential. The fear of creating inflation due to money flows prevents the RBI from depreciating gradually. It should be understood by policy makers that ad hoc and arbitrary measures create a lot of distortions, anomalies and aberrations in all areas. This can be easily avoided by deciding action programmes for every possible scenario both on past experience and future expectations.

This is akin to having and maintaining a fire fighting equipment and fire fighters or a Rapid Action Force on standby even as there are no fires or disturbances on a daily basis. This group of persons in RBI and Finance Ministry should have the sole duty and objective of having a watchful eye on all parameters that influence exchange rates and make it conducive to have a policy of right management by allowing and creating the correct responses and actions.

It is important for the Indian economic situation that the players in the financial market, the Reserve Bank of India and the Government of India undertake an in-depth evaluation and introspection of their respective roles in ensuring a vibrant foreign exchange market. This is more relevant when conditions are stable. In all cases of so called volatility, the responses have been varied and actions taken have hurt the citizens. Due credit has been taken for results in the form of stability, but it has to be explored whether better methods are available other than choking the supply and demand of foreign exchange which has resulted from the free play of market forces.

There is an old Indian saying *"Na Khoopakhananam yukte vahnina grahe"*. "There is no use of digging a well when the house is on fire".

Modern cities adopt modern fire-fighting systems. The objective of the fire-fighting force is to put out the fire. This has to be done swiftly, with as little pain as possible. The desired equipment and adequate water should be near at hand.

It is the responsibility of the fire-fighter to put out the fire and rescue lives. He is not the person who needs to go into the cause of the fire, whether it was arson, negligence or natural. The competent and efficient fire fighter just puts out the fire.

One of the pretexts for keeping the rupee from depreciating when it ought to is its effect on the cost of borrowing by the Government of India in foreign currency and its payment of interest. It is certainly a good reason as any additional expenditure incurred prevents it from having the resources for executing its allotted functions.

But keeping an exchange overvalued is also harmful to the economy. The Government of India must decide that it can prevent depreciation only when it can manage inflation. The economy is punished by inflation and the people are again choked by not allowing depreciation.

If Government of India does not want depreciation to take effect, then once and for all it must decide to stop borrowing in foreign currency. It must finance all its requirements only from the domestic market. This will give an unfettered role to the market. The choice for the Government has to be that it has to factor, the cost of depreciation into its budget.

Interest Rate and Exchange Rate Premia

Why have exchange rate premia fluctuated widely in the last seven years? The premium was as low as one to two per cent annualised during certain periods. This indicates that forward sales by exporters were higher than demand.

During some periods the annualised premium was as high as 12 to 14 per cent. This indicates that forward demand by importers was higher than forward supply.

The exporters' behaviour can be explained as follows:

Let us say, in January, the exporter has a contract for exports for delivery in the month of March, say to the extent of US $ 200,000; then he has two choices:

One, book the exchange for March delivery or two, wait till the date of shipment and book his US$ on that date.

Suppose the US$ was at Rs. 31.37 in January and the annualised premium was five per cent, then the rate offered for March would be Rs. 31.63. The exporter would get the rupee equivalent of Rs. 63,26,000 for booking in March.

As the rupee behaved in the spot market like a dead man's heartbeat, i.e. remained at Rs. 31.37 for over 30 months, exporters who waited for natural depreciation would have got only Rs. 62,74,000 when the date of negotiation arrived.

The exporters started to sell forward and sent the premium downwards. Premia occurs not only on interest rate differential but also by the demand for $ from importers.

Normally, Indian importers expect natural depreciation. But when the rupee was rock steady, importers realised that they would be better off waiting for the actual date of payment than book forward. Hence they kept off the forward market.

The net result was—exporters encashed premia and importers stayed off.

When the rupee started to depreciate on fundamentals, in the spot market, importers rushed in for cover, while there was no corresponding supply from exporters who stopped selling forward and began to rue their opportunity loss.

From 1991, this cycle has been repeated in three to four situations when the rupee has depreciated suddenly.

Depreciation and Inflation Rate Differentials

Exchange rates should depreciate depending on the inflation rate differential between the two countries.

In today's foreign exchange market, exchange rates can appreciate because of capital flows or in the short term export proceeds increase over import remittances.

In the first four years since 1991, the export growth rate in rupee terms was astoundingly large. With liberalisation of the economy, there were also induced and natural capital flows.

The Reserve Bank of India consciously took a decision to absorb all surplus foreign currency earnings from the market and added the same to its reserves. Thus short term appreciation was prevented by management.

At the same time, there was no letup in inflation. The inflation was between 8 to 11 per cent per annum in the period 1991 to 1995. The rupee ought to have depreciated on the inflation differential. Probably due to the steep depreciation in 1991, it did not make a big difference in exports. But at a certain point of time it did make an impact and the rupee depreciated suddenly from Rs. 31.37 to Rs. 34.5 and held steady for some time.

A simple desk research will reveal that the depreciation from Rs. 31.37 to Rs. 42.66 today is the difference in the inflation of US and India during this period and there is a potential for further depreciation. As we are in a managed market economy today, it is gratifying to note that the exchange rate reflects this differential.

Forward Markets and Interest Rate Differentials

Today in India, it is necessary to examine the process of how interest rate differentials reflect in the forward exchange market.

Given the array of interest rates, as also the lack of consistency or certainty in their movements, one would like to query as to what should be the interest rate that should be benchmarked against the other country's interest rate.

For a bank, the interest rates available for overnight balances, for three months and for six months are different.

As banks, institutions or individuals are not allowed to deposit funds in the foreign currency on term basis, the only interest rate then would be the Overnight Rate or Call Rate as it is in India.

For arriving at a base, the interest rates within the country should behave on economic factors. Another important factor is that interest rates must hold within a pattern.

This is incumbent only on the Reserve Bank of India's ability to absorb short term surpluses and provide short term liquidity not only in theory but also in practice and management.

Another prerequisite is that the financial market must equip themselves with the requisite education, organisation and discipline to ensure that interest rates operate within a band. Changes in interest rates ought to reflect the impact of aggregate supply and demand of money in the entire economy and also in individual markets within it.

The next issue that surfaces is that the Indian financial sector, particularly the Banks, should have the necessary resources to meet the requirements of maintaining liquidity and stability in the daily money as well as forex markets.

At present, the market depends entirely on the Reserve Bank of India to absorb net surpluses or provide the net liquidity in foreign currencies. RBI has been intervening both in the spot as well as in the future markets. What is noticeable is that the RBI and financial markets were not able to stabilise interest rates in the various segmented markets. The reasons have been more management factors than economic factors.

The market can maintain premia at interest rate differentials as long as RBI will intervenes as frequently as necessary in ensuring so. In reality, the Authorised Dealers, Bankers and the financial system should perform in a way that premia naturally reflects the interest rate differential.

The Tarapore Committee went into this issue in depth and recommended as follows:

> Convertibility would logically ensure that the forward premia in forex market reflect interest rate differentials between overseas and domestic markets. The Committee recommends that as part of exchange rate management greater attention should be focused on ensuring that forward exchange markets reflect interest rate differentials.

This requires banks to keep balances abroad. At the moment, there are very limited options for the same. Ideally, it is the market which has to provide the equilibrium. As explained earlier, peculiar situations may arise when there is a premium on forward markets, when there are more sellers than corresponding buyers and vice versa.

Financial System's Ability to Provide Stability in Interest Rates and Forex Forward Markets

It has to be examined whether Indian banks have any reason or incentive to keep funds abroad. The cost of capital for Indian Banks is now in the range of 14 per cent. This is what they have paid to raise capital under Tier II requirements.

How can banks keep funds abroad at overnight rates of around three per cent per annum in foreign currency when their cost is 14 per cent in rupee terms? The same logic holds good if they choose to borrow. Any Indian bank cannot borrow at nine per cent in the call money to invest overnight in the international market at three per cent.

Historically, the rupee has depreciated at a little less than 4.6 per cent per annum, compounded, since 1991. The market, which reflects demand and supply has not depreciated over periods of time. But it has depreciated suddenly by up to 10 to 14 per cent within a fortnight. This was again followed by a prolonged steady period for 12 to 18 months.

Given this trend, there is no opportunity for Indian Banks to earn their return as a spread over interest or a return on capital by keeping balances abroad. In this situation, the true interaction between the Indian and foreign currency can take place only on the basis of the spot market.

In situations of sudden depreciation or volatility, stability can be achieved only when the financial sector has the required depth in terms of substantial foreign balances. Another requisite would be capital account convertibility to the extent required for meeting the future requirements.

Allowing the keeping spot balances abroad or by borrowing overnight from overseas financial markets may be necessary till such time equilibrium is restored both in the spot market as well as in the future markets in India. This would be the ideal situation in a market economy. In a managed situation, the RBI has to achieve stability by intervening in the spot and forward markets. The market has operatives who act with an entrepreneurial objective or act with greed. The RBI acts with an altruistic objective in national interest and is governed by Statute as well as a mandate.

The freedom for banks to keep balances abroad is crucial in the management of foreign exchange and the interest rate. At the same time, freedom has also to be provided to banks to borrow from overseas markets both for the short term and long term. This freedom has to be provided to them in a phased manner. The Tarapore Committee had recommended a time frame beginning with 1997-98. A time has come for the RBI and Government to implement the committee recommendation in this respect.

It is more important that the banks and the financial system acquire the experience and expertise in managing both the foreign exchange and the interest rate, which hitherto has been with the Government and the RBI. The strengthening of the financial sector should acquire a priority status. The requisite education, organisation and discipline that have to be inculcated into banks and the other financial institutions in this regard must be carried out forthwith.

How is this to be achieved? This can be voluntary or by mandate. It is said that autonomy is taken and not given.

After the desired policy is stated and necessary freedom given, in a voluntary atmosphere, the banks will exercise options to park their surplus funds abroad. Even then they would not like to lose on this account. Hence, they will park balances only when they have an opportunity for superior return over their cost of funds.

Under today's conditions of stability, it would be difficult for banks to park funds abroad. They would certainly exercise their options when there is volatility or when there is an opportunity for a higher return when a natural demand for forward is present.

A natural conduct will emerge after banks assimilate the techniques and master the nuances of markets. Indian Bank Management has responded effectively whenever an opportunity has been made available to them.

It is not possible to achieve this by mandate, as banks would lose their current revenue on their deployable funds.

What is a Crisis and What is Not?

A discussion, dialogue and debate have to be generated on what is a crisis and what is not?

This is better discussed during calmer times, stable conditions than during a "crisis" or a "purported crisis" or a "real crisis". A crisis is a crisis whether real, pronounced or unnoticed.

The description of events or happenings as "crisis" and acting and reacting on those events as a crisis could be a gross error. The actions emanating as reactions to crisis will be far more stringent, reactionary and arbitrary. When this comes from authorities like the RBI and the Government, it has a wider acceptance.

If it has emerged that it is not a crisis at all, and this is the difference that all managers and leaders have experienced, that it always is easier to judge when the event is over and dealt with, than during the event itself. The actions or action not taken during such events have a telling effect on organisations and individuals. Some may have lasting effects. Some may cause unearned gains at the cost of unanticipated losses to others. The question of economic justice comes into play.

It is therefore, always advisable, be they managers of organisations or managers of the economy, that great effort and pains have to be taken to ensure that crisis do not occur at all.

Events that can be foreseen cannot be grouped in the category of crisis. A crisis is by nature an unforeseen or unpredictable event. Even then, the economy's managers have to prepare themselves to deal with events, situations and happenings, which can be called crisis.

It follows that, in a democracy we must have people and institutions who are unaffected by the crisis, act as impartial observers and offer advice and support.

It is unfortunate that our media, commentators, politicians or all hues and their advisers, take a rupee depreciation as a loss of virility and value of the country. The exchange rate only reflects the loss of virility or strength that the country has already experienced due to high inflation and the result of wrong policies and actions. Added to it is the din created by ideologues, who include sworn enemies of the market, who have every right to express their opinion under the Constitution of India, but who nevertheless make an impact on public minds.

A rupee depreciation is therefore sensationalised. A large number of persons who are actually affected, that is the exporter, importer, or the investor cannot take decisions calmly based on reflection. Sensational statements in the media and rank confusion in markets often result from the talk of uneducated minds. A depreciation of 5 per cent to 6 per cent in one week is also a matter worthy of attention and gets widely reported. A steady depreciation over time goes unnoticed

More important, wild and unconnected reasons and opinions are made available for the consumption of the public. Ignorant people then put forward theories which are not founded on basis of economics or good commercial sense.

Add to that, economists and retired Central Bankers expound theories which are true theories but they do not analyse the inherent imperfections that reside in our organisations. But operators operate in the hard realities of the marketplace. That is why markets and markets alone reflect true information in terms of prices.

A systematic and organised effort has to be initiated by the Government and the Reserve Bank to educate citizens, their representatives, management of banks and institutions, market participants and, of course, the traders and investors in the processes of determination of exchange rates and interest rates.

Added to this, a quiet and efficient initiative has to be generated to prevent future crises, by systematic and purposeful action in the present. This can include correct political, administrative and management initiatives for action.

A determination has to emerge during each period of intense activity or volatility as to whether it is a crisis or just another event to be managed.

The management initiative in foreign exchange should be to contain the impact on domestic interest rates. Domestic fund flow has to be maintained to ensure stability. Exchange rate will then reflect the fundamentals determined by the market.

Reflections on Arbitrage and Speculation

An essential difference has to be made between arbitrage and speculation.

Arbitrage is an entrepreneurial activity in the financial sector which moves resources from that of a lower yield to a higher yield. Arbitrage is therefore a genuine economic activity which allocates the resources. It is an exercise in choices. "Arbitrage is speculation without risk".

In growing markets like India which have been heavily compartmentalised and segmented in the past due to restrictions and controls, arbitrage opportunities are enormous. They provide market players good margins and possible huge profits. This is a welcome sign as it will be temporary. Given spread of education and encouragement of competition, arbitrage opportunities will narrow down as resources spread evenly across choices.

Arbitrage is not something that is encouraged but will happen. In an entrepreneurial society data, information and knowledge converge in an individual. Given the necessary freedom to operate, the person will always look for opportunities to maximise the return on financial resources under his or her control and command. During various discussions that were emerging in the media, there was a mention that "arbitrage" was being "frowned" on by the authorities.

This matter is to be discussed frankly. A pure arbitrage is a gain to the economy. It results in economic efficiency. When current resources are committed to those giving a higher yield, it is a good development. The problem arises when arbitrage is confused with speculation. Speculation is a part of a market economy. It has been looked down on in India.

There is no doubt that during volatility speculation creates problems. Therefore, it has to be speculation that has to be managed, controlled or eliminated, if at all, in the interest of the nation, and not arbitrage. There is no natural scope for the speculation in a steady or fixed market. All "prescriptions" to control volatility have been in the physical markets. Whether they are increase in CRR, or increase in interest rates of imports or mandates to bring in foreign balances, or to keep it abroad for corporates and banks, they are still ad hoc and arbitrary, even though carried out with good intentions.

Speculation that occurs can be curbed more effectively by other means. Speculation in the spot market can be cured by supply, for which RBI at the moment has abundant balances. The speculation that occurs in the forward markets is one which requires to be watched. It is here that operators can exercise options to buy or sell in the forward markets that can cause volatility. It is well known that movements in the forward markets do affect the spot market.

For example, a merchant when he wants forward dollars, he is quoted a price which he can accept or not accept. But when one bank offers other bank dollars and is accepted in the forward market, it creates a price. During periods of volatility, if the bank speculates that the rupee will depreciate it can buy dollars on the forward market and push up the price. This generates an upward spiral.

Theoretically, if all importers decided to cover forward purchases in one day, the demand can be of US Dollar 10 billion for various forward positions, with no corresponding supply, as exporters can chose to hold off. One cannot force dollars out of exporters' positions.

It must be noticed that spot markets do not observe the tendencies of the forward markets during periods of volatility.

The RBI in such a situation can consider the following steps:

- Intervene in spot markets only when it goes out of the REER band.
- Allow forward sales and purchases at market prices so that players take positions depending on their individual views on the market and their respective transaction costs.
- Under ideal conditions, there is no need for RBI to intervene in forward markets. It should nurture the markets to do so. As long as it supplies the current dollars to the spot markets, the market will be able to resolve the genuine demand of the forwards.

The RBI should not resort to steps like impounding CRR, but can take a judicious decision to improve interest rates by operating the bank rate, but preferably open market rate.

If future speculation gets out of hand, then RBI should prescribe margins for purchases. Imposition of margins can be from 10 per cent to 25 per cent in case of inter-bank transactions and from 10 to 100 per cent in the case of merchant transactions would be in order.

These margins should be mandated to be deposited with the RBI till the contracts are performed or cancelled. Since margins require cash, speculative actions will get curbed as also barriers for actions generated in panic.

The ideal time for intervention for imposition of margins would be when annualised premia based on interest rate differentials would be 200 basis points above normal.

The RBI can also curb speculative sales of dollars by imposing a margin on sales when it is 100 basis points below normal.

Stability in interest rates will always result in stability in the movement in exchange rates. A conscious move should be made for stability in interest rates. At the moment there is an obsession with the stability of the exchange rate.

The Government of India and the Reserve Bank of India should decide a clear and firm policy as to whether they prefer stable interest rates or a "steady" foreign exchange rate. By "stable" interest rates one does not mean a fixed rate over a long period of time, but working within a band in the course of the day and the week.

Reasons for Unstable Forex Premia

Bankers, educationists, statisticians, researchers, economists, policy makers, players in the foreign exchange market, exporters and importers and investors who would care to go into the question of the wide variation in exchange rate premia would find it easier with the following pointers:

The market solely depended on RBI for supply and demand of foreign currency. The authorised dealers were not allowed to park foreign currency abroad and not allowed to borrow overnight from abroad. Interest rates in India were gyrating wildly due to a variety of reasons from 1991-1998.

Real interest rates have been high in India. Authorised dealers and banks did not have capital account convertibility. Sudden and unanticipated changes in monetary policy and liquidity management initiatives created some imbalances at times.

The behaviour of exchange rate has not been natural with inflation differentials but its effect got reflected over a period of time in sudden bursts. It would be gratifying to note that exchange rate stability was achieved in a reasonably short time, after equilibrium was restored.

Stable Forex Premia

Stable forex premia which reflects interest rate differentials first and foremost requires stability in interest rates. Interest rates should reflect proper differential between inflation and interest rate, and a truly market oriented interest rate where aggregate supply and demand match along with proper setting of bank rate and open market operations rate by the RBI.

It requires banks and authorised dealers to be provided freedom to keep balances abroad. It requires curbing of speculation which is promoted by motive for unearned income driven by greed, by appropriate measures.

It requires depreciation of the rupee to be managed in line with inflation differentials as systematically as possible. This can be managed by many policy options like prepayment of Government external loans, discouraging short term capital flows by interest rate management as also limited capital convertibility for Indian citizens.

A debate has to be initiated among the political leadership on the question of "stability" in interest rates in India, as it is more beneficial to Indian people than aiming for a "steady" foreign exchange rate.

A clear distinction has to be made between market failures caused by externalities and failures caused by weaknesses inherent in Indian organisations in terms of management, education, organisation and discipline. These weaknesses have to be removed over a period of time. It would be then easier to deal with externalities.

In the last four months forward premia have been at equilibrium with interest rate differentials. Is it due to better management or due to stable interest rate?

It would be interesting to study foreign exchange markets in developed countries where larger intra-day fluctuations in spot market take place whether forward prices also respond instantaneously.

Impact of Exchange Rate on Our Economy

There appears to be very little understanding among policy makers, economists, central bankers, bankers, economic editors, communicators, consultants and other persons who are not actually affected by the exchange rate. The effect of exchange rate is real on the persons, the individual, the firm or an organisation that actually buys and sells foreign exchange for legitimate use.

There are whole sub-sectors which can grow viable or non-viable for export or import on a given day or a given time based on the exchange rate for that period. The measure of macro and micro economic impact of exchange rate on each transaction or each group of commodities or each sub-sectors or a class of individuals is too enormous to go into in one paper or at one go.

The essence of a perfect market is that all information converges into the price. It is open for examination whether the Indian market is at all perfect. If it is imperfect, then the exercise for pushing it to a rear perfect market has to be a continuous one.

It is to be emphasised that the role of State in India is overwhelming and the State cannot abdicate its responsibility in ensuring economic efficiency. The difference between success and failure lies there.

There is no foundation for stability if the entire sum total of transactions is left to the market under present Indian conditions. This is more so where the three essential ingredients, education, organisation and discipline are not present either singly or severally. The most essential ingredient i.e. self-discipline is necessary to be inculcated at all levels. Till such time, we may have to "muddle through" towards our goals and ideals.

The rupee has depreciated from Rs. 31.37 to Rs. 42.82 per US$. The graph does not contain heavy fluctuations at certain points when there was a sharp depreciation on an intra-day, intra-week or intra-month basis.

These are spot prices. Forward prices have varied wildly during bouts of depreciation.

There were periods of prolonged "steady" prices. The longest one was from 1993 to 1995 which was called the "dead man's heartbeat" by analysts and traders.

As per normal economic behaviour, the trend is towards depreciation of the rupee on the basis of inflation rate differentials.

Conclusion

There is a need to study the exchange rate and its movements in the spot and forward markets with a view to analyse past trends.

The exchange rate will always behave on the basis of demand and supply of the foreign currency in relation to domestic currency. The demand and supply are constantly observed by operators and should be continuously studied for future applications.

Knowledge on the operation of interest rates and the foreign exchange market should develop in the country—among operators, buyers and sellers, institutions, RBI and the Government as much as individuals, planners, policy makers and analysts, law makers and participants in the Government.

A study and analysis of the operation of interest rates and their impact on foreign exchange forward market should be done and interested parties enlightened about its mechanism.

Unless interest rates are aligned properly, reflect fundamentals and operate within bands on economic parameters it would be difficult to envisage that exchange rate forward premia will truly reflect interest rate differentials.

A determination has to emerge that the factors that go into the movement of exchange rates are to be managed efficiently. The Real Effective Exchange Rate (REER) should be explained in detail to market operators and the people.

Volatility has to be defined in Indian conditions. Responses to volatile conditions are usually cursory, rapid, hasty, ad-hoc, discretionary, erratic, stubborn, unacceptable, irrelevant, laudable, overdone, respected, underestimated, etc. depending on the degree of volatility, its timing and the set of individuals that are contributory to its conditions and those who respond to it.

But the foreign exchange rate always is a reflection of demand and supply and will settle at the rate of interaction of demand and supply (*see* graph below).

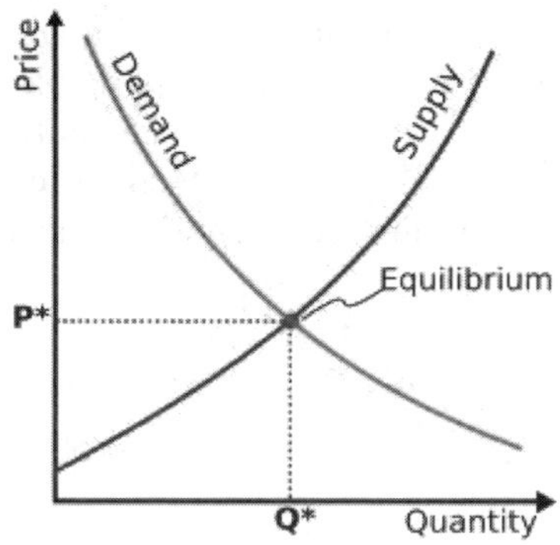

Given controlled conditions, the ability to respond effectively must lie with the persons who control the economy. Equally, under managed conditions the managers must effectively manage the exchange rate. The results of actions taken or not taken, therefore depends on the persons who control or manage. In a market economy, the market determines the rate and the effect of the market has to be borne by the affected persons and no one else is responsible.

In Indian conditions today, it is ideal that the exchange rate is managed towards the desirable and the optimal with an objective that the market economy can take over from the managed economy with the least destabilising effect.

NOTES

1. This paper was written when India had bouts of volatility in exchange rates after the 1991 realisation and peculiar behaviour of exchange rates contrary to theory in economics.

2. The sharp fluctuations in premia stopped once the money markets became stable after 2001.
3. The depreciation and appreciation of the rupee have been unrelated to inflation differentials or interest rate differentials. It has fluctuated more due to capital flows than due to changes on trade account.
4. It would definitely be a subject for extensive documentation and research if interest rates do influence capital flows which could in turn influence exchange rates in the future.
5. Today's forex market reveal a remarkable maturity that forex premia reflect interest rate differentials. The Financial Market has developed the depth in correlation between market rates of interest and the premia in the forex market.

Nine

Financial System and Multiple Interest Rates

[1999]

The decision of freeing interest rates and leaving it to the market was adopted since 1991. It is presumed that the adoption of a policy of leaving interest rates to the market is with the objective of allowing Liberty, which is enshrined in our Constitution. It is also for the most laudable objective of introducing the concept of economic efficiency. Application of wisdom will reveal that though the principle of market economy was introduced with the sole objective of economic efficiency, the interest rate structure following liberalisation is operating contrary to this principle in specific areas, and operating successfully in some areas.

Interest rate behaviour from 1991-1998 does not reflect economic efficiency. Interest rate policies adopted by the Government, (as also not having a policy at times) the Reserve Bank of India and the operators and financial intermediaries have introduced an element of substantial gain to one section of the population at the expense of another at different times. In a market economy it is "no person is worse off without another person being better off".

This element is now examined in the context of two features of the interest rates in the market. The banking system and other financial sector entities, insurance and provident funds were loaded with securities issued by Government in the regimented area. These were called the SLR (Statutory Liquidity Ratio) investments. The banks were required to invest 37.5 per cent of their total liabilities in the assets "approved" securities. Provident Funds and Life Insurance Corporation were required to invest 100 per cent and a certain high percentage of their respective assets in these "approved" securities.

Impact of Changes in Value of Securities on the Banking System

In the regimented era, these securities were offered at interest rates lower than the "market" rates. Data will provide the exact rates in comparison to the rates of deposits raised from the public or lending rates as the case may be. In some instances these were at rates lower than the rates of deposits from public. When this practice was followed the effect on the overall economy was balanced. Even though the banks were getting a lower yield on these investments, the depositor was not hurt as the rates for fixed deposits were stable. The banking system's loss was recouped in charging a proportionally higher rate of interest on the "commercial borrowers" whose borrowings constituted about 45 per cent of the assets of these banks. This proportionate increase was borne willingly by the borrowers as getting the required finance itself was a privilege. The cost of borrowing is naturally passed on to the cost of the product and ultimately to the consumer. The "benefit" was that the Government had a lower "outflow" on account of interest and therefore had lesser need to tax, borrow or print notes to the corresponding "saving" in interest.

The blow to the banking system was not during this period, but began when the "market" process began. Government securities have currently a market only in the banking system. It is natural that the public would not buy Government securities as they had a comparable choice to park their savings at higher rates with banks and other financial intermediaries.

When North Block in conjunction with the Reserve Bank of India, which manages issue and redemption of and tracks the ownership of India's public debt, decided that the Government will henceforth issue its securities at "market rates", one problem of banks was solved i.e. they would not lose on the interest portion of their securities investments on all future investments made by them in Government securities.

The reduction of SLR requirements progressively and wonderfully by the RBI from 37.5 to 25 per cent of deposits and interest pricing at higher levels of 13 to 14 per cent which were a few points higher than the general interest level on savings from the public provided banks with stable earnings. What was more significant was that CRR was reduced from 15 to 10 per cent in stages.

In the meanwhile, RBI moved to a direction of better management of banks. The income recognition norms and valuation of securities marked to market were moves, rapidly introduced. This caused the largest upheaval in the banking sector. Some banks announced huge losses and others managed to scrape through. It would also be a good subject for research in economics and management to study the banking sector's performance in the year of announcement of these measures and as to what percentage of their "losses" could be attributed to depreciation in the values of securities.

An identical position also is held by banks in Bonds issued in DFIs like IDBI, IFCI and ICICI which have coupon rates of 7 to 8 per cent. This list also includes some State Government and other institutional securities. These were all forced investments under the SLR regime. These institutions continue to enjoy these low rates paid out while corresponding matching assets have long been realised. In effect, it is now a transfer of net income from one portion of the financial sector to another. This is economic injustice which has to be removed forthwith in the interest of the financial sector and the citizens of the country as a whole.

The banking system and also the public have lost heavily in this imposed investment. The original ideology or philosophy appeared to be to provide "cheaper" finance for the "long term", "productive" industrial projects.

The banking industry in India is described today with an absence of vision. This vision has to be necessarily provided. The root cause of this state of affairs is absence of profitability. Only when profitability is restored, will the banking sector continue to be vibrant.

Profitability can be restored only when the Banks are provided opportunities to earn a sufficient income from the difference in interest paid to difference in interest earned. Given the necessary management inputs, current bank managements are in a position to realise this objective.

In the context of losses incurred on revaluation of securities, since 1992, the Chief Executives of the losing banks were trying to explain to the public that the losses were notional. What was likely was that these banks were not marking the securities to market, had not shuffled their portfolios when interest rates, even in the directed interest regime were rising, and of course, a subject not now relevant here, were taking income from non-performing assets into their profit and loss account and keeping non-performing assets as performing assets in their balance sheets. It is now presumed that the banks that did not announce a loss but actually began to excel in the performance from that year had low non-performing assets and others had no low yielding Government securities in their portfolio.

To explain further, if a bank had Rs. 2,000 crores worth of Government securities which were yielding 6 to 7 per cent of the face value and Rs. 8,000 crores worth of Government securities at current yields, the Rs. 2,000 crores when valued at face value appeared as Rs. 2,000 crores. As per the new norms for marking to market, the value of the securities would have dropped by 25 per cent Rs. 500 crores. Any person with knowledge of accountancy would know that when you write down an investment you credit the asset and debit the profit and loss account. This writer does not have specific data bank-wise and hence it has been concluded on a notional basis.

Two things emerge. Why did some banks have such a huge portfolio and some not? Why did some shuffle and some not? All banks were owned by the Government. Though they were under one ownership, the managements were having their own methods and strategies, areas and choices of operations. They were largely conforming to directions both by Government and RBI.

Some banks were more profitable than others. So instead of showing a larger profit, some banks cleverly managed to do this shuffling as well as managed a lower valuation. In a socialist era making profits was frowned upon. The other banks were not as profitable and had poor management also in their investment sections. So they had to keep up with other banks and "show" a profit. So they "managed" to "somehow" show a profit while their securities devaluation was concealed in the inflated assets values. Since they held them to maturity, in other words, they were not compelled to sell them, but simply held on to them, they could technically value them at face value. Both were not wrong.

In the free market era, the Reserve Bank, as it should be, is the authority for the Banks. Once these norms were announced they had to be implemented by all banks. When these differences showed up, the owners of the bank, that is the Government, stepped in and improved the capital. The capital was infused by issue of recapitalisation bonds which were subscribed to by the respective banks. The Government technically borrowed from the same bank to invest in the same bank, as capital. This exercise continued over two to three years in the reform era. In later exercises, the banks when returning to profit wrote down the capital also when they could meet the capital adequacy requirements.

The submission is now the whole market is punished by the interest rate policy. If the earlier investments were not forced or pre-empted, there would have been no reason to protect the market. The market should take its own decisions and prepare to meet its consequences and obligations. But when pre-empted securities of a very high amount are in the system and when you convert it to market and they are your own entities, the Government could consider the step of entering into swaps by extinguishing the old securities at face value in cash or by swap.

The argument would be that, what would be gained by the banks would be lost by the Government. The answer is when the ownership is 100 per cent; the loss of the bank is actually equal to the loss by the Government as it is solely responsible for the assets and liabilities of the bank. A loss to Government is a loss to the people of this country. The argument is that the bank should be punished for its earlier mismanagement. Again a punishment meted out to your own entity is like punishing yourself. A larger issue is that the punishment meted out for the Government's and entity's wrongdoing is now met by the community of people and more likely the innocent customers of the bank and the public at large for the drag this entity imposes on the entire system and the Government.

The Government has to be concerned about the health of the banking system as also the fitness of banks owned by Government. Successive Governments have misused the system and abused the system for particular ends in the past during its ownership and in the directed economy. The Government should now restore the banking system for its logical purpose in a society and a market economy. It is bound to bring in specific remedial measures for past ills perpetrated singly or collectively.

The banking system cannot easily extricate itself out of the lower interest rates on its past investments. This is because the Government and RBI had issued long-dated securities, some of which will mature 5 to 10 years from now. The asset liability mismatch was created at the time when fixed deposits were ordinarily not made for more than three years to five years. Now the banking system's yield on this asset is lower by five per cent which is again reflecting itself in the overall yield on securities.

This can be solved only by a drastic drop in all rates of interest which is not feasible unless a sound policy is in place and inflation is in control. This is not envisaged in the near future. Therefore innovative steps are called for.

Though it will make no difference to RBI, it will make a world of difference to the banks as their balance sheet valuation of securities goes up dramatically. The method adopted which is referred to as Yield to Maturity will have a different valuation as against the actual market price of a security or another security which is "marked to market".

With the Financial Institutions, the Government and RBI can take an approach which may hurt institutions for the near term but still they can be made to oblige in the interest of the financial sector. They can be asked to settle all loans below 10 per cent to be settled at par. There will not be a financial squeeze as this money would return to the market.

The RBI can give a special window to them to borrow from RBI at say 9 or 10 per cent or allow them to raise Euro or Swiss Franc or Japanese Yen loan under a special cover or umbrella. The current profitability of financial institutions in such cases may not decline much.

If such a situation is managed say, within the first six months of next fiscal, the overall borrowing programme of the Government will be managed with substantially lower market rates. This is a saving to Government of India which can be diverted for social purposes or reducing the revenue deficit.

Interest rates have to behave within an orderly band. This will be beneficial to citizens as well as operators in the financial sector. Anomalies created out of past structures are best done away with at one stroke. This can be done by RBI alone if necessary, if it wants the interest rate across the whole spectrum to reduce without pain.

As the reliability and reputation of the corporate sector improves, customers will have comparable choices to move from lower yields from bank deposits to higher yields from other securities. Bank's responsibility will be to handle transaction money and provide across the counter service in all financial transactions speedily, efficiently and be profitable.

An Analysis of the Current Rupee Loans of the Government

- The Table reveals the outstanding loans of the Government of India.
- In column 2, the interest rate also called as the coupon rate is listed. This list reveals the range in the interest rates of loans outstanding.
- It is obvious that all the loans which are below the coupon rate of 9.5 per cent were issued prior to 1991.
- Column No. 3 is the description of the loan.
- Column No. 4 is revealing the earliest date of maturity. It may be noted that some of the loans are due 5-10 years from today even for the lower interest rate securities.
- The list has been arranged in the order of interest rates from low to the higher level.
- Column No. 5 reveals the outstanding amount.
- Column No. 6 is the sub-total of each range of interest rates. The first group is from 5.5 per cent - 8 per cent and the amount outstanding is Rs. 9788.09 crores.
- Column No. 7 is the market value of securities based on an YTM of 11 per cent. Again this is not an expert calculation and the actual prices can be accessed from publications available in the debt market.
- The Column No. 8 is the most important to be noted. This is the depreciation in the value of the security and represents the cumulative loss for the holders of the security from the date of issue.
- By application of logic, the depreciation will turn into a profit on the redemption of the respective loan.
- The loss in terms of "current yield" is not calculated and by itself amounts to a substantial sum incurred every year. The above table and notes give a bird's eye view for policy makers to review the impact of outstanding low interest securities on the financial market.

Details of Current Rupee Loans of the Central Government

Sl. No.	IN %	Name of Loan	Earliest Date of Maturity	Budget Amount	Total	Market Value of Securities Mark to Market @ YTM of 11%	Depreciation of Securities on Date	
1	2	3	4	5	6	7	8	9
1	5.50	Bank C. Bond, 1999	—	72.63		36.32	36.32	
2	5.50	Loan, 1999	30.04.1999	275.19		137.60	137.6	
3	5.50	Loan, 2000	11.04.2000	392.23		196.12	196.12	370.03
4	5.75	Loan, 2001	01.07.2001	230.84		120.67	110.17	
5	5.75	N.D. Loan, 2001	20.12.2001	42.16		22.04	20.12	
6	5.75	Loan, 2002	15.07.2002	388.58		203.12	185.46	
7	5.75	Loan, 2003	12.05.2003	378.43		197.82	180.61	496.37
8	6.50	Loan, 2001	01.07.2001	93.61		55.32	38.30	
9	6.50	Loan, 2002	16.10.2002	310.25		183.33	126.92	
10	6.50	Loan, 2003	26.07.2003	396.45		234.27	162.18	
11	6.50	Loan, 2004	20.06.2004	411.96		243.43	168.53	
12	6.50	Loan, 2005	01.10.2005	464.97		274.76	190.22	
13	6.50	Loan, 2000	01.07.2000	420.11		248.25	171.86	858.01
14	6.75	Loan, 2006	15.05.2006	788.78		484.02	304.76	
15	6.75	Loan, 2007	22.11.2007	621.49		381.37	240.12	544.88

(Contd.)

1	2	3	4	5	6	7	8	9
16	7.00	Loan, 2009	25.05.2009	1197.44		762.01	435.43	
17	7.50	Loan, 2010	12.05.2010	1456.22		992.88	463.34	
18	7.50	Loan, 2001	21.07.2001	304.27		207.46	96.81	995.59
19	7.75	Loan, 2002	24.05.2002	64.56		45.49	19.07	19.07
20	8.00	Loan, 2011	27.04.2011	1477.92	9788.09	1074.85	403.07	403.07
21	8.25	Loan, 2005	11.10.2005	664.79		498.59	166.2	166.20
22	8.75	Loan, 2010	13.12.2010	500.22		397.90	102.32	102.32
23	9.00	Loan, 2013	24.05.2013	1999.33	3164.34	1635.82	363.51	363.51
24	9.50	Loan, 2008	20.02.2008	672.48		580.78	91.70	
25	9.50	Loan, 2004	01.06.2004	320.59		276.87	43.72	135.42
26	10.00	Loan, 2014	30.05.2014	2333.26		2121.15	212.11	
27	10.25	Loan, 2012	01.06.2012	1755.13		1635.46	119.67	
28	10.50	Loan, 2005	21.05.2005	470.22		448.85	21.37	
29	10.50	Loan, 1999	15.05.1999	34.15		32.60	1.55	
30	10.50	Loan, 2014	29.10.2014	1755.10		1675.32	79.78	
31	10.75	Loan, 2000	11.06.2000	206.76		202.06	4.70	
32	10.75	Loan, 2001	05.08.2001	52.77		51.57	1.20	
33	10.80	Loan, 2008	22.07.2008	361.81		355.23	6.58	446.96
34	11.00	Loan, 2008	23.05.2008	6976.68				
35	11.00	Loan, 2002	11.05.2002	2951.98				

(Contd.)

1	2	3	4	5	6	7	8	9
36	11.00	Loan, 2001	21.10.2001	5.69				
37	11.00	Loan, 2004	15.05.2004	12.43				
38	11.00	Loan, 2003	23.05.2003	192.94	18146.99			
39	11.25	Loan, 2005	11.06.2005	1338.23				
40	11.25	Loan, 2006	05.08.2006	109.59				
41	11.30	Loan, 2004	27.10.2004	539.56				
42	11.50	Loan, 2006	12.05.2006	5259.55				
43	11.50	Loan, 2015	21.05.2015	4173.50				
44	11.50	Loan, 2011	05.08.2011	3745.36				
45	11.50	Loan, 2010	11.06.2010	7152.80				
46	11.50	Loan, 2009	15.05.2009	7997.74				
47	11.50	Loan, 2007	05.10.2007	4356.97				
48	11.50	Loan, 2006 II series	21.10.2006	26.02	34699.32			
49	12.00	Loan, 2011	21.10.2011	3386.79				
50	12.50	Loan, 2007	25.03.2007	1209.77				
51	12.60	Govt. Stock, 2000	03.03.2000	1000.00				
52	12.75	Govt. Stock, 2002	05.08.2002	1000.00	6596.56			
			TOTAL:		**72395.30**			**4901.42**

Source: Receipts Budget 1992-93.

The chart above was prepared from the 1992-93 budget. The author has no reliable information on other securities outstanding in the approved security list where the coupon rate is less than nine per cent. Based on this data, one can visualise the book losses sustained by the subscribers who have subscribed for Government loans in the regimented era. It is significant to note that more of these securities are now traded in the market. They are in the "purchase" list of RBI, although occasionally they have been found in the "sale" list under the "open market operations".

With the general rates of interest declining, the Government and RBI or RBI alone is in a better position to do the financial engineering as is deserved.

The RBI can adopt a multipronged strategy. If it wants a gradual approach it can purchase these securities under OMO. For instance, it can give a special window only to weak banks after their portfolio is analysed and encourage them for a swap. It can buy for instance all the securities more than five years and swap it with treasury bills. The banks can then take their own decision on buying other securities.

Remedies and plan of action in respect of investments devalued under approved securities

- A decision has to be taken in principle to adopt an innovative approach in handling this issue without detriment to the Government of India, the policies and practices at Reserve Bank of India, the monetary and credit policies - current and future with an objective to place the financial sector on a sounder footing.
- Government of India should adopt a special measure either through the Reserve Bank of India or by itself to enable banks to get rid of low coupon securities which were imposed on them earlier. The process can be simple and gradual or sudden and orchestrated. This action will enable the banks to have a tremendous boost to their current profitability and their balance sheet.
- The decision involves that, in the first instance, RBI can buy back all securities with the banks at a coupon rate of less than nine per cent at par. This will boost the banks balance sheet by a few thousand crores. Again, this exercise can be

restricted to the banks who are most affected. As banks will be forced to buy other securities to keep their SLR ratio, the securities market for higher coupons will become active and interest rates will get lower in the market.

- The same exercise can continue for the other institutions either by RBI buying the same and holding the same to maturity or by persuading institutions to redeem them earlier at par. To compensate them for the notional or actual loss incurred, they may be provided some special refinance at lower rates especially for infrastructure related financing from the RBI as a one time measure. The losses on interest may amount to Rs. 120 to Rs. 150 crores per institution for next two to three years which is easily bearable by them. Nothing can be done about State Government securities except RBI being aggressive in buying them under OMO. A discussion on restructuring State Government loans is being discussed separately.

Benefits

The restoration of health of the banking system in general and that of the "weak" banks in particular will relieve the Government of India the responsibility of capitalising the banks through the budget. In fact, a quick restoration of the profitability will grant many advantages including a better price for the Government on its holdings, better credit rating for the banks and the country leading to lower interest rates and restoration of confidence.

This process of financial engineering does not involve any additional outgo for Government or RBI. What GOI will be doing is converting a long term loan into a short term loan for a small portion of its outstandings. The resulting profit to banks are much higher as their balance sheets will get shored up by reversing of earlier losses arising due to the implementation of the Securities Marked to Market policy. This results in meeting the Capital Adequacy Ratio.

- As the present interest rates on outstanding GOI Securities range from five per cent to 14 per cent, Government Securities will have a narrower band from say 8 to 12 per cent. The author has proposed extinguishing of the higher coupon securities held by RBI to reduce Government outgo. (*See* Chapter V).

- A proper interest rate structure and good management can result in net profit earnings of as high as two per cent on assets. This will be amounting to net profits of Rs. 20,000 crores for the banking system as a whole which can result in income tax (corporation tax) revenue of Rs. 7,500 crores. This revenue is more useful for meeting Government expenditure than borrowings. Further, the Government will recover a substantially higher portion of its earlier investments in banks and help reduce the fiscal deficit in a more orderly way. This is again achieved due to the balanced credit and monetary policy of the Government and RBI and not due to an expropriatory policy which gives less to depositors and charges more to borrowers.
- If the Government and RBI do not exercise these choices, the imbalance in the system will continue till such time the securities mature. For example if bank A is holding Rs. 100 crores of securities which are now valued at Rs. 60 crores, then it will recover its full value on maturity which is five to ten years from now in some cases.
- Again, an issue may surface that these are things that occur and the banks will have to "face the consequences" of their earlier failures. One is at a loss to explain how the Ministry can point out the defects of entities under its own ownership and management publicly while the preferred approach should be to resolve it internally.
- If budgetary allocations of more than Rs. 10,000 crores can be made for recapitalisation; albeit by borrowing from the same entity there is no reason why some financial engineering can be made outside the budget.

Conclusion

A decision in principle has to be taken for a one time exercise to help banks, insurance companies and Provident Funds to get rid of the securities from their Portfolio imposed under the forced "SLR" securities era. It is absolutely necessary as a reform and administrative measure. It is the only conclusive way to effect a quicker improvement in the performance of the financial sector, especially their "weak" banks.

Anomalies created out of past actions cannot be wished away nor should it be allowed to be a drag on the system. The measures suggested in the paper require bold and innovative initiative on the part of GOI and RBI.

Essentially, they are no different from the various "damage control" or "crisis management" steps taken during the reform period. Measures taken will help the "weak banks" and this in turn will strengthen the whole system.

The Government of India and Reserve Bank of India are capable of innovation and they have demonstrated it in various fields. This is also a piece of innovative strategy which can be crafted and refined as necessary. It is hoped that with the above inputs, Government of India, RBI and weak banks operate together in the interest of further development of the financial sector without great cost to the public.

- A one time exercise to help banks, insurance companies and Provident Funds to get out of the securities imposed under the forced "SLR" securities era is absolutely necessary as a reform and administrative measure.
- It is the duly conclusive way to effect a quicker improvement in the performance of the financial sector.
- The focus on financial sector should be temporarily shifted from "growth", "deposits", "savings" and "credit" to profitability. The rest of the objectives will be achieved naturally by the market and encouraging the enterprise innovation and entrepreneurship. The principles of education, organisation and discipline should be inculcated in the persons responsible in financial markets.

> Today is always the result of actions and decisions taken yesterday. Yesterday's actions and decisions, no matter how courageous or wise they may have been, inevitably become today's problems, crises and stupidities. Yet it is the executive's specific job–whether he works in the government, in a business, or in any other institution - to commit today's resources to the future.
>
> Peter F. Drucker, *The Effective Executive*, p. 104

The banking and financial sector have some inherited areas in assets and liabilities, management practices, ideology and economic environment. These will continue to act on them even as they are in the present. Unless it is dealt with effectively, the future cannot be tackled.

NOTES

1. When this paper was submitted in 1999 the banking sector was having bouts of poor profitability.
2. When major changes were announced in provisioning, the true profitability as well as valuations of assets came forth. Some banks had Profit and Loss Accounts, which showed a huge provisioning for loss of assets.
3. Eventually all nationalised banks, State Bank of India and private sector banks began to ride a wave of higher profitability due to massive growth in the economy, higher savings in the economy and better deployment of resources.
4. This has augured well for India. Indian banks thrived even as global commercial banks went under the international financial crisis spurred by the financial debacles in New York based commercial banks, investment banks and the financial sector.
5. The Reserve Bank of India as well as respective bank management deserves the fullest honours and credits for the management of the crucial transition in the Indian financial sector.
6. The experience gained and standardizations make the banking system fit for operations in a market economy.
7. In the current scenario Government securities held by banks have to be reduced and made over to other financial sectors as well as directly by the public as a high SLR or holding of Government securities voluntarily by banks do not augur well for economic efficiency. This matter can be studied further for motivating more policy and action towards an active Government securities market.

Ten

Interest Rate, State Governments and Market

[1999]

The Government of India has been following a policy of providing assistance to the State Governments in the form of loans. This is in addition to the provision for sharing of tax revenue, provision for grants and other forms of assistance.

The State Governments have also been allowed to access loans from the market. This is subject to certain directions and restrictions laid down by the Central Government as well as the Reserve Bank of India.

The loans outstanding to the Government of India are of the order of Rs. 2,01,788.29 crores comprising Rs. 1,97,411.45 crores from the States and Rs. 4,376.84 crores from the Union Territories for the year 1998-99. The loans outstanding by State Governments to the market are not known to the author now. It is still substantial and merits study. The budget for 1999-2000 is Rs. 2,04,790.96 crores for State Governments and Rs. 4,661.30 crores for Union Territory Governments.

It is now increasingly revealed that the State Governments are allotting substantial amounts for payment of interest. In the latest budget of the State of Karnataka the provision for debt services has been of the order of 13 per cent of the Plan and Non-Plan Expenditure.

The interest receipts from the State Governments are estimated at Rs. 21,364.92 crores in the revised estimate 1998-99 and at Rs. 25,243.99 crores in budget estimate 1999-2000 against the B.E. 1998-99 of Rs. 20, 795.97 crores.

It is important to discuss the interest rates which the State Governments have been paying and the necessity of integrating these rates with the market rates.

Current Situation

The receipts budget for the year 1999-2000 reveals the following in detail the interest rates paid by State Governments to the Central Government is mentioned here below

Loans which were given in the respective periods mentioned in Col. (I) and now outstanding have an interest rate corresponding in Col. (II).

Period	Interest Rate p.a.
(I)	(II)
1.4.1974 - 31.7.1974	4.75%
1.8.1974 - 31.5.1981	6.25%
1.6.1981 - 31.5.1982	7.25%
1.6.1982 - 31.5.1983	7.75%
1.6.1983 - 31.5.1984	8.75%
1.6.1984 - 31.5.1985	9.75%
1.6.1985 - 31.5.1986	10.25%
1.6.1986 - 31.5.1989	12.00%
1.6.1989 - 31.5.1991	13.00%
1.6.1991 - 31.5.1992	13.50%
1.6.1992 - 31.5.1993	14.50%
1.6.1993 - 01.9.1993	15.00%
2.9.1993 - 31.12.1998	14.50%
1.1.1999 - —	14.00%

One of the most significant decisions in the current year has been the disintermediation by the Central Government in so far as the National Savings Scheme is concerned. In future, 75 per cent of the collections will be provided to State Governments and 25 per cent will be retained by the centre.

The interest rates on National Savings Scheme have been higher than other instruments offered by banks or the interest yield on other sovereign debt. This is an anomaly as the State should have the lowest rate of interest as, from the view of investor, it is the safest investment. The rates offered have been higher than market rates. This has been the main reason for the sharp increase in National Savings. It remains a moot point whether these savings will attract the same amount, at the rates equal to instruments offered by banks.

The questions before us are:

- Whether the State Governments are having a possibility of raising market loans at rates cheaper than those now charged by the Government or by the National Savings Route?
- Whether the State Governments can raise loans from markets in order to repay the Central Government and still save on interest outgo?
- Can this be achieved without altering the market interest rates drastically?
- Will this result in substantial savings to the State Government?
- Will it result in any benefits or Savings to the Central Government?
- Will it result in any benefits to banks?
- Will it result in benefits to citizens?
- Will it be detrimental to savers?
- The answers are positive to all questions and the answer is no to the last question.

Proposition

The Government of India declares a policy that all State Governments repay loans to the Central Government by raising resources from the market.

Scenario When State Governments Go to the Market

Going to the market at this stage is an advantage to the State Governments. The present demand for short and medium term paper i.e. between one year and six years is very high and the market rate is 11.5 per cent to 12 per cent.

When State Governments raise loans solely for the purpose of repayment to Central Government, then there will not be any alteration in the interest rate. This is, of course subject to the Central Government reducing its outstandings to RBI or in market loans simultaneously.

It is possible to save about 1.5 per cent to two per cent of the total current outstandings. The savings could be about Rs. 3,000 crores per annum collectively to all the State Governments.

The Central Government will be having substantial savings in intermediation costs. In addition, when the Central Government redeems its debt in the market, it will be able to raise sovereign debt cheaper as this will technically result in a fiscal surplus. The savings will shift from the people directly into State Government instruments. It will also be easier for the Central Government to henceforth announce a policy that it will no longer provide any loans to the State Governments and State Governments will have to access the markets on their own subject to their capacity to pay interest and repay principal.

Citizens could benefit as they would now have wider choices in investments. They can move from a lower rate in banks to a higher rate in State Government securities. This is, of course, subject to the change in perception, that State Governments are safer than banks. The services to be provided, whether directly or through financial intermediaries, should be better than those offered by banks. More important, citizens benefit from the lower outgo of interest from State Governments who can improve governance or reduce taxes.

Insurance companies, provident funds, mutual funds and banks, will benefit from the exercise as they have a scope for improving interest on their investment portfolio, especially when the rates for Central Government securities are declining due to better fiscal position.

To a certain extent, portfolio investment from FIIs will be attracted to State Government securities. More important, they or other financial intermediaries can profit from trading in securities. They also can service the saving citizen and earn fees.

There is no detriment to savers. They will have a comparable choice for investment. They can always move from a lower yield to a higher yield.

In the instant case "crowding out" will not occur as the process of intermediation is being discontinued. The total debt outstanding will remain the same to the financial sector.

The Need

Whenever any proposal, radical or otherwise, is considered, the first question that emerges is whether there is a need for any action or change.

The process of disintermediation by the Central Government in respect of loans to State Governments is a necessity.

The origins of lending to the State Governments emanated in the control and allocation era. The capital flows in the country were rigidly controlled by the Central Government as a conscious policy. Capital was deemed to be "scarce". Spending for capital projects by State Governments required capital; the only solution was to provide loans.

The programme then deviated into a "Scheme". The National Savings was a source of capital for the Central Government. State Governments were to be "roped in" for the Savings "effort". As a reward they would be given loans corresponding to the "net" collection, meaning the amount which was raised minus the repayments.

The Scheme also had a subsidy component and a timing mismatch (or asset liability mismatch). The Savings schemes were for tenors of one year to seven years but loans were of a longer duration. The net result was that loans ballooned for the Central Government and interest receipts were less than the outgo on the Savings account simply because the receipts were at earlier contracted rates and fresh loans were at higher rates.

After 1991, and with the decision to go with "market" rates, the Central Government then changed its policy and like a banker decided to charge a premium on the interest rates paid to savers for loans lent to State Governments. The State Governments were already hooked to this scheme and could not do without them. The revenue deficits had become so bad that they had to resort to these amounts as a source for the Budgets.

Somewhere along the line, the Central Government did not notice that the real interest rates given on their Savings instruments were higher than "market" rates. The aggressive mobilisation of Savings by State Government aided by dollops of incentives and helped by a little bit of coercion, resulted in massive inflows into Savings. The Government is on record stating that the fiscal deficit has enlarged more than budgeted figures only because of this phenomenon.

If State Governments can pay the Central Government interest rates at 12.5 to 15.5 per cent on loans taken earlier, there is no reason why they should not borrow from the "market" that is all individuals and financial intermediaries.

If the State Governments can raise funds from the market and repay loans, it amounts to an inflow into the Central government and technically becomes a reduction in the fiscal deficit, provided it reduces its borrowings from the Reserve Bank of India or from the "market".

This singular step could result in savings to State Governments on those tenors which are priced at above today's market rates. The savings can be as high as Rs. 3,000 crores per year and over Rs. 30,000 crores over ten years, given the current interest rate and inflation scenario.

If this is not done, a higher outgo from State Governments throughout this tenure will be manifest at the cost of governance and social services.

This will be possible in today's unique scenario as current surpluses in the financial sector will aid this re-engineering and directly assist banks to improve profitability and individuals to aid their yield. The programme will thus satisfy the needs of everyone and therefore a step be in "Public Interest". What is required is to dislodge inertia and not be enveloped by imaginary fears and concerns.

> Be not afraid of anything. You will do marvellous work. The moment you fear, you are nobody. It is fear that is the case of misery in the world.
>
> It is fear that is the greatest of all superstitions. It is fear that is the cause of our woes, and it is fearlessness that brings heaven in a moment. — *Swami Vivekananda*

The Policy

Whenever an idea is expressed the same has to be converted into a policy. Policy decision to discontinue an existing activity has many implications. The consequences have to be analysed.

Discontinuing loans to the States will not be detrimental to the Centre. In fact, it is a major relief. It is an activity that can be discontinued without pain or loss.

The Central Government spends an enormous amount of time and energy in managing this portfolio which can be done by the financial sector at no extra cost.

There is no difference between the State being indebted to the Central Government and being indebted to the people of the country.

Provision of loans is following a conscious decision by the Central Government. It has no constitutional obligation to provide loans to the State Governments.

It would have been a different position if Central Government had surpluses generated on the revenue account, a surplus budget or a negligible fiscal deficit in order to provide loans to the State Government. The Central Government is burdened with debt. At present it has a total debt of Rs. 9,90,263 crores outstanding with corresponding assets of Rs. 5,85,472 crores. Its foreign loans are at book value and if valued at current exchange rate the debt in rupee terms will increase further dramatically. Therefore, the reduction in State Government loans will result in reduction of Central Government's liability to the market.

Any further borrowings by State Government will have to be assessed by their borrowing capacity which is determined again by ability to repay both principal and interest. Loans should not be automatic but taken on the basis of need.

Current political and bureaucratic thinking at State Governments is to disregard prudence when it comes to spending borrowed money for revenue expenditure citing reasons of inevitability.

A conscious decision not to lend any more funds to State Governments will not meet with any problems as long as the State Governments are given a reasonable freedom to raise loans from the market subject to their capacity to repay.

A decision in principle will be required at the highest level on this policy. Such a decision will have widespread ramifications on the polity, on the financial system, on the Government machinery and on the public too. Therefore, the pros and cons of such a policy have to be taken with utmost care and deliberation.

The most appropriate authority to dwell on this issue, of course, can be the 11th Finance Commission.

The Central Government has to take a policy decision. A well prepared Memorandum has to be made available to State Governments for discussion. State Governments have to be assisted to get prepared for the eventualities. Debate, discussion and dialogue both in and out of Government should be mandatory.

It is also beyond doubt that the entire process has to have the stamp of approval of the Reserve Bank of India. The Reserve Bank of India is not only involved in the policy but also in its implementation. Therefore, each step of the process has to be validated by the central bank.

The most important part is that implementation will have to be discussed thoroughly. The implementation itself will be the plan and the policy.

The Plan

Once a decision is taken in principle, it will have to be carried out. This requires a detailed plan. The planning process itself has to have management inputs. The success lies in carrying out the decision and fructifying into tangible results.

> The future is not going to be made tomorrow; it is being made today, and largely by the decisions and actions taken with respect to the tasks of today. Conversely, what is being done to bring about the future directly affects the present. The tasks overlap. They require one unified strategy. Otherwise, they cannot be done at all.
>
> Peter F. Drucker, *Managing for Results*

The Plan has to be carried out with the least destabilising affect. It has to be voluntary. It should not have the necessity for force, compulsion or rancour. The Plan has to be carried out with the requisite qualities of education, organisation and discipline.

The possible constraints and fall-outs have to be discussed well in advance and required infrastructure and requirements generated on a Programme Evaluation and Research Technique.

Requisite institutional support has to be available from the Reserve Bank of India and the leading banks.

The loans carrying lower rates of interest viz. 1.75 per cent to 9.75 per cent, it would be advisable for the Central Government to transmute those loans on an YTM of say 11.25 per cent and forgive the balance of the debt.

If there are say Rs. 5,000/- crores loans outstanding at 6 per cent then the value of the loan on an YTM basis will be, say Rs. 3,200 crores. This Rs. 3,200 crores is to be repaid by the State Government and Rs. 1,800 crores will be written off under a Debt Forgiveness programme.

This will reduce the debt repayment burden of States which they have been claiming for. This can be subject to terms and conditions also.

The Programme

Once it is decided in principle, then the tentative programme has to be decided. It has to be managed. The technique adopted can be the critical path method (called as CPM in Management Theory). This has to be incorporated in budgetary exercise. The total outstanding loans from State Governments, their payment dates, their interest schedules, and interest rates have to be classified.

The decision has to be taken in consultation with State Governments, Reserve Bank of India, merchant bankers, primary dealers and money market dealers as to what type of instrument, tenor, rate of interest and method of holding is to be decided for each State Government. Once decided, the programme can be carried on a calendar basis.

> Action solves the difficulties which action creates. Inaction can only paralyse and slay... The errors of life and progress are more exuberant and striking but less fatal than the errors of decay and reaction. — *Sri Aurobindo*

The Sequence

Should a decision be taken in principle, the sequence of the operations for State to go to the market has to be decided. The State Governments have exposures to the market. In the last five years, State Governments have their loans oversubscribed. The management of the loans is by the RBI.

When an exercise of this magnitude is undertaken, setting a time frame and proper sequencing will have considerable benefits. The time frame can be two years from ground zero. Ground zero is the starting time as decided by the political leadership and the bureaucracy.

The sequencing can be Rs. 2,00,000 crores divided by twenty four. This amounts to approximately Rs. 8,000 crores per month. The instruments should be placed preferably in the middle of the month. The markets will then anticipate these issues and plan for their investments.

As the proceeds will go towards reduction of loans to central Governments and in turn, the Central Government will extinguish its liability, the role of the Reserve Bank in stabilising the market will be crucial.

Through the open market mechanism the Reserve Bank will have to manage the fund flow and keep interest rates at equilibrium. The whole process should go unhindered for 24 months as a structured programme. It can be advanced to 12 months also, when there is no problem envisaged. It then depends on the management at the Government of India and the Reserve Bank of India.

With considerable advance preparation and a major role of the Government of India and the Reserve Bank of India, PDs and the banking system it can be also telescoped into a fortnight. This exercise could save substantial sums over the next two years. The target date can be middle of June 2000.

The Benefits

The first and foremost benefit is to the Government of India. The process of disintermediation gives it a firm grip on the macro-economy. The total assets and liabilities will come down by a like amount, taking management of Central Government finance and economy to a sounder footing.

Its debt rating will go up and sovereign rating of the nation will go up a few notches. This will enable the overall borrowing costs of the Indian nation to go lower. It will reduce the effects of crowding out and also give the Reserve Bank free reign in interest rate and liquidity management.

The Fallouts

As far as one can see there can be hardly any negative fallout. If the programme is not understood fully then there could be some adverse criticism, if unexpected changes happen in the market place. The fallout will be positive to the Central Government, State Government the financial sector and the people if carried out efficiently and completely.

There could be an apprehension on the part of State Governments that they will be exposed to the vagaries of the market. Their fears have to be allayed by the Central Government and the Reserve Bank of India.

The fallout on the SLR regime has to be evaluated by the RBI. It has to decide whether the securities issued by State Governments qualify for SLR.

Innovation and Entrepreneurship

Entrepreneurship is defined as "the activity of shifting of resources from a lower yield to a higher yield". While the individual is always striving towards this goal in his own interest, the state in India has always seemed to do the opposite.

State intervention in all areas has been evident since the late 50s in the Indian economy. The interventionist policies especially since the late sixties have rendered the State into an area which can be termed as the opposite of entrepreneurship that is shifting resources from a higher yield to a lower yield.

Examples are too numerous to quote here. The average yield on Government of India's and State Government's commercial investment has been less than 2 per cent to 3 per cent on an overall basis. Borrowing @ 14 per cent and getting a return of 3 per cent is entrepreneurship in reverse.

Instead of looking for mundane ideas of cutting costs of telephone and travel, the Government ought to look at more potential areas.

Should the Government be innovative and entrepreneurial? Of course, it should.

> "The entrepreneur," said the French economist J.B. Say around 1800, "shifts economic resources out of an area of lower and into an area of higher productivity and greater yield."
>
> Every practice rests on theory, even if the practitioners themselves are unaware of it. Entrepreneurship rests on a theory of economy and society. The theory sees change as normal and indeed as healthy. And it sees the major task in society – and especially in the economy – as doing something different rather than doing better what is already being done. This is basically what Say, two hundred years ago, meant when he coined the term *entrepreneur.*
>
> It was intended upsets and disorganizes. As Joseph Schumpeter formulated it, his task is "creative destruction".

> He postulated that dynamic disequilibrium brought on by the innovating entrepreneur, rather than equilibrium and optimization, is the "norm" of a healthy economy and the central reality for economic theory and economic practice.
>
> Peter F. Drucker, *Innovation and Entrepreneurship*

It now remains to be seen—whether the people in the Indian Government, in the RBI and in the financial system rise up to the occasion? Can they be entrepreneurial?

An innovator transmutes values. In this instance, by making the State governments go to the markets, the Central Government provides an opportunity for investor to directly invest in State Government securities. At the same time, the State Governments are provided an opportunity to go to the market instead of to the Central Government. In the operation of markets it is economic efficiency that will score.

> Government failure arises when state actions fail to improve economic efficiency or when the Government redistributes income to the wrong people.
>
> Samuelson and Nordhaus, *Economics* 15th Ed., p. 769

The Opportunity

There is no time like the present to launch this programme. There is surplus liquidity in the market. The overall interest rate is declining. The inflation rate is unexpectedly low and also much lower than projected at six per cent per annum.

The markets are hungry for instruments. This is especially so of tenors of up to five years. The rates that may prevail could be considerably lower than the major portion of the current debt to the Government of India.

Simplicity

This programme looks incredibly simple. The complexities will remain in the background. The instruments offered have to benefit the investor community at large. They should have the ease of handling, simplicity, sure administration and quality in returns.

The Instruments

Should a decision be taken, in principle, to have the State Governments go to the market with the singular objective of raising money to repay loans to the Central Governments it is necessary to evolve instruments that are simple and easy to market.

The best instruments are Bonds. They should be of a convenient denomination. It can be at a face value of Rs. 1,000.

Bonds can be of two types—with interest payment on an annual or half yearly basis or deep discount where the payment on maturity will include both interest and principle.

The advantage in the Deep Discount Bond is that the clerical work in respect of payment of interest is avoided.

The third form can be in loans. This is the current practice. However, this type of instrument will be suitable only for financial intermediaries or insurance and provident funds.

The required criteria in any form of borrowing: safety, liquidity, earning and ease in trading and obtaining repayment should be incorporated ab initio.

With the implementation of the above programmes or otherwise the scheme for providing loans against national savings raised by State Governments should be discontinued.

Points of view of an economist, academician, an administrator or a politician could differ. There must also be an attempt to present an existing situation in a new light, from the viewpoint of citizens, who sees potential for innovation and entrepreneurship in Government.

Any citizen who deals with public issues understands well the processes in the Government of India and its institutions. Any positive suggestions go through tortuous processes before they are accepted.

The current situation demands innovation and as such conveying an entrepreneurial and innovative idea where control and administration have been the norm is a difficult proposition.

> Hence entrepreneurship is by no means limited to the economic sphere although the term originated there. It pertains to all activities of human beings other than those one might term "existential" rather than "social". And we now know that there is little difference between

> entrepreneurship whatever the sphere. The entrepreneur in education and the entrepreneur in health care-both have been fertile fields-do very much the same things, use very much the same tools, and encounter very much the same problems as the entrepreneur in a business or a labour union.

Types of Market Friendly Instruments

The State Governments can issue basically three types of securities

- Interest Earning Bond
- Deep Discount Bond
- Loans

In the case of the interest earning bond the payout of interest whether quarterly or half yearly will provide the income in cash to the investor. In the case of a deep discount the investment will provide a capital gain. And in the case of loans, it will be equal to the present type of instrument.

The subject matter for further discussion would be

- The quantum of debt issue to be decided for each State Government
- The type of debt i.e. loan, bond with interest, deep discount bonds or loans.
- The management of debt issue whether it will rest with the RBI, the State Government, primary dealer or merchant banker.
- The term of the debt; whether repayment will synchronise with the existing debt repayments.
- The nature of the instrument—whether SGL Physical Certificate or Dematerialised.
- The sequencing of the disintermediation process and time frame by which it is accomplished.

Benefits

The benefits that accrue from having State Governments go to market are self-evident as well as immense. They are

- The highest benefits to State Governments will be savings in interest rates. The savings for one year for all of SGs and UTs could be of order of Rs. 3,000 crores per annum.

- The Central Government will be saved from intermediation and its costs.
- The bankers will have a better choice and yield on their investments.
- The public will have access to marketable debt instruments.
- Overall savings for Central and State Governments can enable them to concentrate resource on social services like education, public assets and governance.
- The goals of economic efficiency and proper redistribution of income can be achieved more easily.

Conclusion

The programme for making the State Governments go to market can be realised with a proper understanding and will to manage the fiscal affairs of the Governments, both Central and State, efficiently. This should be taken on a holistic basis.

> Today is always the result of actions and decisions taken yesterday. Yesterday's actions and decisions, no matter how courageous or wise they may have been, inevitably become today's problems, crises, and stupidities. Yet it is the executive's specific job—whether he works in the government, in a business, or in any other institution—to commit today's resources to the future.
>
> Peter F. Drucker, *The Effective Executive,* p. 104

The impact on macro-economic or budgetary exercises needs to be taken into account. There is no chance of any negative impact on fiscal, financial or commercial transactions only when the proceeds have to be used to retire the market debt of the Government of India.

The potential impact can be positive as the finances of Government of India would provide a better picture. The savings of the Government of India and State Governments on revenue account go into much needed social services.

The present situation is right for undertaking this exercise and achieving the objective. It is hoped that this paper stimulates discussion, debate and dialogue within Government and the financial sector and contribute to strengthening all institutions within this country.

Another major exercise will be on what should be done on the question of loans carrying less than 10 per cent rate of interest. Should they be allowed to continue, should they be paid back or should they be converted to Market rate on YTM basis? This can be decided by the Central Government alone.

Central Government will save considerable sums on interest outgo by virtue of demand for Government paper and improvement in the rating, both international as well as domestic. The programme will be a success as long as the gains perceived from the whole exercises are made available as provisions for attaining the goals in the social sector.

The major issue to be confronted is whether the Government and RBI will be able to visualise and formulate a proper policy and implementation framework, when a decision is taken in principle.

NOTES

1. This was written in 1999 and is relevant more today than ever before.
2. This requires further study and preparation before action. A positive situation today is that data and information which were not available in 1999 are available today and quite exhaustive.
3. The Management Schools and Departments in Universities can take this up as a matter for deeper study and make it actionable.
4. The Ministry of Finance and the RBI could collaborate on this.
5. There is a mechanism where the RBI now interacts regularly with the Finance Secretaries of State Governments. If it is advantageous to State Governments then State Governments could take the lead.
6. This could be presented before the members of the Rajya Sabha to be further articulated.
7. The Economic institutions and think tanks should take this up as a measure to resolve a lot of issues that crop up in India: development of the bond market, liquidity in Government securities and active trading in the securities markets.
8. This will unlock the resources of the Government of India and reduce activity and expenditure at the Central Government and State Governments for all time to come
9. The debt markets in India are now poised for the leap to better performance. The national and international markets will benefit from the Indian transition. The measures will have global impact including how analysts and raters look at the Indian situation.
10. The requirement of debt instruments will be growing in India due to the increase in the investment potential of provident funds, insurance funds and pension funds.

Eleven

Immediate Positions

[2000]

It is very heartening to note that there is a move to work towards integration and harmony in respect of interest rates. The Government of India, Reserve Bank of India and financial intermediaries are now moving in this direction.

Interest rates are the interaction of demand and supply of money. In India, financial markets are fragmented and have many segments. The influence of interest rates in one segment need not influence the interest rate in another instantly.

The following steps are suggested to keep interest rates at equilibrium and closer to principles of economic efficiency in the near future

1. *Primary Issues Only in Treasury-Bills for Next 14 Months:* The RBI (Primary Issue on Behalf of Government) should not issue any long dated securities in the remainder of this year as well as for the whole of next year for Government borrowings. It should be in treasury bills only. This will keep interest rates low. Considerable savings will accrue to the Government of India. Primary issues of Government debt should be taken over by the Government.

2. *Conversion of RBI Lending to Government into Treasury Bills Only:* The entire portfolio of outstanding Government securities held by the Reserve Bank of India should be converted into Treasury Bills. This will save the Government of India hundreds of crores in interest payments. This will also change the outlook of the market and pave the way to lower interest rates. This will confine Open Market Operations to T. Bills only and stabilize interest rates in the Short Term Market.

3. *Open Market Operations in Government Securities:* An effective Open Market Operation with a fixed rate like that of the United States Federal Reserve serves the twin options of benchmarking of interest rates as well as absorbing all short term surpluses as well as in providing short term liquidity more effectively.

Today OMO is not an everyday process. It is based on a reactive principle. Further, OMO should be open directly to all market intermediaries and not confined to PDs.

4. *RBI Should Resort to Two Way Operations on Long Dated Securities:* The RBI can flatten the curve by buying long dated, i.e. securities of more than five years tenure. This needs to be extended to buying of securities of coupon rates less than 10 per cent. This can be done by Open Market Operations. It can put on the sale window treasury bills or securities of less than five years tenor of the same YTM. In essence, the market will hurry to shift to the market securities and will lower the YTM in the market for longer dated securities.

The gilt yield curve will re-establish itself. To make it more specific, if the gilt yield curve is now 9.05 per cent to 12.1 per cent it will re-establish to a more perfect 9.05 per cent to 10.75 per cent. This will be redundant if item number two is adopted.

5. *RBI's Direct Intervention in the National Savings Scheme Segment:* Though belated the Government has taken a positive step in reducing the interest rates on National Savings. The recent reduction in the NSC rate has attracted a wider attention from economists, commentators and the media and it has been acclaimed. Whether Government will further reduce interest rates on NSC, PPF etc. as a sequel to the Bank Rate cut on April 1, 2006 is now not known.

Even as the rates have been reduced there is need for the Government of India to be more dynamic. The issue is not that of reducing the rates now or increasing it later. The issue is that its interest rate on all instruments should be at rates lower than that of commercial financial intermediaries as they are sovereign in nature and should be at the lowest rate in the interest rate spectrum.

Even as the Government has now reduced it is better for the Reserve Bank to intervene more directly. It can use its powers to prohibit all financial intermediaries whether banks, NBFCs, cooperative banks or the like to invest in National Savings Certificates or any other instruments under the National Savings Scheme forthwith.

It is common knowledge that State Governments and their officers coerce banks and other financial intermediaries into investing in National Savings. Even now, State Governments are offering enticements in the form of incentives.

The yield on National Savings is higher than the rate on Government securities. Banks or other financial intermediaries invest in NSCs for a lucrative yield. This is a distortion in financial intermediation.

This is only a suggestion and it is left to the wisdom of the RBI. The RBI must suggest to the Government a dynamic regime on interest rates of National Savings Instruments.

6. *Depth in Inter-Bank Market:* The RBI must create a framework for an interbank term money market. The time is now ripe. The RBI can reduce the CRR by another one per cent as a surprise measure.

Then it can mandate that at least one percentage of the banks deposits should be in other banks on a term money basis of 30, 60, 90, 180 and 364 days basis. This will lead to the deepening maturing of the MIBOR and at the same time will not be inflationary.

When inter-bank borrowings take place, reliance on deposits from public will come down. Banker's concentration will be to fine-tune their earnings. This will lead to maturity of the financial markets. When banks turn their attention to their profitability, they will try to prune their liabilities in line with market interest rates.

Currently organizational behaviour of banks is to offer better interest rates compared to rival banks. This leads to pushing up interest rates which need not be required or warranted.

7. *Developing the Corporate Bond Market:* The Reserve Bank should encourage the creation of a Corporate Bond market. Even as it is the function and obligation of the market to create such an instrument, the Reserve Bank must act in a facilitating role.

Measures to Implement the Corporate Bond Market

(a) All consortium loans of Corporates with a paid up capital of Rs. 100 crores or above or market capitalisation of Rs. 100 crores and above, can be converted into tradable bonds.
(b) All term loans issued by more than one FI by consortium or on the books, outstanding from similar corporates can be converted into tradable Bonds.
(c) All term loans issued to companies who are now facing a cash crunch can be converted into tradable secured deep

discount bonds with an extended repayment period. This can be on the basis that the project is sound and the company can meet its obligations when its current cash flow problems are resolved. This will enable corporates to complete the projects expeditiously.

(d) The issue of securities in terms of long term as well as short term assets need to be addressed ratings and credit evaluation has to be thoroughly institutionalised.

(e) It is to be emphasized here that shedding some assets by banks and financial institutions in favour of the public or other market intermediaries like mutual funds, unit trusts, investment banks and people and companies with large net worth who have investable surplus is not detrimental to their short term or long term interests. In fact, banks should concentrate on their primary activity that is, tending to the transactions in the economy. This should be the primary source of income and earnings as this is their main business. This will save them from chasing capital for the purpose of meeting capital adequacy ratios.

(g) Manufacturing companies, Housing Finance Companies and NBFCs should be discouraged from taking fixed deposits. Instead, they should be encouraged to go for bonds.

8. *Uniformity in CRR-SLR for All Banking Organisations:* All banks, co-operative and regional rural banks should have uniformity in conditions of Bank regulation in the form of CRR and SLR. This will provide equality among all banks who handle public transactions. It will also even out interest rates in the system and at the same time broaden the market for Government securities.

This should extend to all financial intermediaries or entities that raise deposits from public. Certain intermediaries like NBFC, Financial Institutions and housing loan companies raise deposits at various rates which are considerably high. Along with manufacturing companies, these intermediaries should be forbidden from raising fixed deposits. They should be allowed to float corporate bonds which should be tradable. These will be subscribed both by public as well as banks.

9. *Savings Bank Rate:* The savings bank rate is now a controlled rate. It has to move towards a market rate by giving freedom to banks to pay the interest rates on such terms as is viable for them.

In the process, rates will find their own levels for the Savings Bank accounts. In this process, the RBI can announce a future date; say one year from the date of announcement so that banks and customers will prepare themselves.

10. *Export Finance Rates:* Export Finance rates on rupee are fixed at 10 per cent. The margin on lending in foreign currency, e.g., in US Dollars by banks is decided by the Government. In both cases banks are entitled to freedom to fix the respective rates.

11. *Pruning of "Approved Securities":* The securities under the "SLR" should be pruned to accommodate just enough securities that enable banks to comply with the 25 per cent requirements. Every Government security or securities which have already been notified need not be a SLR security. Reserve Bank should remove all securities which are more than five years in maturity from the list, gradually. Any other instrument other than a Government of India Treasury Bill or loan should not find a place in the SLR list. Securities which have been classified earlier should be de-listed. In the long run, SLR securities should be confined to T. Bills up to 364 days only.

12. *Twelve per cent Rate on PF cannot BE Sacrosanct*: Another position is noteworthy to mention. The Finance Minister and Labour Minister have made statements that the 12 per cent returns on Provident Funds are sacrosanct. This has to be addressed from a point of reasoning and logic. The Government cannot adopt a "market policy" and then "fix" "adopt" or "protect" a rate of interest for any section of the population.

The returns in terms of fixed rates of return need not be guaranteed by Government to any section of the population. Economists need to explain in simple language to the public that interest rates are like any other price. They have to go up or down depending on the demand and supply of money.

Again one wonders, how the Government is in the picture. The Trustees of the Provident Fund Organisation are the custodians of the money and it is their decision on investments that determine yield. This income is consolidated and offered as return to the balances on Provident Funds. The Government need not say that 12 or 13 or 11 or 10 is the rate. The Trustees are repositories of the faith of the Provident Fund subscribers. They should be the spokesmen in the interest of the subscribers and not any third party.

Provoking and invoking emotions and insensibilities do not serve the cause of labour or others within a nation.

13. *Benefit of Lower Interest Rates should Accrue to Government First*: Lower interest rates are a feature phenomenon which has evolved over the last 15 months. Primarily, there is also the evidence of a very low inflation rate. The first benefit of lower interest rates should go to the Government, both Central and State, for a variety of reasons. In the first instance, the revenue expenditure has ballooned in the last few years primarily on account of interest payments on a ballooning debt. It is now beneficial to do some financial engineering which benefit both Central Government and State Governments – INSTANTLY. This will save the Government money for the legitimate functions of state and also for the social welfare especially in the region of primary education, primary health and public services.

14. *Choice between Inflation and High Interest Rates*: If the Government wants everybody to have a higher rate of interest, then we would rather have inflation back. It is not the case of business that interest rates should be low per se.

Inflation rates have floated down. The reasons can be attributed to "success" of Government policies or RBI or a variety of reasons. Interest rates have to respond to a lowering of inflation. If they have not responded lower, it means that the demand for money is sustaining the interest rates at high real levels. This also creates undue profitability for intermediaries.

If the Reserve Bank of India, Government of India and economists, pensioners, savers, journalists, commentators and a large portion of the public want interest to remain at current levels and at the same time view inflation rate at three per cent as good and logical then it is the economic injustice of the gravest kind. In other words either interest rate has to come down or inflation rate has to go up

While it is an economic fact that inflation rates remaining at high levels in various countries have come down due to policies or by production, productivity or consumption patterns, a rising inflation rate is a contradiction. No Government, politician, consumer or a Central Bank consciously wants the inflation rate to go up. In the case of Japan, the inflation is zero. The Japanese Government is in an economic quandary. Even if it is comfortable to have the inflation rate up, it cannot force people to spend more or demand more goods. The RBI therefore has to act to nudge interest rates to equilibrium levels in all circumstances and situations.

These are only some steps among many that can be adopted to cause a "shift" in interest rates to a downward slope as is justified now.

Unless proactive and intelligent steps are taken, Indian interest rates across the spectrum may face a problem in having downward shifts in a low inflation scenario. One should not forget the economic principle, that the price of a good will remain at the same level, (inertial level) until something comes and dislodges the same. This is similar to the law of inertia in Physics.

Conclusion

(a) Pushing interest rates downwards should not be the sole objective. Interest rates should be dynamic to respond to the changes in supply and demand of money.

(b) Effective interest rate management by the Central Government, the Reserve Bank of India and market operators is a dire necessity. Maintaining interest rate stability for a day or even a moment is the function of the Central Bank. In a modern society, the Central Bank alone can provide or absorb short term liquidity. Absence of this results in interest rate fluctuations for the moment.

(c) The financial ecosystem is bedevilled with lack of understanding, lack of application of sound theories withholding and delaying action when needed, unfounded fears, occupation with inanities and procrastination. Undue haste by operators, policy makers or functionaries, poor management and an ineffective executive are causes for anomalies, distortions and aberrations in interest rates.

(d) The aim of any Government and the Central Bank should be economic efficiency. It then should provide the conditions for interest rates to remain at ideal levels.

(e) This should be done on principles of economics, management as well as ethical governance, whether by the State, Institution or Corporates. The first two come as science and require cultivation and practice and the last governs the principles in dealing with individuals, human beings and associations which form society.

(f) Interest rate distortions can also take place when operators out of ignorance or due to externalities resort to actions and practices which are contrary to sound economic or business principles theory or practice. Such ignorance has to be addressed through proper education, organization and discipline.

NOTES

1. After submitting 10 papers it was worthwhile to make a summary which required immediate attention and therefore it was entitled immediate positions.
2. The critiques have been done in all the previous papers. This was intended to take up areas which had scope for regulation or improvement.
3. Many suggestions made in this Chapter are still valid today and require extensive study, debate and dialogue.
4. Research will also reveal developments, regulations and practices that have emerged and evolved since the year 2000 and it is important to make the reform and improvements sustainable.
5. There has been considerable reform and progress in the management of savings schemes from 2000 till now.
6. In the case of Provident Funds the rate of interest is now lower at 8.5 per cent and considerable debate and dialogue is developing on the PF interest rate.
7. Creation of a market for Pension Funds is also called for.

Twelve

Action from the Reserve Bank of India

[2000]

The developments in the last two weeks have revealed capabilities for interest rate distortions to take place. Even as the call money rates went beyond range, the long term interest rates remained stable, foreign exchange premia and interest rates across the spectrum remained fairly steady. Unlike the occasions a few years ago, the short term distortions had no effect on any of the interest rates in other segments. This reveals an improvement in degree in the maturity of the Indian financial markets.

The handling of the reverse repo facility by RBI is a display of agility. It can be described as deft handling and deserves commendation.

However, the call money rates going out of range display the following characteristics:

- The Reserve Bank of India does not have the depth of resources to manage daily interest rates within bound limits.
- RBI needs to considerably improve its interaction with the banking system. This is required if its intentions to provide liquidity in money markets have to be converted into action.
- The banking industry has not reached the required level of maturity of advanced markets. Market movements reveal the absence of education, organisation and discipline.

The following merit the attention of the Government of India and the Reserve Bank of India.

1. *CRR and Its Effects on Short Term Interest Rates:* The CRR on Demand and Time Liabilities should be maintained throughout a given period. The system of 65 per cent and Reporting Friday should be done away with. Any system which specifies that the Cash Reserve Ratio can be variable over a period of time can cause distortions. The cash reserve kept by banks must always be fixed.

The question of verifiability of the Demand and Time Liability is purely a management issue and has to be in the background. The penalties for not keeping CRR to the required level also should be reasonable, but bank management should also see that they do not cross their boundary lines.

Till such time that the banking system is able to satisfy the Reserve Bank of India about the quantum of its Demand and Time Liabilities, the Reserve Bank should announce forthwith that CRR should be maintained at the prescribed rate on all DTL for a fortnight following every Friday. After the requisite data and information systems are in place, it should be on a daily basis.

Reserve Bank has declared that it is its intended policy direction that CRR should be gradually reduced. As a special incentive the RBI may declare that CRR be reduced to five or even three per cent on all RURAL deposits by Commercial Banks. This will enable commercial banks to focus on their rural branches for transaction money and savings. As a measure for stability a CRR cut of one per cent can be announced within the next few weeks rather than wait for the October Policy.

The above measures would result in a release of over Rs. 10,000 crores into the system. The multiplier will create resources to the extent of Rs. 40,000 crores in the banking system over the next one year.

The resources generated should take care of the requirements of the growing Indian economy. This also removes discrimination between commercial banks and other rural deposit taking agencies. Following this system, the payment of interest on CRR balances can be done away with.

2. *Government Securities for 2000-2001*: The RBI has seen the devolvement of long term as well as short term securities on itself. This can be traced to the following:

- The banks have seen rise in their credit disbursal which are at more profitable rates at PLR plus.

- They already have surplus securities under SLR which does not cast any obligation to buy any further Government securities especially where they perceive yields as low.
- Asset Liability Matching is now a pre-requisite. Banks are required to match their liabilities with assets for the same period. Basically, if a bank has a short term liability for say, three years, it cannot have an asset maturing in 15 years.
- Any increase in credit demand is good for bankers as it improves their income.
- The balance of the amount can be raised via bonds and loans as usual but well spaced. The total target of Rs. 1,10,000 crores will take away a major portion of the national savings of the year and will prevent interest rates from softening.

3. *Open Market Operations*: The Reserve Bank of India should convert the OMO into an effective two way operation. If necessary, the RBI can keep a gap of 0.5 per cent on the short term securities. Again, the buy option should be given to the whole financial system and not only the PDs. This will enable the banks to take positions at a comfortable level and lead to stability.

To begin with, the Reserve Bank of India can put on the buy list, in the securities in Table 12.1.

All securities over five year maturity with a coupon rate of less than 10.5% at an YTM of 10.5 per cent. This will flatten the long term yield curve. The market will chose to unload the securities in favour of RBI and the liquidity in the system will improve.

To have a balance, the RBI can put on the self list securities less than five years tenor at an YTM of 9.75 to 10.4 per cent. This will enable the operators to "shuffle" their portfolios.

But ultimately the OMO should be in Treasury Bills (14, 91, 182 and 364 days only) leaving the long term to the market. The OMO rate can be set at around 9.5 per cent which is quite above the present level. When Bank Rate is aligned to 9.0 per cent, this exercise will not in the least effect market rates of interest.

4. *Calendar for Issue of Government Securities*: It is better for RBI on behalf of the Government of India to issue more of short term securities. The 14 day auction can be turned into a daily one with an issue amount of Rs. 100 crores. With exclusion of Saturdays

Table 12.1

Sl. No.	IN %	Name of Loan	Earliest Date of Maturity	Budget Amount
1	6.75	Loan, 2006	15-05-2006	788.78
2	6.75	Loan, 2007	22-11-2007	621.49
3	7.00	Loan, 2009	25-05-2009	1197.44
4	7.50	Loan, 2010	12-05-2010	1456.22
5	8.00	Loan, 2011	27-04-2011	1477.92
6	8.75	Loan, 2010	13-12-2010	500.22
7	9.00	Loan, 2013	24-05-2013	1999.33
8	9.50	Loan, 2008	20-02-2008	672.48
10	10.00	Loan, 2014	30-05-2014	2333.26
11	10.25	Loan, 2012	01-06-2012	1755.13
12	10.50	Loan, 2014	29-10-2014	1755.10
			Total >>	**13,079.45**

and Sundays the total amount involved will be Rs. 1,200 crores. Whenever market conditions permit and the Government of India is in need of short term resources, the amount can be increased.

The 91 days auction can be bi-weekly at Rs. 400 crores per issue. This would generate a sum of Rs. 800 crores per week. Eventually, the pay-out may equal the receipts. But the sum outstanding will be Rs. 10,400 crores outstanding on any given day. This quantum would be sufficient for the financial intermediaries for planning their short term resource utilisation. Eventually the market may require a higher quantity of Government securities and the Government and the Reserve Bank of India should cater to this requirement by releasing securities in its stocks or enabling Government to borrow more for productive purposes.

The 182 days auction can be once a week at Rs. 500 crores. This will involve Rs. 12,000 crores outstanding at any given time. The 364 days auction can be once a week at Rs. 500 crores. This will involve Rs. 25,000 crores outstanding at any given time. The market is bound to take this amount easily in a growing economy.

Altogether, the short term outstanding will be Rs. 48,000 crores. In a growing economy it should be ensured by the Government as well as by the Reserve Bank of India that the banking system has sufficient access to short-term securities. A secure investment option which gives a steady return will give incentive to the banking system to perform its true function.

The savings for Government will be substantial at around 200 basis points. The Government need not fear about its repayment problem. Under a modern economy principle, the interest rates have to be maintained at equilibrium by the Reserve Bank. This demands an expertise in handling resources. This stock of short term securities will ensure better management of interest rates.

At the moment, the issue of long dated securities by the Reserve Bank of India is marked by uncertainty. There is no reason why it should be so. The long dated securities should also be issued on a calendar basis.

The ways and means advances can be done away with and instead, short term T. Bills can be issued to meet the same. This can be by special auction as and when needed by the Government. The RBI can take on as much as is not taken by the market to maintain equilibrium.

The Government should not be obsessed with a notion that in the matter of domestic securities it has to have long dated loans. The total savings in an economy committed to Government securities will not change on tenor of outstanding Government securities.

In this light, the Reserve Bank and the Government should consider that all Long Term Government securities presently held by Reserve Bank of India can be swapped for Treasury Bills. It can be done on a single day or over a period of time. Government outstanding to Reserve Bank of India will be the same. Only the instruments will change.

But it will definitely mean a big difference in perception. It will send a signal to the markets that there will be a shortage of long term paper over a period of time. Hence, the overall interest burden of the Central Government will come down.

When the Reserve Bank of India has stock of Treasury Bills of this dimension, management of interest rates and Open Market Operations become easier.

> It is emphasised that Reserve Bank of India need not resort to issue long dated paper in the remainder of this financial year.

The Draft Calendar for issue of Government Securities 2000-2001 is given in the Table 12.2 below:

Table 12.2: Draft Calendar for Issue of Government Securities 2000-2001

1. Every Monday, Tuesday, Wednesday, Thursday and Friday	14 Day T. BILLS	Rs. 100 crores or as much as desired.
2. Every Tuesday & Friday	91 Day T. BILLS	Rs. 400 crores each
3. Every Wednesday	Long term 3 to 7 years only	As decided in advance on a calendar basis
4. Every Thursday	364 Day T. BILLS	Rs. 500 crores
5. Every Friday	182 Day T. BILLS	Rs. 500 crores
6. Saturday	14 Day T. BILLS	Optional for ways and means

Under this programme, there will be potential for planning for the exact outflow and inflow for each day both for the RBI, the Government and the markets.

5. *Statutory Liquidity Ratio—Approved Securities*: It is necessary to prune the SLR list. The Statutory Liquidity Ratio approved securities outstanding are much higher than required by the banks. The problem with SLR securities is that they have been more statutory and less liquid. Banks subscribe to such securities by statutory compulsion. They have been hardly liquid. Liquidity is not over a term, long or medium or short, nor for a year month, fortnight or week. Liquidity should be here and now. It should be for the present day and hour, nay for the minute.

It is suggested that:

The SLR securities list be pruned by de-listing,

(a) All securities other than Central Government securities
(b) All securities with a maturity or residual maturity of more than five years.

Such an action will enable banks to concentrate on short-term securities. The operators in the market other than banks, which is made up of individuals, business organisations, financial intermediaries, institutions and funds will go for long term securities. This churning in the market will reduce overall interest costs for the Government as it can borrow at a lower rate of interest from banks for the short term. At the same time it will provide an opportunity for the market operators to obtain a higher yield on long term securities.

It is, therefore, suggested that the SLR would comprise of the following securities:

(a) All Treasury Bills 14, 91, 182 and 364 days.
(b) All securities with a maturity of less than five years or a residual maturity of less than five years.

The banking system today has an outstanding of Rs. 3,50,000 crores as investment in Government securities. The technical requirement is only Rs. 2,50,000 crores. A sum of Rs. 1,00,000 crores is held as an investment banking option.

Suppose the RBI were to remove securities as mentioned above, then approximately Rs. 70,000 crores worth of short term securities will be required by banks for the current positions alone. This would replace long term securities with short term.

In such a treasury initiative, for incremental investments, bankers would require short term securities only. So it will be easier for Reserve Bank of India to place T. Bills in the market instead of dated securities. This will ease the interest payments of the Government of India.

As there will be a shortage of Government securities of higher interest rates, Funds, Provident Funds and other Financial Intermediaries will have to resort to the secondary market instead of the primary market. This will prevent banks from making losses on securities trading. They would end up with lesser yields.

This alone will result in orderly churning. Ultimately, banks do not have to resort to securities for their income but realise their interest from commercial lending. If opportunities do not present themselves, then the choice they will have to exercise is not to resort to more liabilities by going for term deposits. Instead, let them concentrate on transaction money.

When banks unload the securities which are not on the approved list, it is up to the market financial intermediaries and individuals to absorb the same. It follows that when a security is sold, the value of the security could be higher to the buyer in the form of better yield when he holds that security for a longer term.

This will result in a twin advantage. First, banks will not require to go for additional capital. Additional capital is required only when they increase their liabilities. Second, accent will be on profitability rather than growth in liabilities.

Therefore, attention will be on quality of assets rather than gross increase in business. Disintermediation will thus result in choices for public to invest in Government securities as an option, than resort to bank deposits.

This will meet Reserve Bank of India's objectives that Government securities should be held also by citizens rather than exclusively by banks and financial institutions.

6. *Marketing Government Securities to the Public:* The RBI has been desirous that a wider section of the public holds a higher quantum of Government securities. The time is ripe for a vigorous introduction during this year itself. The issue should be in the form of bonds. The denomination can be standardised at Rs. 1,000 face value.

It would be beneficial if the tenor is 3 years, 5 years and 7 years to begin with.

The Bonds should preferably be in demat form with the institutions like SHCIL. The investors would prefer this to the current mechanism of Securities General Ledger account because of the convenience. The demat (short form of dematerialised) format is more convenient than the SGL format. In the SGL format, the investor is bound to have a Sub-SGL account with a bank.

Demat format will make it very convenient for trading by any individual, company, bank, financial intermediary, mutual fund, DFHI and the Reserve Bank of India.

The Bonds should count for SLR, should be eligible for support in market operations via DFHI and major banks and also capable of being held by individuals, corporate, mutual funds and institutions.

The pricing of the Bond can be in the range of 10.5 to 11 per cent. This being higher than the Bank deposits, it can be an attraction to the general public as well as all financial intermediaries.

The marketing can be by auction through PDs and then distributed through the financial system. The target can be Rs. 500 crores per week from October through March on a calendar basis. The total sum raised will be Rs. 12,000 crores.

Securities in the segment of zero coupon and deep discount bonds could be more popular with the investing public as well as convenient for management by the treasury and PDO. In a trading segment, zero coupon bonds could be very easy to trade as the value of the bonds will go up incrementally on a daily basis.

It will also resolve the problem of stripping of the interest and record date for interest payments. Enclosed Notes will explain how the zero coupon bond or deep discount bond will be better for management of taxation related issues.

Disintermediation will result in banks offering financial services for gain rather than futile chasing of deposits. Overall savings in economy will improve as and when effective returns are provided by borrowers to citizens who save.

7. *Bank Rate:* The bank rate has to be revised upward to provide stability for the interest rate structure. The bank rate is a rate at which refinance is available to banks. In India it is not really refinance, but the banker getting back his own money.

In the current context, the Indian banking system can be considered weak. Banking organisations suffer from management deficiencies and lack education, organisation and discipline.

In the analysis of the developments in the past six weeks, the refinance at bank rate went up to Rs. 15,000 crores. This drained the Reserve Bank's ability to manage the short term market. The bank rate should be set at such a rate that it does not give leeway for banks to borrow at bank rate and invest the same in short term or Government securities. Raising the rate to 9 per cent will prevent the banks from doing so.

Another reasoning for the increase in bank rate in a comparative or relative sense is that the US interest rate has increased by two per cent over one year. The US inflation rate continues to remain low. But in India the inflation rate has gone up by two per cent. Inflationary conditions are latent in India on several counts. The differential in inflation rate is bound to result in a depreciation of the rupee over this year or over.

Under today's conditions in the Indian financial market, keeping the bank rate at nine per cent makes it a fair price for lending as a last resort.

Even while doing so, the Reserve Bank of India should be careful that it has the Open Market Operations in place to provide stability for interest rates on an intra-day as well as near term basis.

When this is done, the market should not construe that it is a signal for all rates to go up. Most of the time, RBI feels that

> Bank's actions should be stimulated by talk and persuasion. It is more effective when it is done by regulatory action.

The RBI's action on 21 July 2000 is laudable and should be followed by another rate increase of 1 per cent.

8. *Withdrawal of Surcharge of Interest on Advances Against Imports*: The Reserve Bank of India recently slapped a "surcharge" of 50 per cent on interest on borrowings made by importers. This needs to be withdrawn. This move does not really affect the demand for foreign exchange by importers.

The quantum of surcharge is also not rational. The 50 per cent sounds more like a whim. An institution like the Reserve Bank of India should be objective.

Currently, there is no limit of time to charge interest rate surcharge.

A decision has to emerge from the Reserve Bank of India to define what constitutes "temporary".

Whenever it is a "temporary" measure, it would be advisable that the tenure of the requirement, direction or order is contained in the notification itself. For instance, it can be "This will be valid till 3[1] August 2000". This would be orderly and efficient executive action and not arbitrary.

There is no reason to believe that a mere imposition of surcharge will act as a curb on the import activity. Any import activity is planned very much ahead of the time of imports. As the landed cost of any import is depending on its need and marketability, it is doubtful whether any surcharge on import will act as a deterrent for us on foreign exchange.

The volatility in foreign exchange market arises because of supply and demand imbalances and inadequacies in the management of foreign exchange.

It is therefore urged that this tool need not be used in managing foreign exchange volatility as it is an unjust punishment for the importer without serving the intended purpose. It constitutes an economic injustice which goes against the Preamble of the Indian Constitution. In a scenario of interest rate deregulation, this surcharge will also amount to an unintended earning to commercial banks.

In the light of the above, it is hereby requested that the RBI withdraw this surcharge with immediate effect and it is also prayed that such a surcharge need not be imposed again whenever there is exchange market volatility.

9. *Types of Government Bonds for the Public, Interest and Taxation Issues*: The question of payment of interest and the valuation of Government bonds is a matter engaging the attention of policy makers. The matter can be currently resolved by issue of deep discount bonds. This issue is engaging the attention of policy makers.

The matter can be currently resolved by issue of deep discount bonds or zero coupon bonds. Zero coupon bonds do not involve payment of interest over their maturity. Therefore, there is no question of interest income for the investor.

The gain here is the capital appreciation of the bond over the period of investment. In an illiquid economy, such a gain can be realised only on redemption of the bond. At the time of redemption as per accounting practice and as per Income Tax law, it becomes a Capital Gain. The Capital Gain becomes payable only on maturity and realisation of the Capital Gain.

In a liquid market, the bond will appreciate on a daily basis. Therefore, the bond will be more liquid than the one where interest payment is involved. There will be no accounting problem for the Government as in the case of loans where coupons have to be issued on the basis of issue.

Whenever the bond is bought and sold in the market, the difference becomes a short term capital gain. This amounts to an earning equal to interest and will be treated as income for the year.

Liquidity will be assured when market players move from lower yields to higher yields. Liquidity also happens when the holder sells the security and invests the proceeds in alternative investments expecting a higher yield.

Liquidity is assured when yields are marginally higher than bank's Fixed Deposit rates.

10. *Liquidity Adjustment Facility—LAF:* The Liquidity Adjustment Facility launched by the RBI is in the throes of the learning curve. In the light of observations made hereto, the following also may be noted:

Liquidity Adjustment Facility is a contortion. What is sought to be achieved by the LAF can be easily obtained by an efficient operation of the Open Market Operations. The amount of liquidity at the disposal of the Reserve Bank of India is finite. Therefore, it can provide just enough as it would like to let go at the moment.

The Discounting facility at Bank Rate is available only to individual banks. It works under boundary conditions.

The Open Market Operations have to be universal. Open market operations will have to work on a two way basis during the course of the day if at all equilibrium is to be maintained.

Both Repo and Reverse Repo work on the principles of providing securities for cash or for providing cash for securities. In Open Market Operations, the difference is that securities are bought and sold at a single interest rate. The key in Open Market Operations therefore is as long as the Reserve Bank of India is able to maintain the equilibrium, the banking system then is not afraid of taking on demand liabilities, as it always has an avenue of investment for the day.

What makes this possible also is that no bank can increase liabilities beyond a point. Capital adequacy norms require to be met.

For the system as whole therefore, there is no liquidity problem in that the Reserve Bank of India DOES absorb all the surplus cash of the day and also meets the requirements of the day fully.

The market as a whole therefore takes the OMO rate as the guide for its money market activities.

It is up to the Reserve Bank of India and the operators to work out the synergy required to make this possible.

11. *Commercial Paper*: The Commercial Paper Market has witnessed a pricing which is less than the PLR rate and less than Government Paper. This is interpreted as a trend that commercial borrowers have greater strength. This is not a fact. This trend is because there is no sufficient supply of Government paper of that tenor. This can be made good by issuing T. Bills of sufficient quantity as highlighted in the main paper.

Ordinarily, Commercial Paper should be struck around the PLR rate if not higher. PLR rate in India is for loans. Short term loans in India are predominantly Cash Credits. Commercial Paper is backed by recourse to the lender under OCC.

Corporates were gaining at the expense of banks. While one bank was a willing subscriber to CP in the absence of alternate demand, another banker was a loser, as the OCC limits even though earmarked would not be utilised.

OCC limits need not necessarily be at PLR. Therefore, if the contracted rate was say, 14.5 per cent, the Corporates gained funds at a lower rate from the market. This causes opportunity losses for banks who actually support the client. The necessity of providing more short term Government paper to the market need not be emphasised again.

Therefore, the RBI should also take a decision that only CPs "without recourse", that is, without a comfort from the bank having the Cash Credit to the client can be raised from market. CPs should be serviced out of cash flow only and with a suitable rating from the credit rating agencies.

This will restore true pricing for CPs and restore equilibrium for short term corporate instruments. Indirectly, Government will gain in the availability of short term funds at lower prices.

12. *Open Market Operations*: An effective OMO should have two way quotes. Ideally OMO should be in short term securities i.e. T. Bills only leaving the long term securities to the market. Till such time, the RBI can act to even out the guilt-yield curve by specific and strategic action. One such specific action is to buy out long term securities which have a coupon rate less than today's market interest price, which is equal to the issue price of today's securities. This action would help the holders to have liquidity which was not available to them hitherto.

Conclusion

Management of the short term fund flow in the economy requires a higher degree of organisation and management than formulation of policy. Equipping for this is a tireless and unrelenting work of continuous upgradation of facilities and operators who respond to the needs of the market.

However, interest rate distortions and aberrations need not be the order of the day just because of inadequacy of technology or operational needs. What is needed by the Reserve Bank of India and market operators is a closer look at the operations and a thorough understanding and comprehension about the function of interest rates. Interest rate movements act as signals indicating variations in demand and supply of money in particular segments.

In this process, the Government of India as a very large borrower and also as a custodian of public interest, needs to take a view on interest rate movements as indicators. The Government currently appears concerned about interest outflow. However, it does not seem to have mastery on the subject of interest rates.

The result has been an economic injustice of the highest order as interest rate movements have been quite contrary to established developed perceptions and have hurt both borrowers and lenders.

There is a need for better understanding and comprehension on the subject. Government policy should be directed towards the free interplay of forces of demand and supply. Institutions, markets and operators need to be guided by policies aimed at nudging interest rates to equilibrium levels in respective market segments.

NOTES

1. This paper was submitted in July 2000. It highlighted the action required by RBI.
2. Over next seven years, RBI has acted in many segments and this has proved beneficial for the financial sector and the Indian citizen.
3. Some actions can still be carried out.
4. In many cases RBI has expressed intentions to do some actions mentioned in this paper, but it has been constrained by inadequate responses from Government and market.
5. Bankers and academics can take a cue from this Chapter and encourage research and study.
6. This can enable the Government and the RBI to better action oriented steps.
7. The RBI has developed a transparent, democratic and informed way to develop policies and action instruments. It frequently calls for public comment on its proposed agenda for action. It must be responded to by bankers, stakeholders, academicians and citizens. This will prove beneficial in the medium run.

Thirteen

Forex Volatility and Interest Rates

[2000]

The Reserve Bank of India has taken several steps in managing foreign exchange "volatility". Most significant among them are imposing a surcharge on import finance, withdrawal of Refinance Limits, Raising of the Bank Rate and increase in CRR.

The most unexpected and new measure in its armory which has not been used before is to raise short term interest rates by using the REPO mechanism to absorb short term money. It has chosen to raise the 4-day and 5-day interest rates to as high as 14 to 15 per cent.

This paper seeks to highlight the futility of such a move for the sole purpose of managing foreign exchange rates or volatility.

Foreign Exchange Rates are Prices Arising out of a Phenomenon of Demand and Supply

It is a well known fact that the rates of foreign exchange are determined purely on demand and supply of the same. The effects of demand on foreign exchange are not only for the cash markets i.e. for the day but also due to the intricate mechanisms prevailing in the banking and financial markets. Future demand also has an influence on today's price. Therefore, when a demand for a good is unsatisfied by current supply, the price has to go up. In this instance, it is the US Dollar, which is commanding a higher price.

It is now well settled by the RBI statement on Foreign Exchange markets and pronouncements of the Government of India that the RBI as well as the Government of India asserts that the value of the rupee is "market determined".

One fails to understand that, if it is really so, why should the RBI resort to "measures", "orders", "directives" and in journalistic language "diktat", "fiat" and "hard talk"? RBI steps that have been taken were not required under the circumstances.

It is not a new experience that the rupee has depreciated. It was bound to be; due to reasons which are economically sound. The manner of depreciation is also not new. In the last 10 years, the rupee has been in a stupor for months together, even in the midst of changes in fundamentals. The rupee has a tendency to sleep as if in a coma. The trend has been described ably by foreign exchange dealers as "a dead man's heartbeat".

Unfortunately, everyone in this country, particularly, editors, commentators, columnists, economists not to forget, policy makers and the country's economy managers are noticeably silent during this period. The persons affected by exchange rates, exporters, importers, forex traders and bankers are the only persons who are on tenterhooks. This is because the rupee has a tendency to wake up from its coma and suddenly fluctuate vigorously.

This is the main issue before the economy today. The RBI frowns on speculation and volatility and directs the proceedings. In the process it unleashes specific steps which are ad hoc, arbitrary and unnecessary. And finally the rupee is at rest again having found its equilibrium level. A scientific assessment needs to be done to analyse specific actions of RBI.

The conclusion would be that domestic interest rates need not be disturbed to address the issue of foreign exchange price fluctuations, volatility or speculation.

Exchange Rate Fluctuations and RBI Policy

Reserve Bank's action should not be to alter short term or long term interest rates targeted at specific segments.

Any Central Bank in the advanced world uses intervention only as a special or emergency tool. It does not seemingly take concern of movements in foreign exchange rates. But without exception they maintain the stability of short term interest rates. The Reserve Bank must understand the futility of raising short term interest rates.

If the return on holding a dollar exceeds.0125 paise per day, then no amount of mopping of funds by RBI will be of avail. Therefore, the differentials have to come down by market operations. Normally, the banking system takes care of itself. In times where demand is in excess of supply, the banking system cannot hold on to interest rate differential.

Even otherwise, when supply is in excess for spot, the price tends to go down. This is where RBI intervention has been done effectively. The Reserve Bank of India's action on short term interest rates leaves one stupefied on the issue whether it considers the law of economics suspended over its activity or area.

The raising of short-term interest rates has no influence in determining the equilibrium value of the rupee in the short term. Nor does it address the issue of volatility or control thereof. A simple portrayal of the supply and demand curve gives the equilibrium rate under a given situation.

As is conveyed by two eminent economists in the world Prof. P.R. Brahmananda and Prof. Jeffrey Sachs, RBI should not be overly worried about the rupee depreciation. The RBI should not have any difficulty in deciding whether it wants external stability which will be at the cost of interest rate disequilibrium or whether it wants internal stability at the cost of external exchange rate disequilibrium.

It is to be made clear that the RBI should effectively manage with the two choices before it. It needs to publicly discuss options available, gather opinion and more important, convert itself into an organization which is effective in its interaction with the market. Most important is its job of guiding the markets to organization and discipline on a foundation of education.

There appears to be a general feeling that RBI "measures" "orders" "diktat" "hard talk" and "guidelines" are ones which influence markets. Nothing can be farther from hard facts. There can be no reasoning or proof that can be provided that the equilibrium value of the rupee has rested from such measures.

The only way that RBI can do is to prove otherwise. Where is the application of fair, unbiased and representative data and information to prove the point that it is RBI or its steps alone that is providing stability or the conditions thereof?

When RBI's decisions are devoid of reasoning and logic the consequence is that one class of citizens is favoured at the cost of another class. This is the worst form of economic injustice, which goes against the preamble of the Constitution of India. Like everything else in India, justification of action can be made for a variety of causes and reasons and everything that is done is said to be done in "good faith" and in "public interest".

Issues on Intervention

What is the difference between normal buying and selling of foreign currency by the Reserve Bank of India and "intervention"? It is no surprise to markets or the public or to commentators, opinion makers, media and analysts that the Reserve Bank buys and sells currency regularly. This is evident in the "increase" and "decrease" in reserves which are published in the *Weekly Statistical Supplement*. Therefore, the Reserve Bank of India has to evolve its own policy, codes and practices for the quality of interventions.

It is obvious therefore, under "steady" market conditions the buying and selling of the Reserve Bank of India goes without comment. What does invite attention for intervention is "sudden" or "unanticipated" depreciation of the rupee. An intervention has to be separate from "buying" and "selling".

Here the Reserve Bank of India has in the last nine years of its operations in the Foreign Currency area has consistently performed in one area. It has effectively "intervened" to prevent an appreciation of the rupee. The only exception has been when there were specific bouts of volatility.

From an independent viewpoint, a mere addition to reserves is not necessarily a sign of strength. It also indicates that the foreign resources which are assiduously wooed are not dispersed into the Indian economy as these are meant to be.

The Reserve Bank of India utilised the resources garnered from the public or from the issue of currency to purchase foreign currency. Considering the size of the economy it has very limited resources of its own. The Government of India has virtually no savings of its own and is a perpetual debtor. Therefore adding to foreign currency reserves and maintaining them is done at a huge cost to the economy which has not been debated, measured or evaluated to date.

Reserves whether of foreign currency, or food grains, or water are meant to be used for specific purposes and occasions. Reserves do not belong to the Government of India or to the Reserve Bank of India. Reserves are out of people's money. These do not represent the savings of the Government of India or the capital of the Reserve

Bank of India. They have been created by issuing money or utilising money impounded by law.

Very few understand the difference between the Reserve Bank of India and the Government of India. One ignorant columnist impetuously remarked that the reserves held abroad belonged to the Government! Politicians as well as others consider a depreciation of the currency as a measure of virility lost! The confusion is compounded when words and phrases which are used in common or journalistic language can mean quite differently in the refined areas of finance.

Therefore, words have no meaning unless they can be translated into action. And action to be right or appropriate requires to be directed, refined and be capable of being carried out with the right persons at the job.

In this context the Reserve Bank should have its own action plan which meets the desired end or results. An evaluation of characteristics of intervention is therefore necessary internally to qualify for a series of steps for action.

Actions from Reserve Bank of India

The Statement of the RBI specifically stated that it may "directly or indirectly" intervene in the market for settling of foreign currency. There is only one intervention by the Reserve Bank of India that is direct. There is no such thing called indirect in the activity of buying and selling. By indirect, RBI implies actions and measures outside the activity of buying and selling.

By convention and practice the Reserve Bank of India is not a banker to corporates or individuals. Therefore its sales and purchases are from banks or authorized dealers only. As an institution which is created by law in public interest, the Reserve Bank of India deals with situations which demand public interest. The Reserve Bank of India has to determine how it needs to act when there is a demand or need to supply of a particular good, in this case foreign currency. This needs to be in public interest which is the benefit of the largest number of citizens at a given time.

The Reserve Bank, therefore, has to act. As its actions or inactions have a long and lasting impact on the market and therefore on the lives and businesses of the people, its actions have to be right and appear to be right.

Therefore this could be in the best public interest if the RBI targets the market as a whole and not specifically to that the requirements of the oil section or the Government of India debt repayment. The RBI need not have stated so if it could act as it conveyed. However, in a market economy the action of the Reserve Bank of India has to be subtle and not active or reactive.

Debt repayment is on a known schedule. It is for the Government to take care of its interests. Great influence is being exercised by media, analysts, commentators including learned former Governors and officials of the Reserve Bank of India. Opinions do matter and must be valued as extremely valuable by the Central Bank. What could be damaging are presumptions and assumptions, particularly attributed to the Reserve Bank. It is good that the statement has mentioned specifics in this regard. Future statements and speeches from RBI should incorporate such points for conveying clarity to the members of the public.

In comparison, EURO has depreciated over 15 per cent compared to US$. It is noteworthy that ECB has not altered interest rates specifically to arrest this depreciation.

Powers and Functions of RBI

One has to concede:

- That RBI cannot pre determine a particular value
- It cannot announce the timing or the price of intervention in advance
- It has to act in a manner that does not confer any benefit on one set of citizens to the detriment of another
- Its actions must be transparent
- Its actions are subject to scrutiny and analysis
- Its decisions on price cannot be questioned on appropriateness
- Its authority is unquestionable when it acts in public interest

In the exercise of its functions and authority, the RBI has **to decide.** Decision is a managerial as well as executive function, especially so when interacting with the market.

The RBI should involve standards which prevent buying and selling under ordinary circumstances. In such a case quality of intervention will improve tremendously.

RBI should Develop a Buffer in Forex Operations

The Reserve Bank of India needs to have a buffer between itself and the market that can provide signals of quantitative and qualitative movements in foreign exchange. The Indian Foreign Exchange Market is relatively mature. It has enough rivalry to provide comfort to citizens. In the last 12 months a remarkable level of stability has been achieved in forward premia.

The Reserve Bank of India should create an array of buffers to intervene effectively.

It is already using the State Bank of India to intervene. Qualitatively this needs to be addressed. The State Bank of India is the largest forex operator in the market. Therefore, it has privy to most of the information on heavy inflows and outflows. It meets the needs from the market as well as takes it from the market.

It is suggested that a special desk in SBI be activated solely for intervention. This desk should be part of the treasury team. However, its demand and supply management from this desk should be with authorized dealers and not from customers. This will make it a wholesale operation. RBI buying or selling through this desk should be for marginal supply or demand and operations should be subtle. RBI should evolve standards which prevent buying and selling under ordinary circumstances. In such a case, quality of intervention will improve tremendously.

In addition to State Bank of India, RBI can encourage EXIM bank of India to be a trader in foreign exchange. In India, foreign exchange trading for the sake of it is not done because of capital account restrictions. A beginning can be made by introducing a substantial corpus, say Rs. 4,000 to Rs. 8,000 crores as preference capital into Exim Bank. The Exim Bank can be the buffer for evening hour, the leads and lags in forex transactions. Again, Exim Bank forex transactions should be to Authorised Dealers only.

Discount and Finance House—another buffer which can be built up is the DFHI. The DFHI can be the integrator between the forex market, money market and the GSEC short term market. This is very crucial for the future. Being a public institution it can develop a treasury desk which will act as a buffer. More important, the desk will help active trading and avoid speculation. The DFHI can also use the trading desk to develop an apprenticeship programme to develop traders with integration skills. Such traders will be in demand from banks and financial institutions who can also develop promising personnel on deputation for two or three years.

In addition to above, all Institutions can also have Forex Desks with limited capital account convertibility. Development of a buffer of at least three billion US dollars as reserves with these three desks will make RBI day to day intervention or buying and selling redundant. Instead of dealing with the market the RBI will be dealing with these three agencies in its subtle intervention.

Intervention of RBI

At the times of volatility, RBI should intervene by tenders or auctions. The RBI is already doing the same for the T. Bills and money market operations. The advantage of a tender or an auction for RBI is that it can accept or reject the prices at its will. It is always advantageous for RBI to sell dollars for TOM and SPOT by tender as this will enable authorized dealers to project their "genuine demand".

As a multitude of operators will be bidding, the RBI can adopt a "cut off" price just at the time of the tender, or auction, thus will have the time to assess market demand which operates through the tender mechanism. This will make the intervention qualitatively superior.

Reserve Bank should understand that the law of supply and demand is immutable. If it considers the exchange rate as beyond what it considers as acceptable, the one and only thing it can do is SELL.

The quantity of selling can be:

- A fixed or variable quantity per day on cash basis.
- A fixed or variable quantity per day on TOM and SPOT basis.
- A fixed or variable quantity for forwards, but restricted only to the first month.

The quality of selling can be:

- Intervention in the market through SBI
- Intervention in the market through five major authorized dealers
- Intervention in the market by selling to all authorized dealers. Invitation of bids for purchases by tender

- The best possible intervention by RBI could be to buy and sell at a single price throughout the day irrespective of the quality that may flow in or out.

The timing of intervention can be at:

- Opening hours if the price opens up high during opening
- Middle of the trading day if price exhibits sharp increases during the middle of the day
- Closing of the day if there is unsatisfied demand and pushes up prices for the closing as well as for the next day which are reflected in premia.

Ordinarily the Reserve Bank should not sell or buy on forwards. Exceptions can be when first month premium crosses 200 basis points over the regular interest rate differential.

The Reserve Bank of India must note that the cost holding a dollar is only Rs. 0125 paise per day. Any holder of dollars can afford to hold a dollar at that cost if the volatility or expectations crosses 5 paise to 10 paise per day. In a market appreciation of 12 paise in a day the realization for one paise amounts to 100 per cent per annum.

RBI and Stability

The key to RBI activity is to be the balancing wheel that will make fluctuations in price minimal. Given a choice between external "stability" and interest rate stability at home, central bankers all round the world keep domestic interest rates stable especially for the day.

Therefore, at this juncture RBI need not be harsh on the market. It has to be harsh on itself and critically examine its policy, codes and practices and more important its functions.

After a reflection within, it is hoped that all the measures taken or proposed to address short term volatility can be deemed inappropriate and irrelevant. Thus the RBI can concentrate solely on supply and demand as the variables for determining price of foreign exchange.

The Reserve Bank of India must therefore internally separate its Exchange Reserve Management function from its function of providing order for foreign exchange markets.

Conclusion

There is a need for extensive examination of the measures taken by RBI. These should be tested by hypothesis or case study to prove that domestic interest rates need not be tampered when there is a fluctuation in foreign exchange rates whether normal, abnormal or due to specific externalities.

A dispassionate analysis by way of discussion, dialogue and debate as well as application of fundamental principles in economics and management will reveal that there are better ways to manage the foreign exchange market as well as the domestic interest rates.

Any steps towards a market economy institution as well as operators require sound policies and executive action, which by nature are different from those in command and control economy.

Reserve Bank of India should desist from making any changes on domestic interest rates specifically to contain Foreign Exchange Fluctuations or Management of volatility or speculation in Foreign Exchange. As a response to volatility, the Reserve Bank should efficiently balance supply and demand at such levels as desired by it from time to time.

Summary

1. The law of demand and supply is immutable. The market presently needs supply, where marginal supply for the short term is available only with Reserve Bank of India. The quality, quantity and timing of intervention by RBI must be determined and improved to meet market requirements and contingencies.
2. RBI need not resort to any measures it has recently taken or proposes to be taken. It must therefore restore order by retracing of steps taken in the last few weeks. RBI should be ready with its position on rupee value should it again appreciate after intervention.
3. RBI should restore conditions for the interest rate equilibrium to 9.5 per cent to 11 per cent in the Gilt yield curve. RBI can improve bank rate to 9 per cent.
4. Current situation requires medium to heavy intervention. RBI can use opportunity to suck out excess liquidity from

the system. Drawing down reserves at appropriate times have several advantages and current level is no cause for concern. The Reserves belong to the public for appropriate use. "External" stability is a relative value. Distortion of interest rates in domestic commitments deliberately destabilizes the internal financial markets which has worse consequences. Its meaning becomes a shade of opinion. Internal growth is concrete. Therefore without internal stability external stability becomes meaningless.

5. What defines "public interest"? It is the largest benefit to the largest number of people at a given time. The Reserve Bank cannot deliberately dole out economic injustice. The Reserve Bank must have a balancing wheel for foreign exchange which does not interfere with domestic interest structure.
6. The actions of the Reserve Bank must be subject to rigorous internal and external scrutiny by application of fundamental principles. Experience gained from this exercise should be applied to practices which will manage exchange rate appreciation and depreciation without resorting to the type of measures which have been applied in the last one month.
7. A massive education campaign should be directed particularly to media which is prone to hype situations. Reserve Bank of India and Government of India should have adequate public relations expertise in conveying positions. If RBI wants to, then it can impose margins. This can be 100 per cent on SPOT and TOM. 50 per cent on Merchant Transaction for First month and 20 per cent on banks purchases. The RBI and sensible operators should attack the speculator and not the market.

NOTES

1. This paper was written when there was intense volatility in the Rupee US Dollar pair and had a deep effect the financial system and the market.
2. The measures taken by RBI did not address the situation. It caused widespread damage to the stakeholders in the financial situation.

3. This paper was written impetuously that RBI should have more prepared and well informed choices and instruments to address volatility. Volatility could be caused by a variety of factors and then speculators could make it worse.
4. The functioning of RBI and the system is more refined since then and RBI has more calibrated responses to changes in the foreign exchange rates.
5. This requires further reflection and study within Ministry of Finance, RBI, Financial Institutions and Institutes specializing on this subject. This will lead to harmony in financial as well as foreign exchange markets.

Fourteen

Government of India

Debt Issue Calendar a Golden Opportunity

[2001]

The Union Budget has announced that the net borrowing programme of the Government of India is estimated at Rs. 1,18,000 crores in 2001-2002. The estimated redemptions are Rs. 42,000 crores. This implies that the gross borrowings are in the region of Rs. 1,60,000 for the financial year.

The necessity for a calendar of issue of Government Debt is now recognised. The Deputy Governor and Executive Directors of RBI have made distinct pronouncements that the Calendar for short term Bills is in place and that of the long term debts is under serious consideration.

The present economic environment provides an opportunity for providing a calendar in advance even before the commencement of the financial year. This paper discusses a Draft Calendar and its implications.

Policy Issues

The issue of Primary Securities of the Government of India is now "managed" by the Reserve Bank of India. The Reserve Bank's primary function is to maintain stability in the interest rates in the economy for the 'short term'. It has a variety of choices and instruments to do so.

It must be noted that in the transition from a controlled to a market economy, interest rates became volatile at times. The market was fragmented and this resulted in anomalies, distortions and fluctuations in both administered as well as market rates of interest.

The Reserve Bank of India has nudged its policies towards stability in interest rates. Its overwhelming concern with "external stability" that is maintaining equilibrium in foreign exchange rates has spilled over into manipulating short term interest rates. This is not a practice in a mature economy. This policy has to be reviewed with an action plan that "external stability" can be managed without disturbing the equilibrium in domestic markets.

The recognition also has to be augmented with the instruments and action on the part of Reserve Bank of India. The Bank Rate can only be a signalling device. It cannot provide the fund flow or absorption on a "daily" or "hourly" basis that is required to keep interest rates for the day at a single rate. This can be done only if there is an "efficient" Open Market Operation. This efficiency can be managed only if the Reserve Bank of India has "sufficient" resources at its command to manage short term supply as also its ability to absorb (and not necessarily "suck out") short term funds in the market.

The present policy framework does not allow this situation to be managed. This is because both Reserve Bank of India which manages the Debt Issue and Government of India and the Ministry of Finance are obsessed with having more of long dated issues than short dated ones.

A maturity profile of debt for an individual, firm, Corporate or any other organisation differs from that of the Government of India. Government of India should be aware that it is a Sovereign.

A Sovereign debt or outstanding has greater value to the market ostensibly for the reason that a Sovereign can honour its contract better than any other functionary.

A Sovereign debt therefore should be more liquid and when it is more liquid it has to have a naturally lower interest rate than that of other securities. In today's global markets some corporates seem to have better confidence of investors than securities of some Governments. But the difference is marginal. In India corporates could borrow money for the short term at interest rates lower than long term securities of the Government.

The State should not look at short term securities as having a redemption problem. This is a weak state of mind and comes from fear and insecurity. The State which is also sovereign should not be afraid of issuing short term securities at desirable levels.

The market which has been accustomed to long term issues is viewing these issues as not so desirable instruments to hold. The principle of Asset Liability matching which is increasingly adopted by Banks and firms are required to match the tenure of their assets and liabilities. Individuals and institutions that are committed to the long term may choose long term securities. Banks who were the prime investors will no longer look at long term securities as a choice of investments and would always prefer short term securities.

The Government of India should be cognisant that its borrowing programme has a "crowding out" effect on markets. When it prices the interest rate on its securities at a higher level to "complete" its borrowing programme the effect on short term and long term interest rates disturbs its citizens. This problem will continue till Government of India is able to curb its "dissaving".

One cannot understand why Government of India views issue of short term securities as a liquidity problem. It is only in the first instance that it appears that it will have a liquidity issue. When it fulfils the total issue on a calendar basis then the liquidity problem is addressed by Government of India and Reserve Bank of India jointly.

One, it is a management problem. The execution of the issue and its redemption involves more work at Reserve Bank of India. This has to be addressed. Even as there are some costs the results will outweigh those costs.

Second, is the issue that Reserve Bank of India has to manage the interest rates. The dynamics of market are different from a command and control economy. This requires sensitivity to the fund flow of the market.

While the top management of Reserve Bank of India has to simultaneously watch several parameters the Government of India's focus also cannot be narrow. Therefore debt issue management has to be isolated from the macro view of the economy.

The Government of India could save a lot of amount by better management than by policy. This can be proved only when current theories can be applied.

Policy makers as well as the executive should take a serious look at options to save enormous amounts in interest outgo. A net savings of Rs. 2,500 crores per year is feasible.

A Summary on Policy Could be

1. Government of India take over from RBI management of primary issues and the SGL. This will be a major policy decision and implementation should be immediate. The Ministry of Finance should initiate its own Debt Management Agency (called the Treasury in United States of America) which will monitor the issue of primary securities as well as settlement of its redemptions. It will have practical problems if it does not have knowledgeable persons to do so. Reserve Bank of India can depute its current officials till the transition is over within a fixed time frame say, three years, from the date of its decision to do so.
2. Reserve Bank of India top management should insulate itself from the primary issue market. Of course, it has to recognise the effects of Government's borrowing programme. Its concentration has to be to stabilise the domestic short term rates by the instruments at its command.
3. The emphasis on long term debt is no doubt valid from the Government's point of view. A midway correction has to be effected where the market's requirement of short term securities is met effectively.
4. The Treasury Bill Market should be taken away from Securities General Ledger to Depositories. The conduct of auction of Treasury Bills can be temporarily given to the DFHI till RBI and Ministry of Finance are able to sort out organisational problems. If DFHI is a more effective agent in managing the auction as well as the fund flow, then it can continue to do so. SHCIL & ISDL are competent to be depositories of T. Bills with proper safeguards and continuous monitoring by Reserve Bank of India.

   The announcement for issue of long term market has always been discretionary. The markets have always been uncertain as to when and in what form of securities auction of Long Term Securities would take place.
5. The function of stability of short term markets need not wait for mechanisation and the GRTS. In India mechanisation and computerisation could be unstable during implementation. The policy environment should

provide for stability even under current conditions by utilising existing resources: physical, personnel and money. This is because the most precious of all resources is time, and losing time is a loss both to Government of India as well as markets.

6. RBI should not participate in Primary issues at all. At no time, there should then be a situation of "devolution".

The Government of India which is having the executive function over the State and Reserve Bank of India as an institution created by the people should manage their functions in respect of Government Debt as well as interest rates.

This requires policies which can be executed. The executive should be in a position to manage. Management is the delivery of results stated in the policy. Of what use is a Policy when the executive is ineffective, inept, inefficient, indolent and incapable?

Government Policy should be that of order. If it characterises disorder and disarray then it does not mean an effective State. The prime function of a modern State is to promote 'Economic Efficiency'. Therefore, it cannot show characteristics of inefficiency. Even as it has a task to borrow from the market, which means the people of India, it has to do so with least destabilising effects. Taxation and borrowing by a State has to be equated with the evaporation of the water of the sea. Levels of interest rates in the market should not be destabilised. As the Government's budgeted borrowing and budgeted redemption is certain the programme should be on a calendar basis.

The Reserve Bank has to carry out a weighty mandate. It has its main task, stability of short term interest rates, in a market economy. Its resources obviously are limited because it cannot be the sea, where the water levels can be maintained. The market is the sea and the Reserve Bank of India at best a reservoir. With its limited resources RBI should impound and release funds which ensure that markets maintain an interest rate which does not fluctuate during the course of the day beyond limits.

Government Debt Calendar

Keeping the above in view, a Draft—Government of India—Debt Issue Calendar 2001-2002 as Annexure 1 and Long Dated Securities Due for Redemption as Annexure 14.2 below.

Annexure 14.1: Government of India - Debt Issue Calendar 2001-2002

I DRAFT I

Type	TBILL14	TBILL42	TBILL182	TBILL364	GOI2YR	GOI3YR	GOI4YR	GOI5YR	GOI7YR	GOI10YR	GOI15YR	GOI20YR	GOI25YR	GOI30YR	Total
Month															
April, 2001	12000	0000	4000	2000	1000	1000	1000	1000	1000	1500	300	300	300	300	35700
May		5000	4000	2000	1000	1000	1000	1000	1000	1500	300	300	300	300	18700
June			4000	2000	1000	1000	1000	1000	1000	1500	300	300	300	300	13700
July			4000	2000	1000	1000	1000	1000	1000	1500	300	300	300	300	13700
August			4000	2000	1000	1000	1000	1000	1000	1500	300	300	300	300	13700
September			4000	2000	1000	1000	1000	1000	1000	1500	300	300	300	300	13700
October			2000	2000	1000	1000	1000	1000	1000	1500	300	300	300	300	11700
November				2000	1000	1000	1000	1000	1000	1500	300	300	300	300	9700
December				2000	1000	1000	1000	1000	1000	1500	300	300	300	300	9700
January,2002				2000	1000	1000	1000	1000	1000	1500	300	300	300	300	9700
February				2000	1000	1000	1000	1000	1000	1500	300	300	300	300	9700
March				2000	1000	1000	1000	1000	1000	1500	300	300	300	300	9700
118000 **169400**	12000	13000	26000	24000	12000	12000	12000	12000	12000	18000	3600	3600	3600	3600	**169400**
27320															
15000 **160320**															
9080															

	Every	Every	Every	Every	1st & 3rd	2nd & 4th	1st & 3rd	2nd & 4th	1st	2nd	3rd	4th	1st	3rd
Week														
Monday	1000	500				500		500	1000					300
Tuesday	1000	500			500		500			750				
Wednesday	1000	500	1000	500		500		500			300			
Thursday	1000	500										300		
Friday	1000	500			500		500			750			300	
Saturday	1000													
	6000	2500	1000	500	1000	1000	1000	1000	1000	1500	300	300	300	300

All figures: Rupee crores

Annexure 14.2: Long Dated Securities Due for Redemption

Sl.No.	**Percentage**				
1.	5.75	GOICL	2001	1.7.01	230.84
2.	5.75	"	2001	20.02. 01	42.16
3.	6.50	"	2001	1.7.01	93.61
4.	7.50	"	2001	21.7.01	304.28
5.	10.75	"	2001	5.8.01	52.77
6.	11.00	"	2001	21.10.01	50.69
7.	12.70	"	2001	27.2.01	820.85
8.	13.31	"	2001	17.11.01	848.03
9.	12.08	"	2001	28.6.01	900.00
10.	11.75	"	2001	25.8.01	8,078.36
11.	13.85	"	2001	25.3.01	1,500.00
12.	13.75	"	2001	25.5.01	2,000.00
13.	13.55	"	2001	27.11.01	2,000.00
14.	10.85	"	2001	29.7.01	5,000.00
15.	11.55	"	2001	2.7.01	2,500.00
16.	11.55	"	2001	2.7.01	2,898.72
					27,320.31

Treasury Bills Outstanding Estimated **Rs. 15.000 crore**
As on 31.3.2001
All Above Figures are Estimates. Actuals May Vary.

The Calendar

The calendar has been made on broad assumption. It can be calibrated to Indian situations and conditions. The broad principles would remain the same. The amounts can be altered by the Debt Issue Managers. Banks liabilities comprise of current accounts and savings Bank which require matching short term asset that are less than a maturity of 364 days. Their Asset profile also takes into account 1 year to 7 year maturities.

It is well known now that Reserve Bank does not issue these maturities even when there is a huge demand from Banks. It persisted in issue of long dated securities at prices of 11 per cent even as there was a demand for short term securities at 9.5 per cent. The calendar ensures Government has a total issue and outstanding of Rs. 85,000 crores in short term securities which will fulfil the need of the market the average; saving throughout the future will be in the region of Rs. 1,600 crores every year.

The average difference between a T. Bills Rate and Long Term security in India is about 2 per cent or 200 basis points. If its outstanding on securities of maturity less than 5 years is around Rs. 80,000 crores then its annual saving would be around Rs. 800 crores on a perpetual basis.

The Debt issue calendar provides for an equally divided loan raising programme security wise. This is except for the 14 day Treasury Bill which is provided for in April itself, the 42 days Treasury Bill which will run for Seven Weeks and the 182 day Treasury Bill which will run for 26 weeks.

After the initial period, respective redemptions of Treasury Bills will start. Therefore, net raising will be in this year and remain in perpetuity. This can change if the issue amount per day is altered. This will provide an on-going liquidity for the Government on a continuous basis for Rs. 9,000 crores. This will take care of ways and means, contingencies and repayments which arise in the future.

The programme is heavily loaded for the near term for the present. This gives an orderly maturity profile for the entire Government programme. It will also save considerable outgo in interest as shorter maturity profiles will have greater subscriptions and hence will result in Government getting attractively priced outcomes. This will get calibrated in the coming year when it will shift to forward maturities. The borrowings programme is heavily loaded for the first two months. This provides an opportunity for Government to avoid Ways & Means Advance as well as conduct its disbursal on Plan account in advance. The advantage lies that investments on Plan account get fructified earlier.

This also provides the buffer for redemptions. It will also enable RBI to hold sufficient quantity of 14 Day and 42 Day T. Bills for an efficient Open Market Operations. The RBI has to price its Open Market Operations rate. This will be the most crucial decision for stability. The OMO Rate has to be fixed for the day as a single two way quote - buy and sell at one rate. This can be 1 to 1.25 per cent over Bank Rate. For effective control it can be for any security with a residual maturity of less than 10 days. This will ensure liquidity in a constant rate.

The Reserve Bank can help the situation by a sharp reduction in CRR by 2 per cent in April and May. This will enable banks to utilise about Rs. 20,000 crores out of their DTL instantly on T. Bills which can later graduate to other higher yield securities. A multiplier effect will generate as much as Rs. 90,000 crores without inflationary effect.

The SLR regime can be altered slightly. The Reserve Bank can specify that 5 per cent of outstanding DTL can be invested in maturities less than one year and the balance in less of residual maturity less than 5 years. This will bring forth Rs. 2,50,000 crores into this range within a period of five years. The long dated securities will then be held for investment value by banks or can be turned over to long term investors.

The long term securities are issued in smaller quantities more regularly over the year. This will enable easy subscription and orderly market for long term investors. This schedule will establish a perfect gilt yield curve. Whenever factors are available in the market that cause long term changes, rates get calibrated of their own first in the secondary market which then will reflect on primary.

The Reserve Bank can maintain perfect equilibrium for the day by offering a buy/sell rate at the same price for T. Bills primarily of the short term 14 and 42 day or of residual maturities less than those days.

The market will then park all short term funds in T. Bills thereby enhancing value in the money market. An opportunity is there to present all issues of less than 5 years in zero coupon bonds. This will make it investor friendly and easily tradable. All issues over 5 years can be interest bearing. The secondary market will be active in all issues. At present only few issues are liquid.

If a Bank Holiday happens to be on the day of the schedule, then the auction can be on the previous day and not later. In this programme, RBI should dispense with Government of India Ways & Means Advance. If Government requires additional funds then it can issue additional quantum of T. Bills. RBI should calibrate secondary markets in such a way that such borrowings do not alter short term interest rates.

It would also be advantageous if RBI converts its present investments in Government Securities to the extent of Rs. 80,000 crores entirely into Treasury Bills.

This calendar fulfils the needs of the market more adequate and needs of Government without conflicts. Government of India finances should be strong enough:

- To withstand "shocks" or externalities.
- To keep its commitments "external" or "internal".
- Not to resort to "beseeching".
- To keep its contracts of payments and repayments.
- The Borrowings are shown as Rs. 5,080 crores more than budgeted.
- To eliminate ways and means advances or provides for contingencies.

Each redemption of debt is paid for and not "rolled over". A borrower and lender are two opposites in a market. A lender chooses to shift his yield from lower to higher and a borrower chooses to shift his cost from higher to lower. A Central Bank has to be neutral and provide the conditions for the rate to be at equilibrium. Under this Calendar system opportunity is provided for investors to plan their investments. In the Secondary Market shorter end maturities will always be liquid. Liquidity implies realising money without loss of the principal.

The purpose of a debt calendar is to take out the uncertainty of issue to markets. Money moves in market very fast these days. The first opportunity for markets is to park surplus money in Government securities.

When one operator has a surplus the other could have a need. Trading of securities thus provides an opportunity for holders of money to move from a lower return to a higher return without loss of principal. In a modern market 'LIQUIDITY" means ability to sell one's asset without loss of principal.

A calendar provides a reasonable guide to markets. Markets will then anticipate their surplus funds and make provisions accordingly. They can also plan reinvestments from redemption, shuffle their portfolios and play for their liquidity. It can enable institutions, corporates, societies and investors other than banks to plan for investments in Government securities out of their fund flows thus widening the base for Government securities.

Banks will tend to invest in shorter maturities and life and pension funds in longer securities. Therefore, the calendar will facilitate an orderly churning of their securities by both banks and other institutions.

Conclusion

Government borrowing has a tremendous impact on money markets. Orderly conduct of borrowings removes uncertainty. Secondary markets will respond well to structured offerings.

The State is an instrument of the citizen it serves. Therefore, all its policies and programmes should be in public interest. The Reserve Bank of India is an institution with a particular mandate. It should be an orderly function of the Reserve Bank of India to provide liquidity to sovereign debt as well as maintain stability of interest rates for the day.

Both are to be governed by principles of economic justice. The proposals contained in the paper merit the immediate attention of Government of India and RBI.

NOTES

1. This paper was inspired after information on how developed countries had debt issue calendars and responses from the financial system and investors to it.
2. Government of India relied raising loans on Expenditure - Capital and Revenue. The loans were announced when necessary in an ad-hoc manner. To an extent this would upset money markets in a narrow market.
3. Reserve Bank of India plans Government of India borrowings now in a better and systematic way and market operators, raters and investors have predictability in the manner and quantum of Government redemptions and borrowings.
4. An article in Finance and Development magazine of the IMF also gave clarity on the need and practicality of the Debt Issue Calendar and hence the title.
5. There is a need for breadth and depth in the money market and hence will be evolutionary.

Fifteen

Open Market Operations

[2001]

Open Market Operations can be defined as a continuous action on the part of a Central Bank in buying and selling Government securities with a purpose of maintaining stability in short term interest rates within a nation.

Open Market Operations therefore require several conditions:

- There must be sufficient amount of Government Securities outstanding of short term maturities.
- The Central Bank must hold them in sufficient quantities.
- The Central Bank must provide as much quantities to the market as demanded by it for the day.
- The Central Bank must provide as much quantities to the market as the market offers the same to it for the day.
- It must do so without interruption, obstacle or hindrance in the course of a working day.
- It must decide the OMO rate, which is the rate of interest at which it will price the Government security for the day.
- It must have operational efficiency by having "frontline troops", sound management and executive effectiveness.

The value of such an operation is evident in a modern economy. The United States has the largest amount of fund flow in the world both in and out of its economy. The City of London handles the largest flow of money in the world. Interest rate is a price reflecting the demand and supply of money at a given moment. Given such fund flows which are in torrents and very unpredictable, how do markets maintain interest rates at fairly stable levels?

If one looks closely, it is not markets which maintain interest levels - but Central Banks of all major economies. They do so by absorbing all surplus funds and releasing them when the market requires so that interest rates remain stable in their "respective nation states"

This has resulted market efficiency of the highest order.

The Indian Scenario

The Indian financial markets were totally under the command and control of the Government of India and the Central Bank of the country, The Reserve Bank of India. The command and control money market was fairly placid where interest levels were decided depending on the situation. There was no market orientation in any segment. Fund flow was directed either by the State or the Reserve Bank of India.

The transition to market economy has been "chaotic". The transition from control was done gradually. Specific segments were freed over a period of time. The instruments that were available in text books and not used during the command and control era were gradually re-introduced. Where they were done so on sound theory, the organisation, education and discipline that are required for orderly functioning of markets was missing either at the Government, Central Bank or market operators.

Therefore, market movement defied normal behaviour of market because it was not seamless. The result was interest rates had distortions, anomalies, aberrations and volatile movements.

A certain semblance of order has emerged in the markets in the last 30 months. It is moving towards harmony and integration is taking place in the market.

Open Market Operations in India

The Reserve Bank of India is very well aware of Open Market Operations as a tool. It does occasionally indulge in it. But most of the time it was one way; that is, reducing its portfolio of Government securities and putting it into the market.

Going by the information provided by Reserve Bank of India it can be concluded:

- Open Market Operations are not a daily feature
- It does not give a two way facility

- It has done so only in long dated securities
- It does not have a fixed OMO rate
- It is not doing the same for stabilising internal short term interest rates
- It does not have sufficient short term securities in its portfolio
- The Government of India does not have enough short term Treasury Bills outstanding to enable an efficient Open Market Operations
- The speed and efficiency of Reserve Bank of India operational Managers to maintain liquidity by the minute instead of the day is in doubt.
- The requisite infrastructure could be missing to ensure interface with the market to have efficient Open Market Operations.
- The Reserve Bank of India is not seized of the issue of "internal stability" as against its priorities in meeting "external stability" that is, preventing undue volatility of India's rupee against currencies of the world, particularly the US Dollar
- The market is not integrated in between operators and between operators and RBI
- The Government of India does not have a sound policy in place on interest rate regime for its outstanding to the market.

However the deficiencies noted above cannot be viewed in isolation nor is it a criticism. It merely describes the state of affairs. The intentions are clear. Only a plan of action and methodology are missing.

It must be first agreed in principle that an efficient Open Market Operation is necessary for the Indian markets. Secondly, once it is accepted a commitment must be available to put into action.

This paper will examine the necessary plan of action for an efficient Open Market Operations in India.

1. *Availability of sufficient amount of Government Securities outstanding of short term maturities*: An efficient Open Market Operations require a sufficient amount of Government Securities in the form of Treasury Bills outstanding. They must be mostly in 14 day, 42 day, 182 day and 364 day Treasury Bills. The calendar

should ensure a daily primary issue and almost a daily redemption of earlier issued securities. This is an absolute necessary precondition for the existence of an efficient Open Market Operation.

There can be no fixed criteria as to the amount. The term sufficient will vary depending on the short term fund flow in the market. But at the moment it is too low to carry out an efficient operation. The general conditions of the market today dictate that at least Rs. 80,000 crores should be the total outstanding value of short term T. Bills.

2. *The Reserve Bank of India must hold them in sufficient quantities*: The Reserve Bank of India must hold sufficient quantities of T. Bills to service the market.

3. *The Reserve Bank of India must provide as much quantities to the market as demanded by it for the day*: The market has its cycles of temporary surpluses and demand as it constantly shifts resources. The Reserve Bank of India must make available as much quantity that is demanded during the day. This will maintain interest rate equilibrium when there are temporary surpluses in the market.

4. *The Reserve Bank of India must purchase as much quantities from the market when the market offers the same to it for the day:* When market has temporary shortages of money it should be able to offer its holding to the Reserve Bank of India for cash. Normally it is for utilisation towards a higher yield till fresh resources flow in or unloading of excess holdings made temporarily.

5. *It must do so without interruption, obstacle or hindrance in the course of a working day*: Money moves in large volumes even during the course of a day. The market operators therefore operate at high levels of efficiency between themselves and between markets. The purchase and sale operations therefore have to take place during the entire working day between different persons and organizations. If equilibrium is provided only at the end of the day on the principle of "net" surplus or "net deficit" for the day, intraday fluctuations will be common. Therefore, the Reserve Bank of India must be ready to operate throughout the working day. It can of course prescribe rules and conditions for the same. Eventually the market will even out during the day and its interface with market will become more orderly and gradual. This constant interface will also enable Reserve Bank of India to gauge the moods of the market and "sense" fund flows on a regular basis.

6. *The Reserve Bank of India must decide the OMO rate, which is the rate of interest at which it will price the Government security for the day:* This is the most crucial aspect of the Open Market Operations. Since it is a two way process at a single rate it is the equilibrium that is maintained by the economy for the day. If it is wrongly priced then the reflection will be on the whole economy. The two way price is not weighted towards borrowers or towards lenders. It stands at midpoint. The entire market will respond to a just equilibrium by pricing the return for money or capital to the borrowers or lenders as the case may be depending on transaction costs or risks. In the United States it is not an individual who decides it but the Federal Open Market Committee. This is a democratic way of decision on rates.

7. *It must have operational efficiency by having "frontline troops", sound management and executive effectiveness:* The Reserve Bank of India is an organisation created by Parliament to meet a specific mandate and carry out specific functions. Any function has to carry out a purpose and should deliver the desire results. Management as a practice should deliver results. This requires an effective executive.

Modern economies and societies depend on institutions to provide them the specific service that people need.

Operational efficiency requires trained executives to ensure that execution of a particular operation is carried out to the desired level of efficiency.

The efficiency and excellence therein will then provide the required service to the markets and thereon to the people.

Without operational efficiency the Open Market Operations will not deliver the desired results. The RBI must address itself to the task of Open Market Operations as its core function and assign executives to accomplish it. Education, organisation and discipline should be present as ingredients throughout the organisation that gives a platform to its operational section in this area.

Conclusion

The interaction with the market acquires a different connotation compared with diktats, orders, guidelines, terms and conditions and regulations. It is pure buying and selling to maintain equilibrium for the day. As there is an absence of injustice it will be economic justice at the purest for all the people of this country.

The sign-posts for efficient Open Market Operations are given in this paper. The Government of India and the Reserve Bank of India must work closely to launch it and ensure its success. Therein lies the delivery of Governance.

Tables

Value of Treasury Bill on a Given Day at YTM of 8 per cent p.a.

Redemption value (Rs.)	100
Interest Rate/Annum	8%

14 DAYS T.BILL

Balance Days	Value (Rs.)	Balance Days	Value (Rs.)
14	99.6941	6	99.8687
13	99.7159	5	99.8905
12	99.7377	4	99.9124
11	99.7595	3	99.9343
10	99.7813	2	99.9562
9	99.8031	1	99.9781
8	99.8250	0	100.0000
7	99.8468		

42 DAYS T.BILL

Balance Days	Value (Rs.)	Balance Days	Value (Rs.)
42	99.0878	27	99.4117
41	99.1094	26	99.4334
40	99.1309	25	99.4550
39	99.1525	24	99.4767
38	99.1740	23	99.4984
37	99.1956	22	99.5201
36	99.2171	21	99.5418
35	99.2387	20	99.5636
34	99.2603	19	99.5853
33	99.2819	18	99.6070
32	99.3035	17	99.6288
31	99.3251	16	99.6505
30	99.3468	15	99.6723
29	99.3684	14	99.6941
28	99.3900	13	99.7159

(Contd.)

Balance Days	Value (Rs.)	Balance Days	Value (Rs.)
12	99.7377	5	99.8905
11	99.7595	4	99.9124
10	99.7813	3	99.9343
9	99.8031	2	99.9562
8	99.8250	1	99.9781
7	99.8468	0	100.000
6	99.8687		

NOTES

1. Values have been computed for the 4th Digit dividing the year as 365 days.
2 This chart is provided to give an idea that equilibrium is maintained by the Reserve Bank of India only when it chooses to buy or sell at a single rate.
3 As the total outstandings are not for a single date but over a period of time the value of Tbills vary depending on its residual maturity.
4 The Open Market Operations will be successful only when the rate is stabilised for a given range of maturity.
5 Since the interest of Central Bank will be to maintain short term stability, it has to use its resources to stabilise the rates for the day of operation.
6. While the market operator provides two way quotes the Reserve Bank necessarily has to quote a single rate to the market operator.

Value of Treasury Bill on a Given Day at YTM of 8 per cent p.a.

Redemption value (Rs.) 100
Interest Rate/Annum 8%

182 DAYS T.BILL

Balance Days	Value (Rs.)	Balance Days	Value (Rs.)
182	96.1640	148	96.8581
181	96.1843	147	96.8786
180	96.2045	146	96.8992
179	96.2248	145	96.9198
178	96.2451	144	96.9404
177	96.2654	143	96.9610
176	96.2857	142	96.9816
175	96.3061	141	97.0022
174	96.3264	140	97.0229
173	96.3467	139	97.0435
172	96.3671	138	97.0641
171	96.3875	137	97.0848
170	96.4078	136	97.1055
169	96.4282	135	97.1261
168	96.4486	134	97.1468
167	96.4690	133	97.1675
166	96.4894	132	97.1882
165	96.5098	131	97.2089
164	96.5302	130	97.2296
163	96.5506	129	97.2503
162	96.5711	128	97.2711
161	96.5915	127	97.2918
160	96.6120	126	97.3126
159	96.6324	125	97.3333
158	96.6529	124	97.3541
157	96.6734	123	97.3749
156	96.6939	122	97.3957
155	96.7144	121	97.4165
154	96.7349	120	97.4373
153	96.7554	119	97.4581
152	96.7759	118	97.4789
151	96.7964	117	97.4997
150	96.8170	116	97.5206
149	96.8375	115	97.5414

(Contd.)

Balance Days	Value (Rs.)	Balance Days	Value (Rs.)
114	97.5623	73	98.4252
113	97.5831	72	98.4464
112	97.6040	71	98.4677
111	97.6249	70	98.4889
110	97.6458	69	98.5102
109	97.6667	68	98.5315
108	97.6876	67	98.5528
107	97.7085	66	98.5741
106	97.7295	65	98.5954
105	97.7504	64	98.6167
104	97.7713	63	98.6380
103	97.7923	62	98.6593
102	97.8133	61	98.6807
101	97.8342	60	98.7020
100	97.8552	59	98.7234
99	97.8762	58	98.7447
98	97.8972	57	98.7661
97	97.9182	56	98.7875
96	97.9393	55	98.8089
95	97.9603	54	98.8303
94	97.9813	53	98.8517
93	98.0024	52	98.8731
92	98.0234	51	98.8945
91	98.0445	50	98.9160
90	98.0656	49	98.9374
89	98.0866	48	98.9589
88	98.1077	47	98.9804
87	98.1288	46	99.0018
86	98.1499	45	99.0233
85	98.1711	44	99.0448
84	98.1922	43	99.0663
83	98.2133	42	99.0878
82	98.2345	41	99.1094
81	98.2556	40	99.1309
80	98.2768	39	99.1525
79	98.2980	38	99.1740
78	98.3191	37	99.1956
77	98.3403	36	99.2171
76	98.3615	35	99.2387
75	98.3827	34	99.2603
74	98.4040	33	99.2819

(Contd.)

Balance Days	Value (Rs.)	Balance Days	Value (Rs.)
32	99.3035	15	99.6723
31	99.3251	14	99.6941
30	99.3468	13	99.7159
29	99.3684	12	99.7377
28	99.3900	11	99.7595
27	99.4117	10	99.7813
26	99.4334	9	99.8031
25	99.4550	8	99.8250
24	99.4767	7	99.8468
23	99.4984	6	99.8687
22	99.5201	5	99.8905
21	99.5418	4	99.9124
20	99.5636	3	99.9343
19	99.5853	2	99.9562
18	99.6070	1	99.9781
17	99.6288	0	100.0000
16	99.6505		

Value of Treasury Bill on a Given Day at YTM of 8 per cent p.a.

Redemption value (Rs.)	100
Interest Rate/Annum	8%

364 DAYS T.BILL - Part 1

Balance Days	Value (Rs.)	Balance Days	Value (Rs.)
364	92.6114	352	92.8375
363	92.6302	351	92.8564
362	92.6490	350	92.8753
361	92.6678	349	92.8942
360	92.6866	348	92.9131
359	92.7055	347	92.9321
358	92.7243	346	92.9510
357	92.7432	345	92.9699
356	92.7620	344	92.9889
355	92.7809	343	93.0078
354	92.7998	342	93.0268
353	92.8186	341	93.0458

(Contd.)

Balance Days	Value (Rs.)	Balance Days	Value (Rs.)
340	93.0648	299	93.8496
339	93.0837	298	93.8689
338	93.1027	297	93.8883
337	93.1217	296	93.9076
336	93.1408	295	93.9269
335	93.1598	294	93.9463
334	93.1788	293	93.9656
333	93.1978	292	93.9850
332	93.2169	291	94.0043
331	93.2359	290	94.0237
330	93.2550	289	94.0431
329	93.2740	288	94.0625
328	93.2931	287	94.0819
327	93.3122	286	94.1013
326	93.3313	285	94.1207
325	93.3504	284	94.1401
324	93.3695	283	94.1595
323	93.3886	282	94.1790
322	93.4077	281	94.1984
321	93.4268	280	94.2179
320	93.4460	279	94.2373
319	93.4651	278	94.2568
318	93.4843	277	94.2763
317	93.5034	276	94.2958
316	93.5226	275	94.3152
315	93.5418	274	94.3347
314	93.5610	273	94.3543
313	93.5801	272	94.3738
312	93.5993	271	94.3933
311	93.6185	270	94.4128
310	93.6378	269	94.4324
309	93.6570	268	94.4519
308	93.6762	267	94.4715
307	93.6955	266	94.4910
306	93.7147	265	94.5106
305	93.7339	264	94.5302
304	93.7532	263	94.5498
303	93.7725	262	94.5694
302	93.7918	261	94.5890
301	93.8110	260	94.6086
300	93.8303	259	94.6282

(Contd.)

Balance Days	Value (Rs.)	Balance Days	Value (Rs.)
258	94.6479	218	95.4398
257	94.6675	217	95.4598
256	94.6871	216	95.4798
255	94.7068	215	95.4997
254	94.7265	214	95.5197
253	94.7461	213	95.5397
252	94.7658	212	95.5597
251	94.7855	211	95.5798
250	94.8052	210	95.5998
249	94.8249	209	95.6198
248	94.8446	208	95.6399
247	94.8643	207	95.6599
246	94.8841	206	95.6800
245	94.9038	205	95.7001
244	94.9235	204	95.7201
243	94.9433	203	95.7402
242	94.9631	202	95.7603
241	94.9828	201	95.7804
240	95.0026	200	95.8005
239	95.0224	199	95.8206
238	95.0422	198	95.8408
237	95.0620	197	95.8609
236	95.0818	196	95.8811
235	95.1016	195	95.9012
234	95.1214	194	95.9214
233	95.1413	193	95.9415
232	95.1611	192	95.9617
231	95.1810	191	95.9819
230	95.2008	190	96.0021
229	95.2207	189	96.0223
228	95.2406	188	96.0425
227	95.2605	187	96.0627
226	95.2804	186	96.0830
225	95.3003	185	96.1032
224	95.3202	184	96.1235
223	95.3401	183	96.1437
222	95.3600	182	96.1640
221	95.3800	181	96.1843
220	95.3999	180	96.2045
219	95.4198	179	96.2248
		178	96.2451

(Contd.)

Balance Days	Value (Rs.)	Balance Days	Value (Rs.)
177	96.2654	136	97.1055
176	96.2857	135	97.1261
175	96.3061	134	97.1468
174	96.3264	133	97.1675
173	96.3467	132	97.1882
172	96.3671	131	97.2089
171	96.3875	130	97.2296
170	96.4078	129	97.2503
169	96.4282	128	97.2711
168	96.4486	127	97.2918
167	96.4690	126	97.3126
166	96.4894	125	97.3333
165	96.5098	124	97.3541
164	96.5302	123	97.3749
163	96.5506	122	97.3957
162	96.5711	121	97.4165
161	96.5915	120	97.4373
160	96.6120	119	97.4581
159	96.6324	118	97.4789
158	96.6529	117	97.4997
157	96.6734	116	97.5206
156	96.6939	115	97.5414
155	96.7144	114	97.5623
154	96.7349	113	97.5831
153	96.7554	112	97.6040
152	96.7759	111	97.6249
151	96.7964	110	97.6458
150	96.8170	109	97.6667
149	96.8375	108	97.6876
148	96.8581	107	97.7085
147	96.8786	106	97.7295
146	96.8992	105	97.7504
145	96.9198	104	97.7713
144	96.9404	103	97.7923
143	96.9610	102	97.8133
142	96.9816	101	97.8342
141	97.0022	100	97.8552
140	97.0229	99	97.8762
139	97.0435	98	97.8972
138	97.0641	97	97.9182
137	97.0848	96	97.9393

(Contd.)

Balance Days	Value (Rs.)	Balance Days	Value (Rs.)
95	97.9603	54	98.8303
94	97.9813	53	98.8517
93	98.0024	52	98.8731
92	98.0234	51	98.8945
91	98.0445	50	98.9160
90	98.0656	49	98.9374
89	98.0866	48	98.9589
88	98.1077	47	98.9804
87	98.1288	46	99.0018
86	98.1499	45	99.0233
85	98.1711	44	99.0448
84	98.1922	43	99.0663
83	98.2133	42	99.0878
82	98.2345	41	99.1094
81	98.2556	40	99.1309
80	98.2768	39	99.1525
79	98.2980	38	99.1740
78	98.3191	37	99.1956
77	98.3403	36	99.2171
76	98.3615	35	99.2387
75	98.3827	34	99.2603
74	98.4040	33	99.2819
73	98.4252	32	99.3035
72	98.4464	31	99.3251
71	98.4677	30	99.3468
70	98.4889	29	99.3684
69	98.5102	28	99.3900
68	98.5315	27	99.4117
67	98.5528	26	99.4334
66	98.5741	25	99.4550
65	98.5954	24	99.4767
64	98.6167	23	99.4984
63	98.6380	22	99.5201
62	98.6593	21	99.5418
61	98.6807	20	99.5636
60	98.7020	19	99.5853
59	98.7234	18	99.6070
58	98.7447	17	99.6288
57	98.7661	16	99.6505
56	98.7875	15	99.6723
55	98.8089	14	99.6941

(Contd.)

Balance Days	Value (Rs.)	Balance Days	Value (Rs.)
13	99.7159	6	99.8687
12	99.7377	5	99.8905
11	99.7595	4	99.9124
10	99.7813	3	99.9343
9	99.8031	2	99.9562
8	99.8250	1	99.9781
7	99.8468	0	100.0000

NOTES

1. The Reserve Bank of India has since then conducted Open Market Operations. It has sold securities into the market and also bought securities from the market in the last seven to ten years.
2. The suggestions made in this chapter have not been recognised yet. In USA the Open Market Operations are a continuous operations and absorb and release the daily liquidity in the market at a pre determined rate called the OMO Rate. This is done in Treasury Bills.
3. In India, the initiative should be taken have Open Market Operations in treasury bills.
4. The above suggestions are not exhaustive. It should be possible for RBI and Government to have a mutually acceptable approach towards Open Market Operations as defined in USA and implemented by the Federal Reserve.
5. Open Market operations now in Treasury Bills can be a very good strategy to reduce interest costs to Government of India. This can also be the easiest route to the benefits of the next stage of the convertibility of the rupee.

Sixteen

Interest Rate Decontrol in a Free Market Environment

[2001]

The Mid Term Credit and Monetary Policy for Oct 2001 is a remarkable document. It reflects careful thinking and remarkable articulation. The management of Reserve Bank of India deserve congratulations on the policy framework and its orderly implementation.

The Reserve Bank of India and the Government of India have a long history and record of intervention in the interest rates. Specific segments have been targeted for lower or higher interest rates. The whole principle of a "market" rate of interest was ignored for well over three decades.

The Government of India decided in principle to move to market rates of interest since the early 1990s. The Reserve Bank of India has acted on this gradually since 1991. This transition has been marked by several aberrations, distortions and anomalies. The interest rates in particular segments have behaved erratically.

The year 2001 has been a remarkable year as it has shown the stability in interest rates in segments. The Reserve Bank of India has moved clearly in the direction of market determined rates. It is also cognisant of its role as a Central Bank and steering the interest rates with a watch on the fund flow and the cash flow in the economy.

The Reserve Bank of India has still direct control on the rates of interest to be paid or charged on some segments which remain to be freed to the interaction of demand and supply in the market.

There are very few segments remaining, in which the Reserve Bank of India has continued to exercise direct control on the rates of interest to be paid or charged.

They need immediate attention. Taking action will complete the task set for removing all control and direction over interest rates for particular segments.

Decontrol of Savings Bank Interest Rate

The Savings Bank interest rate still remains fixed by the Reserve Bank of India. Currently it is at 4 per cent per annum. In the direction towards decontrol it is appropriate that the Reserve Bank sets free the Savings Bank interest rates and allow it to be determined by the Banks themselves. This could be done immediately but the date of implementation could be April 01, 2001.

The time is ripe for control of the interest rate for Savings Bank. Currently it is the only mandated interest rates for savings of depositors. The rest of the deposit rates have been decontrolled. The highest advantages will accrue when it is done in the present economic and monetary conditions.

Savings bank comprises both of cheque and non-cheque accounts. Therefore, they are the crucial instruments in the garnering of the savings of the economy as citizens deposit their earnings as well as expend from these accounts. The two crucial elements have to be noted in Savings Accounts. They are the reason for the existence of banks in so far as individuals are concerned and the service element. The interest paid on savings bank and the interest earnings banks realise from deployment of those funds minus their costs comprise the core earnings of banks.

There is no substitute element in a savings bank account. It cannot be equated with deposits or with investments. They perform a basic and much wider and larger service. The Reserve Bank of India and Commercial Banks should pay more attention to this sector. This sector has been denied the attention it deserves in terms of customer service, as an important conduit for fund flow. The deficiencies arise in paying attention to the customer, counter services, clearing services, payment services, efficiency and excellence.

With competition, a visible change has taken place for bank customers. Branch automation has helped to reduce queues and transactions are completed faster. The introduction of ATMs has provided conveniences to customers. The Indian economy is predominantly a cash economy. At retail level almost 95 per cent of transactions take place in cash. The arrival of the credit card has not helped matters as the load is on merchants and not on the customers. The predominance of cash in all retail transactions is not providing the economic efficiency, which a cheque economy would provide. The Reserve Bank of India and commercial banks should devote exclusive attention on this area on a continuous basis to upgrade the services of the cheque economy. This naturally would give rise to savings bank accounts for individual customers and current account for business customers.

The service element on savings banks therefore should cover the entire gamut of credits, debits, agency services and special services. The interest on Savings Bank is now paid on the basis of balances at a particular date of a month. This was so in the case of manual maintenance of accounts. In the case of computerized accounts it is to be considered whether the product method is to be applied.

Banks should have the freedom to design the Savings Account product. In all cases minimum balances apply. The differentiation between checking and non-checking accounts is to be examined. Emphasis is again made on the question of decontrol of savings bank accounts.

The Reserve Bank of India may consider that this decontrol be applied from a future date. This is because banks have tended to over react during times of decontrol. Therefore if the decision is taken in principle to decontrol the rates the Reserve Bank may announce a day at least three months hence.

This will enable the banks to have a proper debate, discussion and dialogue within the organization and at inter-organisation levels to arrive at a proper rate for the Savings Bank under the current financial situation. The Reserve Bank should take this decision consciously but without delay. The timing is right to do it forthwith.

Rupee Export Rates

Reserve Bank of India still determines the rupee export credit rates. It is time that this segment is also decontrolled totally and allows banks to apply interest rates as per prevailing rupee interest rates.

The Export Credit rates in rupees have a long history of subsidisation. Earlier it was subsidised by the Government and the Reserve Bank of India. During the 90s it had a transition to directed rates where the Reserve Bank of India fixed the rates for different tenors.

The Banks have also been directed that at least 10 per cent of their loans should be given to the export sector. The facility of continuous packing credit has been extended to provide for procurement of raw materials, managing in process till the export is completed.

The Reserve Bank of India has been generous in providing refinance to banks to a certain extent of their export loan portfolio.

In the easing of interest rates in general, banks have found that recourse to refinance is not necessary and do it only during certain periods when liquidity is an issue. Some banks do it to lower their cost of funds.

In financial markets where fundamentals determine market rates, the idea of Reserve Bank directing the interest rates in any segment should be done away with. This would apply to interest rates applied to exporters too. RBI can operate a rediscount provision for the very short term at attractive rates.

The Continuous Packing Credit now operate with a lower rate of interest at the beginning of the transaction and higher at the end of the transaction. The same can be reversed with normal rates at the beginning of the transaction and lower rates at the end of the transaction.

The rupee rates on exports are fixed irrespective of the creditworthiness and rating of borrowers. When freed, banks may apply differentiation based on risk perception.

The Reserve Bank of India may also direct that ECGC premium be absorbed by banks in their cost and not passed on to borrowers.

Export Dollar (Foreign Currency) Interest Rates

The spread on these rates is determined by the Reserve Bank. It would be appropriate to allow banks to determine the spreads as applicable to other types of lending. This gives banks the freedom to operate commercially.

The Reserve Bank of India has devised an excellent product which has enabled banks to lend working capital to exporters. The PCFC is a foreign currency loan given to exporter under the overall Packing Credit limits. The PCFC is denominated in foreign currency. The cost of PCFC is very low in India.

The Reserve Bank of India has even prescribed the maximum spread it can earn over LIBOR. This is now One percent over LIBOR. The Banks are willing to lend on PCFC to borrowers. The borrowers are shy because even as cash out go on account of interest is lower the advantage of a possible depreciation in the rupee is lost.

The Reserve Bank of India and Banks have not provided fungibility between a PCFC and a PC. The RBI must address the issue of fungibility. Fungibility is to allow the borrower to have a choice between a PCFC and a Rupee Based PC within the currency of a Single transaction PC. At the moment the Continuous PC or the PC against firm orders follow very strict rules as laid down by RBI and also as laid down by the banks themselves as terms and conditions in the loans given by them.

RBI can provide a rediscount facility to Banks. This can be a 7 day, 14 day, 21 day or 42 day special facility linked to the receivables by banks. This could be devised as a special incentive to banks. The RBI can discount $ denominated bills of up to certain pre-determined amounts. This will let out dollar balances for financing export activity for the short term and will have to be paid out of proceeds received by banks.

The opportunity for RBI will be to lay the foundation for an indo-dollar, or indo-euro market which will provide long term stability in Indian money markets, improve bank profitability and also effective utilization of Indian capital. Presently, the Reserve Bank of India is keeping a large balance abroad which is much more than the benchmarks required for keeping official foreign exchange. These are kept at very low rate, as they constitute overnight balances.

Even as the above scheme is developed the Reserve Bank can free the interest rates on Dollar Denominated Packing credit at the earliest.

Decontrol of Interest Rates up to Rs. 2 Lakhs

Interest rates of loans up to Rs. 2 lakhs have been pegged at PLR. This is fair to small borrowers and well directed and with good intentions. But it rebels against the principles of the market economy. It would be better if the Reserve Bank of India decontrols this segment too from direction.

Any Other Interest Rate in any Other Segment

If there is any other segment where the Reserve Bank of India has determined the rate of interest, the same should be done away forthwith.

The Reserve Bank of India must refrain from any directed interest in any segment. If there is any such segment other than mentioned above, the same may be done away with.

The Reserve Bank of India has chosen to direct banks to keep interest rates at the lowest level in the commercial segment. This rebels against the principle of commercial interests.

A small loan will always entail higher cost. It is a well-known principle that costs of retailing are higher than wholesale. It should be left entirely to individual banks as to how much they should charge for each category of loan. The transaction cost of each category of loan will determine the rate of interest charged over the market rate.

The Indian banking sector has been a channel for public policy above the requirements for being commercial entities. In this process a new term "social banking" has evolved. For over three decades banks have provided banking services to the economy including lending to those entities which would have ordinarily been overlooked. However all concerned including bank managements have sacrificed commercial interests.

Ownership by state has not helped improve the situation. The Reserve Bank of India too was influenced by concerns expressed by the State. It is a matter of record that all actions emanating from it from 1960s to 1990s did not reflect the purpose and functions of Central Banking but were exercised as a tool for the State in the extension of its activities in the financial sectors of the economy.

The Reserve Bank should do away with the stipulation of directing interest rate in the segment. The interest rates charged to sector will find their own levels. There may be justifiable fears that the small borrower may be neglected over charged. This will not find any credence in a market economy.

The Reserve Bank should create conditions on how the general public should be eligible for credit. Most of the problems are related to poor understanding of what borrowing constitutes.

- That all borrowings should be repaid.
- That interest agreed on also is a price to be paid for borrowing.

- That interest is something that should be paid on time and come out of the earnings of borrower.
- That the rate of his earning should exceed the rate of interest for which he has borrowed and for the purpose which has been borrowed.
- That the character of money will not change irrespective for the purpose of which it is borrowed.

The frequent cry that is heard from the marketplace that one cannot afford the interest to be paid is often due to borrowing for wrong purposes or that the borrowing does not result in getting a return to commensurate with the cost of borrowing the same. In a market economy the interest rate has to be at the market rate plus transaction cost. It is obvious that retail loans entail higher transaction costs than wholesale loans. The banks should arrive at their own rates on the basis of their capabilities, infrastructure and approach to small lending. This should cover their costs of servicing the loans as well as the risks they entail.

Small loans are local in nature and require skills, which are essential to borrowing. Even as the loan is small, the principle remains the same that the loans should get repaid even as loans should be accessible and affordable. This does not mean that these loans should be provided below their true and fair cost. Otherwise it will be at the cost of other borrowers, or depositors or shareholders.

Reserve Bank should free the interest rates on this sector. The liberalisation in financial markets will ensure credit to deserving and eligible borrowers can be determined through agencies other than commercial banks. For instance, NBFCs and Co-operative banks, LABs and RRBs can be requested to handle small loan portfolios at lower costs than national banks.

The definition of borrowing as small medium or large is a managerial division. A sum of Rs. 5,000 can be very big for a poor person and very small for a large bank. Therefore arriving at a figure of Rs. 2 lakhs as a small borrowing is very subjective. The Reserve Bank should cease arriving at such classification and focus on its core function: Central Banking.

If Banks on their own judgement set a price of interest at PLR it would indicate the credibility of the small borrower. The banks in all probability price interest according to their own judgement by categorising the credit worthiness of the borrowers.

Commitment for the Future

The Reserve Bank of India must commit itself that it will not resort to any arbitrary or adhoc direction on interest rates on any particular segment of the financial sector.

This of course will not apply in the case of an emergency, financial or otherwise. However these emergencies must be well defined within the Bank and in concurrence with the Government of India.

The Reserve Bank should fix and determine only the rates which it uses directly as a signalling device, that is the bank rate and its operating rate, the OMO rate. The interest rates for other segments should be also regulated by its setting the REPO rate and Reverse REPO rate appropriately.

The Reserve Bank, as a Central Bank has the prerogative to set the pricing for any segment of interest rates. This has to be exercised consciously and in public interest. Therefore, any specification of interest rate for a particular segment should not be applied.

The market rate of interest should be carefully governed. The tools at its command and the ability to absorb and provide the flow of money are adequate. The exceptions could be in the case of an emergency, financial or otherwise. These options and tools should be discussed and carefully regarded to be used during exceptional times. They should not be used to deal with market fluctuations. When market fluctuations reveal unusual movements in particular segments, the RBI should launch an investigation and remedy the same by education, organisation and discipline.

Sound management of Reserve Bank Assets, the powerful tools at its command with a well-oiled machinery and a committed executive the markets would behave in an orderly fashion with the instruments of Bank Rate, OMO Rate, Repo Rate and Reverse Repo Rate

Government of India and State Governments also have to upgrade quality of economic policy that will not result in disruption or disturbances in an important factor like capital.

Interest rates will depend on the supply and demand of money in a particular segment. Monitoring the entire financial sector by constant scanning and internal surveillance will involve practices in management within the institutions. These have to be evolved and nurtured well within the institution.

This also involves a regular interaction with the Government. The intensity of interaction with Banks and financial intermediaries will determine the flow of data and information into the bank. The knowledge within the Central Bank and outside will have to be used and transmitted.

The orderly functioning of money markets will then require subtle techniques rather than gross and direct methods. If directed rates disappear well within the next few weeks a good beginning would have been made in readying the financial sector for India's century.

Conclusion

The above steps should be taken forthwith. It will pave the way for a fully market determined rate for all the lending and borrowing segments in the financial sector.

The rates determined by the Reserve Bank – the Bank Rate, the OMO Rate, the REPO rate and the Reverse REPO rate will have to be calibrated and fine-tuned taking into account: The fundamentals: savings, consumption and investment activity in the economy, the rate of inflation, the rates of interest in the global economy for different currencies and the domestic economic environment.

The Reserve Bank of India must provide the framework to educate the polity, bureaucracy, the general public on the nature of the interest rates and their influence. It will go a long way in correcting the anomalies, aberrations and distortions that prevailed for decades and pave the way for an orderly market.

NOTES

1. The above positions are reiteration of earlier communications which have not been acted on.
2. The theoretical aspects of interest rates compared to the actual behaviour in India require more focus and attention.
3. There has been remarkable changes in Policy and practices over 12 years. Banks focus now on CASA (Current Accounts Savings Accounts) than on Fixed Deposits.
4. Savings Bank rates have been decontrolled with beneficial impact.
5. Core Banking and information Technology have made a big difference.

Seventeen

Alignment of Bank Deposit Interest Rates

Analysis and Case for Regulation

[2002]

The interest rates offered on deposit rates are now more transparent than a few years ago. The table below is extracted from a newspaper, which gives comparative rates offered on different tenors by commercial banks.

It can be argued that deposit on bank rates should not exceed the Bank Rate which is the Discount Rate announced by the Reserve Bank of India. Currently, the Bank rate is 6.5%. This is the practice now in developed countries. The Banks in London also do not offer interest rate contract exceeding one year.

Anything above one year is available to the investors in the form of instruments. The interest rates in India have moved lower on one main macroeconomic factor, that is the rate of inflation. The interest rates in India have been characterised by anomalies, aberrations and distortions as interest rates as well as channels of savings and investments were controlled and directed by the State or by the Reserve Bank of India or both.

After 1991, the Reserve Bank of India and Government of India have held the view that the interest rates should be left to the "market". Though this policy was evolved consciously, it resulted in a chaotic situation. Interest rates often gyrated wildly for various reasons.

The gradual easing of directions on interest rates leaves open the question as to how interest rates can be **governed**. The Reserve Bank of India is an institution created for monetary stability. The Government of India and State Governments have not been

Interest Rates on Bank Fixed Deposits

Bank	15-29 days	30-45 days	45-60 days	61-90 days	91-120 days	120-179 days	180-270 days	271-364 days	1 Yrs <2 Yrs	2 yrs <3 Yrs	3 yrs <5 Yrs	With effect from
Foreign Banks												
ABN-Amra Bank	4.50	7.00	7.00	7.00	7.00	7.00	7.00	7.00	7.00	7.00	7.00	3/30/2002
Standard Chartered Grindlays Bank	4.50	6.25	6.25	7.00	7.25	7.25	7.00	7.00	7.00	7.25	7.25	3/5/2002
State Bank of Mauritius	5.25	6.00	6.75	6.75	7.75	7.75	8.00	8.00	8.00	8.00	8.00	7/8/2002
The Hongkong & Shanghai Bank	5.00	5.75	5.75	5.25	6.25	6.25	6.75	7.00	7.00	7.25	7.50	2/20/2002
Indian Banks—Public Sector												
Allahabad Bank	5.00	5.25	6.00	6.00	6.25	6.25	6.75	6.75	7.25	7.50	8.00	8/1/2002
Andhra Bank	5.00	5.00	6.00	6.00	6.00	6.00	6.50	6.50	7.25	7.50	7.75	8/1/2002
Bank of Baroda	5.25	5.25	5.50	5.50	6.00	6.00	6.50	6.50	7.25	7.50	8.00	7/23/2002
Bank of India	5.75	5.75	5.75	5.75	6.50	6.50	6.50	6.50	7.25	7.25	8.00	7/29/2002
Bank of Maharashtra	5.00	5.00	5.50	5.50	5.50	5.50	6.50	7.00	7.25	7.50	8.00	8/12/2002
Canara Bank	4.25	4.25	5.00	5.00	6.00	6.00	6.50	6.50	7.00	7.25	7.50	8/1/2002
Central Bank of India	4.75	4.75	5.50	5.50	6.50	5.50	6.25	6.25	7.00	7.25	8.00	8/1/2002
Co-operation Bank	5.00	5.00	5.75	5.75	6.25	6.25	6.50	6.50	7.25	7.50	7.50	7/29/2002
Dena Bank	4.75	5.00	6.00	5.00	6.25	6.25	6.50	6.50	7.25	7.50	7.75	8/1/2002
Indian Bank	5.00	5.00	6.00	5.00	6.25	6.25	6.50	6.50	7.25	7.25	7.50	8/5/2002
Indian Overseas Bank	4.50	5.25	5.25	5.25	6.00	6.00	6.25	6.25	7.00	7.25	7.50	8/1/2002
Oriental Bank of Commerce	5.00	5.25	5.75	5.75	6.00	6.00	6.50	6.50	7.00	7.25	7.50	8/1/2002

(Contd.)

Bank	15-29 days	30-45 days	45-60 days	61-90 days	91-120 days	120-179 days	180-270 days	271-364 days	1 Yrs <2 Yrs	2 yrs <3 Yrs	3 yrs <5 Yrs	With effect from
Punjab & Sind Bank	5.00	5.50	6.25	5.25	6.50	6.50	6.50	6.50	7.25	7.50	8.00	3/15/2002
Punjab National Bank	5.00	5.00	6.00	5.00	6.00	6.00	6.25	6.25	7.00	7.25	7.50	8/2/2002
State Bank of Bikaner & Jaipur	5.00	5.00	6.00	6.00	6.25	6.25	6.50	6.50	7.00	7.25	7.50	8/1/2002
State Bank of India	5.00	5.00	6.00	6.00	6.00	6.00	6.25	6.25	7.00	7.25	7.50	7/29/2002
State of Mysore	5.00	5.00	6.00	6.00	6.50	6.50	6.75	6.75	7.25	7.75	8.00	6/15/2002
State of Bank of Patalia	5.25	5.50	6.25	6.25	6.50	6.50	7.00	7.00	8.50	8.75	9.00	4/172002
State Bank of Saurashtra	5.00	5.00	6.00	6.00	6.00	6.00	6.50	6.50	7.25	7.50	7.75	8/1/2002
State Bank of Trevarcore	5.00	5.00	6.00	6.00	6.00	6.00	6.25	6.25	7.00	7.50	7.75	7/22/2002
Syndicate Bank	4.25	5.00	5.50	5.50	6.00	6.00	6.25	6.25	7.00	7.25	7.50	8/7/2002
UCO Bank	5.00	5.25	6.00	6.00	6.75	6.25	6.50	6.50	7.25	7.25	7.50	8/12/2002
Union Bank of India	5.00	5.25	5.75	5.75	6.00	6.00	6.50	6.50	7.25	7.25	7.50	8/1/2002
United Bank of India	5.00	5.00	6.00	6.00	6.25	6.25	6.50	6.50	7.00	7.25	7.50	8/12/2002
Vijaya Bank	5.00	5.00	6.00	6.00	6.00	6.00	6.50	6.50	7.25	7.50	7.75	8/8/2002
Indian Bank – Private Sector												
Bank of Punjab	5.00	5.50	6.00	5.00	6.50	6.50	7.00	7.25	8.00	8.25	8.25	8/9/2002
Bharat Overseas Bank	5.00	5.50	6.25	6.25	6.50	6.50	7.00	7.00	7.50	7.75	8.00	8/8/2002
Centurian Bank	6.25	6.25	7.00	7.00	8.00	8.00	8.50	8.75	9.00	9.25	9.25	5/1/2002
City Union Bank	5.00	5.00	6.00	6.00	7.50	7.50	8.00	8.00	8.50	8.75	9.00	7/15/2002
Development Credit Bank	5.25	6.00	6.50	6.50	6.75	6.75	8.00	8.00	8.50	8.50	8.50	8/1/2002
Glube Trust Bank	5.25	6.00	6.50	6.50	7.00	7.00	8.25	8.25	8.50	8.50	8.75	8/1/2002

(Contd.)

Bank	15-29 days	30-45 days	45-60 days	61-90 days	91-120 days	120-179 days	180-270 days	271-364 days	1 Yrs <2 Yrs	2 yrs <3 Yrs	3 yrs <5 Yrs	With effect from
HDFC Bank	5.00	5.50	5.50	6.00	6.50	6.50	7.00	7.00	7.50	7.75	7.75	7/29/2002
ICICI Bank	6.25	5.00	6.00	6.00	6.00	6.00	7.00	7.00	8.00	8.25	8.25	7/31/2002
IDBI Bank	5.00	5.50	6.00	6.00	6.50	6.50	7.00	7.25	7.75	7.75	7.75	8/2/2002
IndusInd Bank	5.25	5.75	5.75	6.25	6.25	6.50	7.75	7.75	8.25	8.25	8.25	8/9/2002
Karnataka Bank	5.00	5.00	7.00	7.00	7.50	7.50	8.00	8.00	8.50	8.50	8.50	5/15/2002
Lord Krishna Bank	5.00	5.00	6.50	6.50	7.25	7.25	7.75	7.75	8.00	8.25	8.25	8/10/2002
Tamilnad Mercantile Bank	5.00	5.00	6.00	6.00	7.50	7.50	8.00	8.00	8.50	8.50	8.50	7/8/2002
The Catholic Syrian Bank	5.50	6.00	6.50	6.50	7.00	7.00	7.25	7.25	8.00	8.00	8.25	6/15/2002
The Dhanlakshmi Bank	6.00	6.00	6.00	6.00	7.00	7.00	7.50	7.50	8.00	8.00	8.50	4/17/2002
The Federal Bank	5.00	5.25	6.25	6.25	6.25	6.25	6.50	6.50	7.25	7.75	8.00	8/5/2002
The J&K Bank	5.00	5.25	6.00	6.00	6.25	6.25	6.50	6.50	7.25	7.25	7.50	8/5/2002
The Karur Vyasya Bank	5.00	5.00	6.00	6.00	6.50	6.50	7.50	7.50	8.00	8.00	8.25	8/5/2002
The Lakshmi Vilas Bank	5.00	6.00	7.00	7.00	7.25	7.25	7.50	7.50	7.75	8.00	8.00	8/1/2002
The Nadugadi Bank	5.00	5.50	6.00	6.00	7.00	7.00	7.25	7.25	8.00	8.00	8.25	8/17/2002
The South Indian Bank	5.25	6.00	6.50	6.50	7.00	7.00	7.25	7.25	8.00	8.00	8.25	6/7/2002
The United Western Bank	4.00	5.00	5.00	5.00	6.00	6.00	7.00	7.00	8.50	8.50	8.50	6/24/2002
The Vysya Bank	5.25	6.25	6.25	5.25	6.85	6.85	7.85	7.85	8.25	8.25	8.25	8/7/2002
UTI Bank	5.00	5.00	5.50	5.50	6.00	6.00	7.00	7.00	7.75	7.75	6.25	8/17/2002

prudent in their borrowing policies and have displayed lack of discipline and self control markedly in this area. They have also shown ignorance in the mastery of interest rates as a factor influencing their financial affairs.

The necessity now is to address how the Reserve Bank can influence the interest rates of the market. The Reserve Bank can do so explicitly as well as implicitly. Explicitly by the instruments at its command and implicitly by education, organisation and discipline that can be conveyed as a regulator and supervisor.

A regulator has been described as follows:

> Regulation consists of government rules or laws issued to control the price, sale or production decisions of firms.
>
> Samuelson & William D. Nordhaus, *Economics*

If interest is a price what prevents the Reserve Bank of India from laying down ground rules for banks to follow their own interest rate-pricing pattern?

This paper makes out a case for direct regulation of interest rates in the near term to align deposit rates into a narrow range.

The freedom given to banks to set their own rates should not result in economic inefficiency. The rates that are set should be fair to both the depositor and the lender. Rates should not be arrived which would result in a risk to the owners of the bank i.e. the shareholders. The Bank should also be safe as a business as it is an institution of society.

The economic questions involved are, given conditions of a market economy and sound governance:

1. What should be the ideal deposit rate for under 360 days from a bank to a customer for a term deposit over or under the Bank Rate?
2. What should be the ideal deposit rate over the 360 day rate in terms of basis point for each year up to five years over or under the Bank rate or the 360 day rate?
3. What should be the ideal difference between one bank and another in terms of basis points over each tenor of deposit rate? Should there be a difference at all levels when they are "market" determined?
4. What should be an ideal response of a bank to cuts in Bank Rates or in a more refined market the OMO rate?

5. What should be an ideal self regulatory mechanism on the pricing of deposit interest rates across the country for a bank or banks of different size of operations?
6. What should be an ideal regulatory framework for Reserve Bank of India to exercise over banks when they price their deposit rates?
7. There should be an ideal regulatory framework for Reserve Bank of India to act on, when it forms an opinion that the bank is not pricing it ideally either in economic terms or in terms of safety or jeopardy to the financial system, citizens or the Bank itself.
8. What is the material that should be available for the Boards of Banks if they are the arbiters and deciders for increasing or decreasing or maintaining the rates of deposits from time to time?
9. What are the macro economic and business phenomena that have to be necessarily factored in the decision making process?

These questions need to be answered by the Reserve Bank of India, Bankers, policy makers in Government, specialists in the subject, media and academicians. There needs to be an active discussion, dialogue and debate by stakeholders, analysts, commentators, correspondents and of course, the citizens who are the persons affected by the decisions.

A general view is provided for the above to enable framing a regulatory policy on deposit rates paid by banks.

Ideal Interest Pricing Pattern

A consensus should emerge in the banking sector itself as to the ideal pricing pattern for the industry as a whole for rates on deposits.

This should be formally launched by the Reserve Bank of India on an immediate basis by forming working groups among banks themselves and culminating in a National meeting or workshop on this subject among banks under the aegis of the RBI.

This consensus should on the basis of discussion, debate and dialogue, free flow of information and ideas, dissemination of existing practices in banking industry, positions stated in banking theory and its application in Indian conditions and other preconditions or necessities that would be taken into consideration.

A consensus needs to be arrived at as to how the banking industry and Reserve Bank of India respond to conditions that emerge in the market place in emerging contexts. The deposit rates need to have a dynamism that aligns with the policy rate determined by the Reserve Bank of India periodically.

The substance of the interest rate pricing should be discussed and not coloured by the qualities that have ruled the Indian banking industry in the last four decades.

Equilibrium in Deposit Interest Pricing

The next idea that should emerge from the industry and the Central Bank is what constitutes the basis of pricing of interest rates in a market economy. How is equilibrium arrived at?

A bank deposit is for a fixed period and carries a fixed rate of interest for that period. The depositor is insulated from changes during this period. In the case of instruments e.g. tradable bonds the interest rate fluctuates in the course of the day as they change hands and therefore interest rates are dynamic in the market. In the case of fixed deposit the interest rates are static.

It can be different during volatile and inflationary times. Banks have to respond to reduction in inflation rates or international trends in currencies and monetary phenomena of trading partners or of world markets.

Given stable conditions the response is made usually to the changes considered by the announcement of the decision makers within Reserve Bank of India on their views on the market as well as the concrete direction set by announcements in the Bank Rate or other monetary policy instruments like OMO, Repo and reverse repo transactions.

Elimination of Adhoc or Inconsiderate Changes

Banks often go on what media terms as interest rate wars. This is definitely not a desirable state of affairs that banks exercise rivalry on the basis of interest rates.

Competition results in a fair situation both to depositors and lenders. But if banks resort to indiscriminate increases in rates of interest on deposits just to attract more clientele or reduces interest rates in its own interest of reducing cost of borrowing or increasing spread due to a semi monopolistic position it exercises, then it would be doing subtle damage to the financial system.

Reserve Bank of India should recognise that the organisational behaviour of banks in this respect is markedly devoid of economics as a discipline, best practices in markets. Sometimes interest pricing is based on decisions coming out of managerial or executive ego. The emphasis on liability creation by banks that is chasing deposits is also responsible for this particular phenomenon.

Ideal Difference between Short Term and Medium Term Deposit Rates

The interest rates between different banks provide scope for comparison. A depositor of one bank will compare the deposit rates of another.

The Reserve Bank of India and the Central Government as well as specialist institutions like NCAER, ICRIER, IGIDR, BTC, ISEC, Universities, academicians, economists, analysts and commentators should vent their opinions and ideas on the nature of interest rates in a market economy on a focused area like bank deposits.

The dictates of economic efficiency will point to rates converging to one rate. Competition and rivalry will be pulls in the reverse directions. A broad consensus should emerge on the difference that should emerge from short term to long term rates.

Organisational Behaviour and Interest Rates

The pricing of interest rates on deposits in India requires a study in the discipline of organisational behaviour. A major issue to be addressed is one of social psychology—the organisational behaviour of banks as well as responses and reactions from customers. Banks are sensitive to public opinion (or so it seems). Often in India, commentators and analysts do not present unbiased neutral views in a given situation.

The Boards of banks as well as their economists and PR specialists should give undiluted articulation on the background of pricing. This makes room for public opinion to be formed on right lines on sound theoretical bases and also leaves less room for criticism and emotional outbursts.

More important, public opinion which is not based on sound theory but based on bias, prejudice and special interests, influences policy as well as causes delays and procrastination in decision making. In a conflict between doing the right policy on interest rates and adverse market behaviour, the politician does not want to get unpopular and the bureaucrat who is better informed on theory is often in a quandary.

A strong central banker alone can give an unequivocal stand. The market should also get trained in self-discipline and sound theory. When practices turn deviant there should be an equal and opposite movement to curb such deviant practices. Freedom should not turn into licence.

Responses to Signals and Market Conditions

When the above aspect is taken care of, sufficient exercises must begin on how the marketplace responds to "signals".

Interest rates depend on pure supply and demand of money as well as monetary phenomena like interest rates and the stability of the payments system.

A conservative stance is called for over the next 18 months to promote and protect stability, integration of the banking system and improvement in its profitability and performance.

Ideal Regulation to Self-regulation

A decision in principle should be arrived to have a consensus on what constitutes regulation in the case of pricing of deposit rates.

Even as it is left to operators, how and when should the Central Bank intervene in the pricing? Should the Central Bank as well as the market be informed of such a change? How should the Central Bank audit a process of decision-making? Can it specify standardised tools in which the decision to arrive at rates is based?

Reporting formats should also be in such a way that the Reserve Bank of India can respond or react to specific moves of banks. It would also help if alerts were provided on the basis of notices to be given to customers at least 2 weeks before the rates come into effect or that at least 4 weeks notice be given to the Reserve Bank of India and the market that there is a contemplation to examine the rate structure. These conditions lead to ideal self regulation.

Education, Organisation and Discipline in Determining Interest Rates

The decision making process on increasing, decreasing or maintaining rates should not be a hasty one.

There should be two processes: one in response to signals and two in conditions of stability or otherwise where the bank should respond or act on its own. In the former case, the decision making process should be rendered faster and should be a standard response. In the case of the latter, it should be a considered and well-deliberated decision.

A conscious decision to increase, decrease or maintain rates should be based on facts, practices and science applied.

The Reserve Bank of India should guide banks into having an acceptable standard practice in both cases and leave the market better educated, better organised and therefore capable of self-control and self-discipline. This leads to economic efficiency on the basis of justice.

The need is now for a concerted effort of all parties, interests and sections to view the subject of interest rates dispassionately. There is no occasion for finding faults but work towards an acceptable standard, which keeps the banking system sound, healthy and capable of delivering the crucial functions for which it exists.

Best practices should be evolved which ensures economic efficiency for the nation as a whole. Interest pricing to be left to the "market" should not imply that the principles of economic efficiency be ignored or the effects of lack of application of sound theoretical principles by market operators left unattended. In a transition phase, the market functionary should be conveyed the principles of education, organisation and discipline by the regulator as well as the Government.

NOTES

1. There is a significant improvement since 2002 on how Bank Deposit interest rates are determined and managed.
2. The Asset Liability Management system within banks is getting mature and robust.
3. An expanded economy and the gradual move towards market economy and market determined interest rates the dominance of Bank Deposits will move towards direct investments in bonds and instruments. Mutual Funds will also play a significant role in the holdings of individuals.

4. There is tremendous scope for refining the bank deposits and redefining the liabilities structure of Commercial banks in India.
5. This topic needs more focus and attention of all stakeholders as the economic efficiency generated due to the mobility of capital and dynamism of interest.
6. In the global market there is hardly any significance for Bank Deposits.
7. In another interesting aspect, the Indian approach in commercial banking which is essentially different from advanced economies could have protected it from the onslaught of the wicked problem which arose out of the financial crisis generated in New York in 2008.
8. The intellectual challenge is to improve continuously towards efficiency without falling into compromises that lead to damage to individuals as well as to the system.
9. Commercial banks are bound to be challenged by investment banks and other financial entities in the coming years in India.

Eighteen

Prime Lending Rate

[2006]

The Reserve Bank of India mention the term Sub-PLR in "Perspectives" of the 'Report on Trend and Progress of Banking in India, 2004-05' is noted and reproduced herewith.

> The benchmark prime lending rate (BPLR) system was introduced to increase the transparency in pricing of credit by banks. In the recent past, however, with the introduction of sub-PLR lending, spreads between minimum and maximum lending rates have increased significantly. Furthermore, the sub-BPLR lending of the banking system (excluding exports, the bulk of which is at sub-BPLR) has also increased substantially-to the extent of over 60 per cent of total outstanding advances above Rs. 2 lakh. Though sub-PLR lending has enabled corporate to raise funds at competitive rates from banks without incurring any additional cost towards stamp duty, dematerialisation costs or fees for issuing and paying agents (IPAs), it is distorting the role of BPLR itself. Many banks have their average lending rate below their BPLR, which is also putting pressure on their spreads. Furthermore, there is a growing perception that there is under-pricing of credit risk for large private sector corporates, whereas there could be over-pricing of risk in lending to agriculture as well as small and medium enterprises.
>
> There is, therefore, merit in reviewing the current procedures and processes of pricing of credit, perhaps through a well-structured segment-wise analysis of costs at various stages of intermediation in the whole credit cycle, and bringing improvement in risk assessment and risk management systems in banks.

The Reserve Bank needs to be more active and more action oriented than mere mention of the anomalies that are arising out of the decisions made by the Banks on PLR and lending their customer's below the PLR Rate.

Directive

- A directive that says Banks should not lend below PLR is to be given.
- It need not tell the banks what the Prime Lending Rate should be.
- It need not take away the banks freedom to arrive at its own Prime Lending Rate.
- It need not take away the banks freedom to lend to any constituent at the rate it chooses to as long as it is at the prime lending rate or above it.
- It need not alter the ability of banks to continue to lend at rates which it considers profitable as long as it is above the Prime Lending Rate.
- This need not take away the banks freedom to invest in securities at the market rate of interest for respective securities whether it is above or below the PLR in its "investment" function. Lending means a loan. The definition of loan is well known.
- At the cost of repetition, the Bank shall not lend to anyone at any time at any place less than the Prime Lending Rate determined by itself.
- The RBI must give banks at least four weeks time before banks take a decision with the assistance of boards.
- Further guidelines can be also given in the interest of an equitable system under Indian conditions. It must be fair and just to all constituents.
- As the Indian banking system is having problem on price due to competition and rivalry the regulator has to step in now with direct intervention to set what is fundamentally right.
- In due course, the market rates and rates of loans will align themselves on the basis of economic and business theory and practice.

Simplicity

- The Reserve Bank of India must give a directive that "no Loan shall be given below the Bank's decided PLR.
- There should not be any variations in PLR. (BPLR, LTPLR etc.)
- RBI does not tell the banks what the Prime Lending Rate should be. This is the position at present.
- However, RBI should conduct workshops and seminars and give guidance to bankers on how PLR should be arrived at.
- This does not take away the bank's freedom to lend a loan to any constituent as long as it is at the Prime Lending Rate or above it.
- It does not alter the ability of banks to continue to lend at rates which it considers profitable as long as it is above the Prime Lending Rate
- At the cost of repetition, there shall be no such thing as a sub-plr and the Bank shall not lend to any constituent less than the Prime Lending Rate determined by itself.
- This directive emanates from ethical considerations. This will not violate the principles of banking or the principles of economics as the current situation is so glaringly doing.
- When RBI gives a specific directive it will be a permanent long term correction in Indian Banking practice.
- It will have a significant authority and will also curtail practice by special interests in the political, social or economic segments who demand interest rates which are different and lower than the market rates.

Implementation

- The RBI must give banks at least four weeks time for the implementation.
- This should give sufficient time for Banks to go to their boards.
- The RBI has been giving explanations and coaching on several aspects of banking and effects of central banking to banks. The same must be done in this case also.
- The directive is given with firmness. It may even be called as a "fiat" by journalists. Unmindful of criticism, it must be given.

- The Indian banking system is not responding to hints, suggestions, mentions and advice. It is trapped by a situation of its own making. The directive will aid and assist the banks and not deprive the Central Bank of credibility nor will it hurt the Banks in anyway.
- The Indian banking system is intransigent or trapped in a social psychology problem. This is due to the inherent rivalry and competition prevailing in the marketplace.
- It is also due to a historic phenomenon in the Indian market place, which is, a surplus of financial capital which has happened for the first time in 1993-94 after decades.
- The Regulator has to step in now with direct intervention to set what is fundamentally right.
- The Banking system will welcome this. Currently the banking system is influenced by smart executives in the financial and corporate world. Banks as a rule conform to the directive or guidelines of the Government and RBI.
- In due course, the market rates, rates of loans will align themselves on the basis of economic, banking theory, business theory, Central Bank policy and demand and supply of money.

Reference

- The reference rates of the Reserve Bank of India are as follows:
    - Bank Rate 6.0 per cent
    - Repo Rate 6.25 per cent
    - Reverse Repo Rate 5.25 per cent
- The PLR of Banks is stated as 10.25–10.75 per cent
- Banks are lending on homes and cars screaming from Newspaper advertisements and Bill Boards, calling every person on the phone and mobile and asking for loans on these segments at 6.75 per cent to 7.5 per cent.
- Newspaper reports regularly convey that Banks are lending to Corporates under pressure of availability of funds in large amounts of hundreds of crores and sometimes to a single corporate at competitive rates between 7 per cent to 7.25 per cent.
- This has found mention in the recent Reports by the RBI—the Annual Policy, the Annual Report, the Report on

Currency and Banking and Trends and Progress in Banking. It has concluded that a significant portion of the lending is at SUB-PLR rates. The RBI directive will have no impact on the banks lending rates or profitability on the negative side. It will be more on the positive side.

- In this scenario, based on the Directive of the Reserve Bank of India, banks could arrive at the PLR of 7 per cent. Individual banks may arrive at 7.25, 7.75, 8.0, 8.25, 8.50, 8.75, 9.0 or even retain their present PLRs. But they will be bound by the direction not to lend below the PLR Rate.
- The action will be that the interest rates they have agreed with constituents will have to be altered so that they are NOT BELOW THE PLR announced.
- It is the borrowers who will be affected when the banks implement the decision. The PLR will have to be aligned with the bank rate.
- Any economic, econometric or logical application of sound banking practice should make the banker currently arrive at no more than 2.00 per cent over the Bank Rate. This will have to be 8.00 per cent when the Bank Rate is 6 per cent. The Bank Rate needs to be the benchmark for the PLR and PLR the benchmark for all loans to customers. There is no need to add B to the PLR as BPLR is now used.
- Banks have clauses in their loan agreements that they can revise the rates of interest depending on 1, 2, and 3.
- Banks, will therefore take advantage of the directive to "align" themselves to a proper method of borrowers hierarchy. The best borrower will get at the "prime" rate and the rated borrower will get at no more than 4 percentage points above Prime Rate.
- In a market economy, any rate at 4 per cent above the prime rate is a risk on principal and return itself (Dr. Bimal Jalan)
- The interest rate, whether on a home loan, car loan, SME individual or a corporate will have to be on the basis of sound banking principles and practice and not on the basis of psychology. Of course, the theory of price is mysterious and no one has been able to explain the rationale of price.
- However, a business has to exist for its customers. Banking is a business. Therefore, the bank should not be subject to

pressures from particular constituents nor from within itself to favour or disfavour particular segments or constituents. Banks should arrive at the eligibility of the borrower and not on the basis of segments. (Dr. Rakesh Mohan)

- In all, the directive, when given will be favourable to the banks and the banking system. It will help banks to improve profitability by re-aligning interest rates in the cheaper segment. Ultimately it is the depositors who have a slight negative discrimination now who will stand to gain both from the safety and the returns angle.

True Meaning

- The word prime should not be abused by an introduction of the terminology sub-prime. There is no such word and therefore, it is a created word in the Indian context. If a particular constituent has to be a beneficiary, he has to be given grants by the charitably disposed donor. Interest rates should not be distorted nor subsidy in interest payments through the banking system.
- An orderly market-oriented system of an emerging super power cannot permit outlandish practices in such an important area as banking. It is therefore incumbent on RBI to correct itself; it is the originator of the term sub-plr.

Benchmark Rate

- The outcome of the Credit Policy with special reference to the evolution of the PLR (Prime Lending Rate) as a benchmark rate.
- The necessity is now to have a Prime Rate which is:
  - Reflecting the borrowing capacity, credibility, credit-worthiness, repayment capacity and character of the borrower who will be eligible to borrow at Prime Lending Rate.
  - That which responds to the signals from Reserve Bank of India when it sets the Bank Rate and the OMO rate.
  - That which is an indicator for the right pricing of the interest rates on bank
  - That which is an indicator and helpful in right pricing of interest for the borrowers from the banking system.

- The Prime Lending Rate should be such that the Bank which decides the right PLR should not lend to any constituent below that rate for whatever segment or tenor.
- A letter was submitted to the Governor of the Reserve Bank of India on the PLR issue on 28.2.2005. A letter dated 5.11.2003 along with a Note was sent to Sri V. Leeladhar, Chairman, IBA.
- The Credit Policy has clearly mentioned that the onus is now on the IBA and it may issue guidelines to Banks. Coming from a statutory regulatory body the IBA was bound to respond correctly and scientifically.
- IBA has not succeeded in advising Banks on practices which will reflect the fundamentals of best banking practices worldwide.
- We look forward to a more constructive role played by IBA in shaping the policies within the Banking system in a progressive, modern market economy.

Pricing and Freedom

- The Reserve Bank of India has held discussion with Bankers on the question of pricing the Prime Rate of Commercial Banks. The evolution of the interest rate structure of interest in the marketplace in India from 1991 to date is noteworthy.
- The term "freedom" to arrive at rates has to be matched by sense of responsibility. The Banking sector in India and the Reserve Bank of India do not need any education on defining what a Prime Rate could be. The fact is that both are caught into a trap where they are found practicing something different from what it could be.
- The Reserve Bank of India has allowed a practice which is opposed to the principle of PLR by introducing a new term called the "Sub-PLR". This was to allow certain concessions to particular segments.
- The Banking sector which had the experience of three decades of direction, control and intervention by RBI has long forgotten the principle of "Prime Rate" and when it was revived by the RBI, it went through the motions of adjustment with the Prime Rate. *The Banking sector froze*

the PLR at a level which was convenient. But when there was a situation where they were able to lend to particular segments at lower rates, began pricing those loans at substantially lower rates than the "Prime Lending Rate". Therefore, the Central Bank of the Nation and the operating Banks themselves are to take the responsibility for verbicide.

- The Central Bank and the Indian Banks have indulged in destroying the meaning of the word "Prime". The Prime Rate by definition and emphasis would be the lowest rate that the Bank would determine and it could offer on a loan to its best customers with the highest guarantee of safety of return of capital. It cannot implement a rate below the prime lending rate to any of their customers.
- The peculiarity of the situation today is that the Banks are caught in a web of their own making—The results of the mistakes, errors and stupidities of the past. The Banks have contracted rates of interest payment on deposits which they now claim result in "costs". They find it convenient to load this on to particular segments. The incremental deposits they are having which are at low costs are being deployed in securities which do not offer any additional returns to them. In the present situation they also take the liberty to grant loans in chunks to their favoured customers at considerably less cost of interest than the Prime Lending Rate.
- The solution therefore requires that the RBI must define the prime lending rate which is sensible by a process of arithmetic and econometric calculation and reach a conclusion on how Banks should price the interest rate on deposits.
- The rate of inflation, conditions in the international money markets, the demand for investment in India or lack of it should all be taken into consideration in pricing of interest rate. RBI must specify right things to be done and then leave it to the Banks to do things correctly.
- It is very important to distinguish between loans and instruments. The interest rate for instruments which are tradable and transferable will get determined on their own. The principles of market efficiency can make instruments priced cheaper than loans.

- It is also very important for Banks and RBI to distinguish between these two. Instruments can be raised only by organizations. Individuals will have to resort to Banks only for credit and take loans based on need and the ability to utilize them effectively. Taking of loans also implies their capacity to employ the amount profitably to enable them to pay interest and repay the principal.
- There is a mistaken notion in Financial Circles about the benchmarking of the Prime Rate. The linkage to cost is a secondary issue. The focus of the Prime Rate should be on the customer who has acquired the credit, capability and character to be eligible for that.
- The eligibility of Prime Rate is for the borrower to transcend from the ordinary. It is a standard. It is an ideal. Prime is goodness. It indicates superiority. It puts a mark on the client as a first-rate, first class borrower irrespective of the segments or lending or class of borrowers.
- The Banking system has ignored the values that are necessary to its conduct by focusing only on the "Cost" issue. Its behaviour can be considered unethical as it has favoured only Corporates (whether first-class or not) and segments (home loans and motor vehicle loans).
- All that is needed by Reserve Bank of India is to use the powers and authority vested in it to restore right conduct to the Banking System and Regulate the Prime Rate.

First, the Reserve Bank is an authority and a regulator. Therefore, it can serve well by intelligent direction to Banks than mere mention in "Perspectives".

The Indian banking system is in the direction to maturity, but a little short of application of intelligent thought.

The root cause of this situation lies not only in the banking system but in Government and the regulator themselves. Government, due to its long direct interference and intervention in the factor markets of which capital and interest has been no exception.

The regulator is to be marked as a willing collaborator with Government, even when it deviates from principles or theory as a humble servant of parliament and the citizens.

The RBI therefore, as an autonomous organization must first correct itself. Who introduced the term sub-plr? It must remove the same from its thinking and stop mentioning it again. It must not just do it, but explain why. It must do it by reasoning.

Please Stop Using the Word SUB-PLR any More

Sub-PLR shabd ko mitha diya jaaye

Once it is accepted in principle, then it must also be broadcast and enforced with vigour amongst all market participants. Customers as citizens must also be explained why it is done. The action is done in public interest.

The Reserve Bank may then choose to do so using its powers as a regulator. It shall be in a concise and precise statement.

> Effective 1st March, 2006 no financial institution or bank or loan giving company shall lend to any of its constituents below its Prime Lending Rate.

This statement is simple and direct. This may be done at the soonest in public interest.

NOTES

1. The term sub-PLR surfaced when there was a surge of liquidity with commercial banks. They had to compete with each other to secure customers for loans.
2. This resulted in corporates in India getting a sweet deal that bankers were vying with each other to provide them loans.
3. Interest rates became a point of negotiation for secure borrowers. Banks started to offer them loans at interest rates lower than the prime lending rate. The term sub-PLR was born.
4. It continued for quite some time. Frequent mention of it was made in the media, in speeches and announcements by bankers. Even Reserve Bank of India mentioned it.
5. In 2008 the sub-prime crisis broke out in USA. The term sub-prime in USA meant weaker customers and here, in India sub-prime rates were meant for better customers.
6. This was an anomaly for some time. Currently, the term is not in frequent use.

Nineteen

Monetary and Credit Policy Current Imperatives

[2007]

The Reserve Bank of India has been lauded for its exemplary handling of the Monetary and Credit policy from the era of controls and direct management to the regulation of the financial sector in a market economy. The area which has not been guided to a satisfactory conclusion is the regulation of interest rates in the financial sector as it should be in a market economy.

This phenomenon is due to the hangover of excessive control and regulation in the 3 decades by the State and its agency, the Reserve Bank of India. Unless the instruments and the management of tools to interest rate movement are regulated thoroughly, the Indian economy will continue to suffer from the inadequacies of interest rate management.

The current situation highlights the requirement. The carefully nurtured integration of India with the world economy has brought overwhelming results. The Central Governments, State Governments and the Reserve Bank of India are probably surprised and mobilized beyond their imagination and planning. They appear to be swept away by the overwhelming forces of the success of the individuals in a market economy.

This requires an understanding, an appreciation. This requires action to be bold and rooted in the principles of political economy. The following guiding principles may help policymakers to manage the current situation to the advantage of the State, its agencies and the citizens of the nation.

1. *The Indian Nation:* Any policy made should be perceived as to be in the interest of the Indian Nation in its entirety. The Rupee

is our national currency. It is imperative that our thinking is not dominated by foreign currencies in the conduct of the affairs of State or the nation or its citizens. The rupee has to be projected as a currency of national and international reckoning. The problems in Indian financial circles are compounded by "thinking in dollar terms". The internationalization and globalization of the rupee have to be taken in a series of small steps. The confidence and involvement of the citizens must be in the national currency. The Reserve Bank of India has been advised by many national and international experts on the handling of currency and finance in any context. In the current context the rupee must have its equilibrium rate of interest which is to the benefit of all its citizens without any bias amongst the following: creditors and debtors, national and international, Central and State Governments, RBI and Financial intermediaries, financial intermediaries and citizens. There is no established mechanism yet to arrive at a "market rate of the rupee" due to the hangover of severe fragmentation of the financial sector over years. We see integration happening. This needs to be accelerated.

2. *Integration from divisiveness:* We still see persistent divisive segments in the Indian financial sector. These have to be defined nevertheless from their scope and functions. The rupee cannot be made divisive. Interest rates cannot be made divisive. The integration has to meet at a certain point. That point is the Reserve Bank of India. The manner in which interest rates are decided in the nation ultimately depends on the gross and subtle intervention by the Reserve Bank of India. There is excessive divisiveness in the Central Government. There is divisiveness between Central and State Governments. Even as the Constitution of India and various enactments act as binding forces, there is no force which portrays integration. Reserve Bank of India is the only agency which commands the respect and the resources to make the national integration of the financial sector a visible and vibrant process. The Reserve Bank of India needs to integrate the financial sector in a visible and invisible manner to overcome the divisive feeling that is present in the financial sector and guide and nurture it to vibrancy.

3. *Praxeology:* Praxeology is the theory of action. Thousands of policy pronouncements, pious intentions, visible goals and directions are given from the State and its institutions. A 100 million

citizens in this nation are waiting for action. The frustrations at various levels in the field are 900 million expectant people who are looking for results. A 100 million citizens who are ready to act are bound. The Indian state and its agencies are stodgy, unmoving, inertial and totally devoid of feeling and sensitivity.

Today, there is a need for rapid responses and not rabid inaction. State and its agencies have to adapt to the new environment and direct action. Action requires a control on the purpose and direction for an effective public policy on interest rates and not just activity. According to Prof Drucker, "waste is an activity which does not produce results." Enormous amounts of waste in the financial and real sectors are happening because action is held up.

4. *Waste in the Financial Sector:* A huge amount of activity in the financial sector is currently wasteful due to inherent Indian practices. Economic efficiency rests on the efficiency of the financial sector. The conduct and performance of the Indian financial sector is exemplary and better than world class. It is systemic issues that plague the financial sector as whole. At the root of this is the regulation and management of interest rates. The efficiency levels that are desirable are yet to be seen. This results in huge losses in the real sector impeding its growth to full potential.

5. *Growth:* Growth implies individual growth. The sum total of individual growth is total growth and not vice versa. The contribution of the financial sector to individual growth is immense. Understanding growth process and determining efficiency are constant and continuing exercises. In the Indian context, the highest growth potential can come from the bottom 40 per cent of the population. Channeling their contribution will be the biggest challenge in the real sector as well as the financial sector. India is ready to do it. Are Indian institutions collaborating and cooperating with it?

6. *Integration with international markets:* It is a well-known condition now that India cannot get isolated from international markets and international conditions. Mediocrity in public life is preventing us from getting a true perspective. Nationalism has to be portrayed and projected at its highest by the State and its institutions. There is no clear signal coming from the State and its institutions that they are coping with this phenomenon adequately.

In the light of the above guiding principles the following imperative steps are requested from the Reserve Bank of India in its monetary and credit policy:

A Reduction in the Market rate of Interest: India cannot be an island of high real interest rates. There are hundreds of explanations on the rate of inflation and its management. Increasing interest rates have managed inflation can be a gospel truth. The monetary and foreign exchange phenomena are now giving an uncontrolled direction. It is imperative to establish control on the market rate of interest. This implies that the rate on Government securities should be in the region of 6 to 6.5 per cent as against 7.8 to 8 per cent now.

Reserve Bank of India must target the interest rates of Government securities at 7. 5 per cent in the near term for tenors more than 10 years. Short term rates can behave on demand supply considerations.

Reserve Bank of India must decide in principle and advise Government of India that there shall not be any long tenor loans issued from now onwards till 31st March 2009. Fresh Government borrowings will only be in Treasury Bills as per the issue calendar devised for meeting the needs of Government.

Reserve Bank of India then should resort to Open Market Operations as is done by the US Fed and other Central Governments to have a "single" buy and sell rate as against the dual system up Reverse and Reverse Repo. Repo and Reverse Repo will then be used only in exceptional circumstances.

Short term treasury Bills deserve a rate of only 4.5 to 4.75 per cent due the current liquidity. Government of India will benefit immensely if the TB Bill rate is 4.5 per cent over the next 15 months.

Deposit Rates of Banks: Deposit rates of banks are skewed in India. Nowhere in the developed world the deposit rates by banks exceed the Bank rate. This phenomenon is peculiar to India alone. Banks do not follow the principles of political economy and economics in the determination of deposit rates. Reserve Bank of India must intervene in the short terms and regulate the rates for all banks for a period of 15 months rigidly. The boards of the Banks and bank managements act whimsically and in an adhoc manner in the pricing of deposit rates as also in the rates of advance.

Regulation of Credit Rates: Credit rates have a correlation to deposit rates. Normally credit rates cannot be higher than 4 per cent over the market rate of interest. In India there is no market rate of interest at all as a benchmark and the benchmark rate of the regulator is not as scientific as determined in global markets. This can be attributed to the phenomena of unprecedented growth and inability to manage data and information in a vast and diverse economy like India.

Currency: The issue of currency by Government of India could be termed as unnecessary and excessive. This is also a prime cause for inflation. Management on issue of currency alone can control the inflation rate. If issue of fresh currency is stopped for the rest of the year, economic consequences cannot be negative. The Indian economy is cash oriented—a substantial cash economy which should be replaced by cheques or debit cards. Another problem is the mediocrity in State has resulted in excessive penalization of tax payers. Tax dodgers are having a field day with a huge unregulated unofficial market in goods, finance and other trafficking including corruption and bribery on a scale unprecedented for the Indian economy to date.

One asks the RBI – what would happen if the RBI issued no currency for the rest of the year as against the planned release?

SLR: The Reserve Bank of India has not addressed the SLR for the last few years. The regulator has the power to decrease the rate of the SLR.

A suggestion: Change the SLR composition to a really liquid phenomenon.

The approved securities are changed only to Central Government securities with a residual maturity of less than 5 years with a target date of 31st March 2007. All other securities are delisted over the next 15 months.

If there are no sufficient securities to match this requirement, Government of India can issue treasury bills and short term bonds and buy back the illiquid long term loans over this period. This will bring in a healthy Government securities market. State Governments and other agencies will be given a better mechanism by improvements in the bond market.

Benefits of Lower Interest Rates to Central and State Government: The Reserve Bank of India should have a more serious and comprehensive look at the outstanding securities of State Governments and Central Government and give a direction to the Bond market.

Initially, Reserve Bank of India must have a "market" operation for Central Government securities and State Government securities to bring in liquidity to long dated securities. A sum of Rs. 10,000 crores to Rs. 30,000 crores may be sufficient in the near term. Reserve Bank of India can operate through the Financial Institutions by providing short term facilities just to bring in homogeneity and liquidity in the Government Bond markets. In the medium term market operators will take over. This will also bring down cost of borrowing for Central Governments. State Governments should come on par based on reputation of their offerings.

A well regulated interest rate regime in the Short Term is the need of the day. Interest rates should be benign and at equilibrium. The capital goods formation in the nation depends on a "reasonable" rate of interest.

NOTES

1. Comments in this Chapter are a repetition of the statements made in the earlier chapters since 1998. These can be considered as a reminder and reiteration for issues that need to be examined.
2. There is scope for fine tuning of credit and monetary policies.
3. All the suggestions are provided in order that there is intelligent discussion on the same for a speedy conclusion of desirable policy and actionable measures.
4. Far reaching consequences including productivity of capital and the establishment of sound financial markets will be positive when all proposals are examined and integrated in the national and world economies.
5. Thinking in US Dollar terms is still prevalent in Government as well as companies. Official pronouncement and tariffs should always be in Rupees and it is the stakeholders to express it in any currency for interpretation.
6. The study on inflation in India is not having any depth. A scenario needs to be established if there is a short term curb on notes in circulation a medium term effect on inflation could arise. This needs to be matched with a reduction in Government expenditure as well.

Twenty

Savings Bank Rate

[2010]

The Reserve Bank of India recently announced that the rate of interest on the Savings Bank Account is intended to be freed. The appropriateness of the timing and the necessity of wider public opinion and debate have also been emphasized.

The current rate of interest which is under control is 3.5 per cent. Recently, banks introduced this rate for the entire period of a month as against a balance for a fixed period.

Core banking technology makes the interest rate on Savings Bank dynamic. Currently, the software of some banks enables automatic sweeps from Savings Banks to term deposits and can revert at a simple instruction when the client wants it back from term deposits.

Savings bank accounts are the primary channel for a citizen's savings in monetary terms. This is the first credit of the surplus of an individual. Millions of individuals who are earning are also part of the unaccounted or parallel economy where the primary saving is still in the form of currency or inventory.

There is a large expression in public about the necessity of financial inclusion. Today, in most cities the number of accounts outnumbers the population. This does not imply necessarily that all citizens are account holders. The availability of resources in India permits the opening of accounts of all citizens. In the undivided South Kanara District, now called Dakshina Kannada and Udipi banking has been widely spread and financial inclusion was practiced decades ago. In the class on banking theory and practice, Prof. B.S. Raman used to have the opening hour with the remarks, in South Kanara, "every child is born with a passbook in its hands".

The focus here is about interest rate on Savings Bank and the direction that is needed to make the transition from a controlled rate. This requires a recall of the economic history and development of this free nation from 1991 till date. The gradual process of liberalization and decontrol has been marked with developments of freeing of interest rates for various segments. They were also marked with distortions, anomalies and aberrations defying the theory of interest rate. These are more fully described in other papers. The last four years have shown remarkable maturity in the financial system.

Control and Regulation

The situation before us demands whether

1. The Savings Bank rate should be removed from control and freed
2. The rate should be decontrolled and regulated
3. The rate should be continued to be controlled by the Central bank in an informed and objective manner.

Scenario 1

The Savings Bank Rate should be Removed from Control and Freed

In the first scenario, the Reserve Bank of India can act in the manner which it has always acted in the segments earlier. The decision in principle is acted on and communicated in an appropriate way. The decision is decided in the announcement of the Annual policy or the periodic one. The decision is conveyed and could come into effect the next Monday or a date is announced in the near future.

In this event, the preparedness and the speed of the banking system could vary depending on the infrastructure and the responsiveness or reactions of bank managements. The market leaders and the proactive managements will be more aggressive. The rest of the banks will follow.

The result would be various degrees of freedom to license. The aggressive banks will use this to lure new deposits into the banks by giving "teaser" or "high" rates. Pricing difference could emerge on the amounts deposited. Conservative managements would use it as an instrument to reduce costs and make the deposit rates in tune with costs.

There could be pricing of various instruments or services depending on the interest rate structure.

RBI should examine thoroughly by inviting studies and reports from banks themselves on the structures of the offerings of various banks. Nationalised Banks who are stodgy and conservative may have less of offerings than maverick start up banks, the private sector banks and foreign owned banks.

In India the impact of interest rates on social psychology is very high. Clients switch accounts at a quarter percent differentiation in interest. It is required by the RBI to make extensive diligence before it makes a decision on decontrol and freeing of interest rates.

There should also be a serious examination within RBI when it exercises the function of control or decontrol within its powers and regulation or deregulation. What the RBI has done all these years is decontrol and deregulation too and the interest rates in the market are mis-priced resulting in aberrations, anomalies and distortions. In the current situation, the pricing in interest rates do not have wide fluctuations or volatility as in the nineties. The distortions are small enough on a large base to cause economic injustice.

This also requires RBI to have exercises on regulation. In the recent case, the arriving of Base Rate and the manner it is to be arrived at and exercised is a regulation. It prohibits banks from lending lower even if the market situation warrants it. This paves the way for self-discipline and market discipline. The true essence of interest rate regulation has been arrived at in the Base Rate directive.

The arriving at that directive also has been the basis of inputs and has been carefully calibrated in the market with great sensitivity, timing and sufficient time for the banking system to adopt it with least disruption in operations. The Base Rate regulation is a good case to be refined into regulation of interest rates in all segments.

This brings us to the point of regulation of interest rates in all segments. Interest rates in all segments need to be regulated across all organizations. National Savings rates, Co-operative banks, Financial Companies and deposit rates of manufacturing companies who announce Fixed Deposits need to be regulated too. In fact, the raising of Fixed Deposits by companies should be banned and they should be directed to issue only instruments like Bonds which could be listed or unlisted depending on the regulation.

The RBI therefore needs to examine the structure of determining the rates of SB accounts in the National Savings Scheme as well as in the cooperative sector. It would be wise not to adopt total decontrol in the current situation.

Scenario 2

The Rate should be Decontrolled and Regulated

It is necessary for RBI to go into the question of how it can regulate the Savings Bank rate. Regulation implies that the management of banks should deliberate on the issue and arrive at the correct pricing. Banks must be objective in their approach and this is prepared in such a manner that the banks seek regulatory approval prior to intimation or subject to examination during RBI inspection for deviations.

Obviously RBI can take several steps to bring this process and do it in public light and convey its positions. The steps that RBI has taken in the past few years have been exemplary. The constitution of an internal group to arrive at the positions is welcome.

The calendar for such an event can be nine months and regulation can take effect from 1st April 2011. This involves a multidisciplinary approach. Banks are large oligopolistic organizations and should not arrive at pricing which is detrimental to clientele. Their organizational behaviour has been found wanting when it comes to the question of their handling interest rates for themselves and their clientele.

Public policy of determining a price should not be detrimental to banks in their exercise of functions or pricing of the deposit that influences their cost of funds and therefore lending rates. Savings Bank rates could be sensitive to public opinion and more so from luminaries from retired senior bureaucrats, former central bankers, economists, editorials and columnists of business newspapers.

There is no better opportunity than this with the explosion of mass media and communications for expressing the theory of interest rates and its application in India. The prevailing of emotion over reason in some sectors. e.g. the pricing of petroleum products can extend to the financial sector at times.

A refreshing public opinion campaign will help and moribund economic, banking and commerce departments of Universities, autonomous colleges and colleges get revived. RBI can devise and commission a national poll with properly framed questions. RBI can also involve all 160 State Universities on the structure of interest rates and invite summaries of discussions and papers.

Healthy discussions involving senior academicians and young minds can help a segment of the population involved in banking services to get grounded on theory and use it well in practice.

India has evolved from a command and control era into one of regulated and free markets. Interest is the price of a major factor, capital. Savings and capital need to be understood among the broadest sections of citizenry.

The case is for regulation and regulation needs to be understood. Can the RBI portray for itself that it is a fair regulator?

Scenario 3

The Rate should be Continued to be Controlled by the Central Bank in an Informed and Objective Manner

The third scenario is that RBI initiates the debate and discussion and on the basis of its observations, vast experience and well designed internal systems and continue to control the Savings Bank rate for next three years.

This implies that RBI can fix a minimum or maximum rate which banks can alter to suit their cost structures or simply calibrate the rate in public interest on an annual basis. The exercise implies bringing in objectivity by linking the same to the rates arrived at RBI in monetary policy exercises and also take into account a balanced view of banks' and public interest.

This would be an ideal choice for RBI after examining scenario one and two. This could also be a wise choice if RBI feels that conflicts need to be addressed for some more time and its administration of supervision of interest rates in all sectors i.e. cooperative and on National Savings scheme is established.

Way Forward

The Reserve Bank should conduct introspection on the freeing of interest rates over the last twenty years. There has been a remarkable improvement in the handling of fund flows and the Reserve Bank of India has played a positive role in the evolving of markets.

The question before us is: is Reserve Bank of India regulating, overtly or covertly, the interest rate structure in the economy? There is scope for study of organizational behaviour of all participants in the financial sector. Recently, even State sector banks were participants in behaviour that distorts interest rates. The lending rate and deposit rates in particular segments within the Bank's borrowing and lending portfolio hardly had a difference of 1 per cent when the bank claims to have a Net interest margin of 2 per cent. This implies Banks routinely play within segments for market share which resembles the distortions in air travel and telephone sector.

The role of Central and State Governments in meddling with interest rate structure is evident in the form of subsidies to the farm and msme sectors. The control of the export credit rate and subvention are examples of continuing focus on sectors which are still handled by the State on the opinion that they deserve this form of grants or subsidy. State Governments offer subsidies to the Farm sector on interest and assist in write off of farmers debts.

The regulation of the SB interest rate will be an important case for RBI and Government of India to restore their abilities of regulation. Another area of regulation is that of Government Savings Schemes and aligning them with "market rates". The behaviour of cooperative sector and NBFCs indicate that they always have to be ahead of Commercial Banks in attracting deposits by offering higher rates of interest and in turn, charge higher rates to the commercial sector. This requires a Memorandum of Understanding with the Government that RBI regulates the interest rates on all instruments of the National Savings scheme as well as other areas in the Financial Sector.

Summary

The RBI has to take a view on control and regulation. The Savings Bank rate regulation requires RBI to do diligence on:

- Objectivity
- Impact Analysis
- Organizational Behaviour of entities in the Financial Markets

- The working, application and practice of economic, social and political theories
- The principles of political, economic and social justice
- Choices before citizens

Reserve Bank of India has chosen an appropriate time for regulation of the Savings Bank interest rate and its intention to move away from control. RBI must initiate a dialogue with banks, discussion within itself and debate in public to arrive on consensus and agreement on various aspects of regulation and its effects.

The Reserve Bank must cognize the effects of removal of control without regulation on a matter of wide public interest such as the Savings Bank rate.

The Reserve Bank must examine its role on observation and regulation on all interest rates by entities engaged in borrowing and lending or borrowing and using the capital or lending of capital from own resources in the economy.

NOTES

1. Since then Reserve Bank of India decided to decontrol Savings Bank rate.
2. The Reserve Bank of India in its current pronouncement is always emphatic about decontrol but has never talked about regulation.
3. The distinction between free, deregulation and decontrol needs to be arrived at in the case of interest.
4. Regulation and control in the context of interest rates have to be in mainstream discussion. India has experienced control and decontrol but not yet regulation in interest rates.
5. Research on interest rate structure will reveal the nuances and intricacies of pricing of Savings Bank interest rates by individual banks.

PART 2

Interest Rates
2011 - 2014
Towards Harmony

Twenty One

Bank Rate

[2011]

Bank Rate as a tool of the Reserve Bank of India was discussed and debated within a working group. This was put on public domain. After it was published, a Response was sent. They are presented with excerpts from the Executive Summary of the report. Reports of the Reserve Bank of India, Speeches and Working Group Reports constitute a rich source for students of economics and public finance.

> The Response to the Report of the Working Group to Review the Framework of the Operating procedure of Monetary Policy in India

EXECUTIVE SUMMARY

The RBI announced the constitution of the Working Group to review the framework of the operating procedure of monetary policy in India (Chairman: Shri Deepak Mohanty) in the First Quarter Review of Monetary Policy for 2010-11. On the basis of a survey of country practices and technical evaluation of the evolution of the current monetary operations in the RBI, the Group makes the following key recommendations;

The liquidity adjustment facility (LAF) with some modifications to be the key element in the operating framework of the RBI.

It is agreed that the LAF should be the key element. The process, though however needs to be dynamic, proactive, interpretative and responsive.

The modified LAF should operate in a deficit liquidity mode and the liquidity level should be contained around (+) / (-) one per cent of net demand and time liabilities (NDTL) of banks for optimal monetary transmission.

Deficit liquidity mode seems to be a negative approach in management. What would be the situation in a "positive" liquidity mode? The containment to 1 per cent of the Net DTL is an objective definition.

How will it be operated on a daily and hourly basis that will have an impact on markets and the circulation of capital? How will it influence rates across all segments of the economy?

The repo rate should be the single policy rate to unambiguously signal the stance of monetary policy to achieve macro-economic objectives of growth with price stability. It will operate within a corridor set by the Bank Rate and the reverse repo rate. As the repo rate changes, the Bank Rate and the reverse repo rate should change automatically.

This is not agreed to. The Reserve Bank of India should adopt the middle rate for the stance. The Middle rate between the Repo and the Reverse Repo should be the daily and hourly rate at which RBI ensures the circularity of capital and maintain equilibrium.

The relative weights of the Repo and Reverse Repo in a given situation need a balance and the Middle Rate. This is equivalent to the Open Market rate announced by the Federal Reserve at predetermined intervals.

The Reserve Bank of India and Government of India like to give unique names to their creations. For the purpose of current discussions let us assume that it will be called the Middle Rate.

The Middle rate should be the single unambiguous signal conveying the "interest rate" policy as part of the overall monetary policy.

The interest rate signal is just a part of the deployment in monetary policy while the major part in a modern economy is to have a control on the issue of currency to the public and manage the money in circulation.

The RBI at its discretion could conduct simultaneous auctions for longer period if the liquidity situation so warrants. However, such actions should be at variable prices as they will be for purely liquidity management rather than for signaling the policy rate.

This particular recommendation is contrary to the current practices in advanced economies. They practice Open Market Operations judiciously. This comment of the Committee is justified in Indian context by a deliberate stand on the part of Government of India and Reserve Bank of India that some steps are taken or some policy maintained particularly in the Indian context due to Indian conditions that warrant such a stance.

The Reserve Bank of India must examine this in greater depth and leap towards a new management programme of the purchase and sale of Government securities in the Open Market. It has to be a part of RBI's action plan that the management of the liquidity in the economy is on the basis of a continuous and hourly operations by front line troops who are guided by able generals. (Samuelson and Nordhaus).

This does not undermine the policy of Reserve Bank to maintain the interest rates as well as absorb or release the liquidity at a particular objective level. What it helps is to even fluctuations of interest rates across the economy on a daily or weekly basis.

An even interest rate creates economic efficiency as a balance between lenders and borrowers and saves huge activities in the markets which are currently redundant in practice and wasteful.

The economic justice that is meted out to both borrower and lender will have enormous productive value in their respective endeavors to get just returns on their savings as well as a reasonable rate at which borrowings can occur for the sake of asset building by individuals and organizations.

Once RBI buys and sells treasury bills on a daily basis at the Middle Rate the activity of auctions become redundant.

They however can be done only for exceptional nature of securities or exceptional situations when the daily limits for operations by troops are exceeded and RBIs objective policy makes it necessary to have a Reverse Repo or a Repo Auction.

In simpler terms the buying and selling of treasury bills is objectively set at a limited rate of say 0.25 to 0.5 of the NDTL of the banking system while the Reverse Repo and Repo auctions can be done for amounts exceeding that for the RBI to assess the market.

Another way of looking at it is that the Open Market Operations can be done with a limited number of chosen Banks while Reverse Repo and Repo can be done with dated securities with all banks having access to the Reserve Bank of India.

The Bank Rate should be reactivated as a discount rate as envisaged in the Reserve Bank of India Act, 1934. It will be the rate at which the

RBI will provide liquidity under a new collateralised Exceptional Standing Facility (ESF) up to one per cent of NDTL of banks to be carved out of the required statutory liquidity ratio (SLR) portfolio. The Bank Rate will constitute the upper bound of the corridor.

Agreed in Full. The Bank Rate will have to be an objective signal for other interest rates in the prevailing banking structure.

When the RBI conducts Open Market Operations banks always have a choice of selling their "surplus" "SLR" securities to meet their requirements till they reach the statutory levels. However, when No. 4 is followed as mentioned above it becomes almost a lesser used facility by Banks.

The Reserve Bank of India needs to activate it in emergency situations alone when Banking sector would lose in the liquidity of any of its assets in an otherwise strong balance sheet.

A facility at Bank Rate therefore gets justified only on say Long Dated securities which the Banks hold for the compulsions in the Indian context and they are reluctant to sell the same at a loss.

The Exceptional Standing Facility must have objective exceptions specified: natural disasters, an attack on the Indian rupee, rapid or nervous flight of capital from the Indian economy, sudden or unexpected requirements of the Indian Government in emergency situations well defined, rapid outflow of portfolio investment and the like.

The reverse repo rate will have a negative spread on the repo rate and it will be the rate at which the RBI will absorb liquidity under the LAF. The reverse repo rate will constitute the lower bound of the corridor.

In the scenario of Open Market Operations the corridor will be more explicitly: the Middle rate will be at the middle of the Repo and Reverse Repo, the Bank rate will be at the border above. It will therefore be above the Repo.

The optimal width of the policy corridor be fixed at 150 basis points and should not be changed in the normal circumstance. The corridor should be asymmetric with the spread between the policy repo rates and reverse repo rate twice as much as the spread between the repo rate and the Bank Rate. With a corridor of 150 basis points, the Bank Rate could be fixed at repo rate plus 50 basis points and the reverse repo rate at repo rate minus 100 basis points.

Objectively, for the Open Market Operations for Treasury Bills of less than 91 days have the Middle Rate needs to be announced for a specific period under the Quarterly Monetary policy or at an independent date announced by RBI following the procedures at the FOMC in the USA (The Central Open Market Committee in India).

If the COMC (Central Open Market Committee) decides on the Middle rate the Repo and the Reverse Repo Rate can be 50 basis points above and below the Middle Rate. In the current context the Open Market Operations will be conducted only in Treasury Bills of less than 91 days.

This requires Government of India and RBI to arrive at a conclusion that the outstanding 91 days Treasury Bills should be of a nominal value of at least Rs. 200,000 crores at any given time.

The amount outstanding as on this day is only Rs. 88106.82 (mentioned in the liabilities of Government of India).

This is to be arrived afresh by the Reserve Bank of India when concluding its observations from the Report. The Bank rate can be 100 or 150 basis points above the Repo Rate in the Indian context. The reasons are explained at the end of this response.

The weighted average overnight call money rate to be the operating target of the RBI. The operating objective should be to contain this rate around the repo rate within the corridor.

The RBI needs to track the Call Money market as an important signal for market rates. It should be merely for interpretation and not a decision to base on.

The Central Open Market Committee should have access to all data, information and knowledge within to arrive at the rate appropriately. When Open Market Operations are conducted the call money rates will be at a steady rate below the Reverse Repo rate.

The borrowing or lending in call money as a necessity for temporary asset management by banks will be efficiently substituted by the buying and selling of Treasury Bills in the market regularly and the RBI s action with the market.

The Reserve Bank should conduct the second LAF (SLAF) on a regular basis.

The LAF should be conducted on a bi weekly basis on Every Wednesday and Every Friday for Repo and Reverse Repo with the pledge of securities other than Treasury Bills.

The purchase and sale of treasury bills by RBI front desk should be done at 30 minute intervals till 30 minutes after the closing of Banking hours with at least 7 selected banks and 3 financial institutions.

Persistent liquidity in excess of (+)/(–) one per cent of the NDTL should be managed through other instruments such as outright open market operations (OMO), cash reserve ratio (CRR) and market stabilisation scheme (MSS).

This is submitted for deep reflection. If OMO is conducted regularly the excess liquidity management occurrence will be minimized if not at all unless under exceptionally good situations of large inflows of desired or undesired capital, or an emergency situation which causes large withdrawals of capital from the nation including flight. The cash reserve ratio must be reduced to 3 per cent and kept there.

The market stabilization scheme devised will also get redundant in the situation of managing the OMO and a better option would be expanding the Capital Account Convertibility in a managed form by Banks.

This will be an improved version of the current management of the foreign exchange flows limited to Reserve Bank of India alone. The banking system should be competent and have the management of 10 per cent of the nation's foreign balances within itself and manage the impact of flows efficiently.

This is possible by including securities of OECD countries, BRIC countries and India's trading partners to be included in the SLR. This will be elaborated later.

Banks should be incentivised to progressively mark-to-market their SLR portfolio to improve the use of OMO as an instrument of liquidity management. The Group recognises that in due course, the accounting standard shall get aligned with the international financial reporting standards (IFRS).

The SLR securities are too weighted to long term securities. The RBI in conference with the Government of India should determine that the SLR securities should never be over 10 years. The meaning of liquidity is essentially that it should be a short term security.

The long term securities obviously will carry a higher rate of interest than short term securities. These needs to be held by other investors who have long term investment plans and also need a higher return: they are Provident Funds, Pension Funds and Insurance funds and also individual savers who look at the long term.

The liquidity for this also to be assured by RBI and Central Government by having a promotion for active trading, jobbing by select organizations and occasional. When an efficient bond market is created and the gilt yield curve is arrived naturally the mark to market will happen automatically.

Governments of India and RBI have not been sufficiently pro-active and determined in the nurturing of an active bond market.

The Reserve Bank of India must consciously reduce SLR from 24 to 18 per cent and keep it there. This should be done at the rate of one per cent per quarter beginning from the next policy.

The Banks must be allowed approved securities of OECD nations and friendly nations as part of SLR.

The approved securities for SLR purposes in India are required to be only Government of India securities with a tenor 10 years and less, of which 50 per cent must be less than 5 years.

To improve liquidity management, a scheme of auctioning of government surplus cash balance at the discretion of the RBI to be put in place in consultation with the Government.

The Government of India surpluses with RBI is contradiction. In its weekly statistical statement RBI states Borrowings by Government:

Rs. 3,13,073 crores (Business Line dt. 04.04.2011). In recent newspaper reports RBI says it has balances from Government which it is finding difficult to handle. There needs to be clarity on the issue.

Why should RBI be concerned about Government surpluses? It is Government's concern. The best current solution is that Government of India pays the amount deposited with it by the Provident Fund Organisation in full on an immediate basis.

The surpluses will then get efficiently deployed and Government of India can borrow by way of Treasury Bills at any time. Another radical option is for Government to prepay all bilateral and multilateral loans whatever be the tenor and interest at one go and be independent of foreign borrowings itself.

A separate submission is made on both proposals to the Secretary Economic Affairs, Government of India.

Collateral pool for reverse repo operation under LAF could be extended to include oil bonds.

Active Bond market will take care of the Oil pool bonds. The Provident Fund Organisation must be encouraged to invest in the same as well as in Tier Two Bonds of Nationalised banks and bonds issued by financial institutions. Oil pool bonds must be marketed to mutual funds and pension fund organizations including the Insurance sector.

The methodology for the RBI's internal liquidity forecast should be strengthened. Information on government cash balances should be put in the public domain with the minimum time lag for better liquidity assessment by market participants.

This is a welcome move. Government of India and Reserve Bank of India along with all its institutions must portray the financial sector well into the public domain.

State Universities, Management Institutes must be extensively involved in this process. Bank managements must encourage the formulation of such forecasting within themselves and put it into periodic peer reviews through the Indian Banks Association.

The Indian Banks Association must be funded by Government, RBI and by Banks themselves to energise itself to the tasks of generating and building economic and econometric perspectives in the financial sector. The Government Cash Balances can be mentioned in the Weekly Statistical statement from next week.

The minimum level of reserves to be maintained on any day by banks with the RBI during a fortnight be raised from the present level of 70 per cent to 80 per cent of the required CRR.

The relaxing of CRR to 70 or 80 pc is a situation not to be tolerated. CRR should be 100 per cent.

CRR should be reduced to 3 per cent and banks should be encouraged to keep up to 5 per cent as an inflation control exercise by paying interest on excess balances.

Banks behaviour in this regard on maintaining of balances should be continuously monitored.

The T+0 transactions for short-term money market segments [collateralised borrowing and lending obligations (CBLO) and market repo] should be extended up to the cut-off timing for customers in real time gross settlement (RTGS) (i.e., 4.30 PM) so that the banking system could square off their CRR position efficiently.

The Open Market Operations must extend to one hour beyond banking hours and so should the interbank market. This will give options for the banks to assess the day and the day to follow.

Pricing of Deposits and Advances

The Committee must be complimented on a finely produced Report. It is highly technical and capable of being understood by the Government, Bankers and operators. RBI should act on the recommendations and translate in into action

There is no light thrown by Reserve Bank to date on the behaviour of the banking organizational in terms of pricing of deposits. The Reserve Bank of India and the Government of India have repeatedly emphasized over a decade and a half that the interest rates are left to the "market".

Following Questions Need to be Raised

- What does RBI imply when it says that the interest rates are determined by the "market"? Deposit rates are determined by the managements of 130 banks in India.
- Is there any internal or external analysis on a continuous basis on the organizational behaviour of banks in respect of pricing of bank deposits?
- Are Bank deposit rates determined on any whimsical or ad hoc basis at times by managements?
- Is Bank deposit pricing a tool for marketing by banks?
- What is the variance in deposit prices in India: by tenor, by quantum, by age of depositor (senior citizens)
- What should be the ideal difference in deposit pricing between banks: 05 basis points 10 basis points 25 basis points 50 basis points
- What is the analysis on the timing of deposit rates? Deposit rates are varied at different times of the month by different banks?

- Is there any regulation needed that deposit rates must be timed in line with the monetary policy?
- Is there any case for regulation of deposit rates than keeping it "free"? i.e. should banks ask the prior permission of RBI before increasing or decreasing deposit rates (or for that matter loan rates).
- RBI has advocated a "free" policy while it has the function of being a "regulator". If freedom is turned into licence by banks, does RBI have any recourse other than issuing "stern" warnings?
- What are international best practices in deposit rates that are absent in India? How can they be introduced?

There are occasions when bankers individually or in herd behaviour do not act in accordance with globally accepted practices in banking which are necessarily sound. Even as decisions are to be made by the respective Boards of banks, the patterns and announcements of bankers resemble the marketplace for detergents rather than the important pricing of a factor which has a far reaching effect on the economy.

The RBI can use a direct instrument for regulation which means it must step into the role of again being a command and control organization for the whole banking system. The RBI does not choose to do so and that is something acceptable in a market economy.

The adoption of the report in making policy and instruments for fine tuning the repo, reverse repo and Bank rate fails to establish a reference for Banks to follow for pricing deposit rates and thereby establishing the range in which interest rates must prevail for depositors and borrowers within the banking system.

- The RBI must use the Bank Rate as a reference point where the Banks should not have the rates for deposits above the Bank rate.
- Deposit rates announced must be from beginning of the calendar month.
- Acceptance of deposits by banks should not exceed the period of three years for the next year and beyond that the interest rate contract should be only one year by following the system of notice deposits.

- RBI must examine the process in pricing prior to bank's announcement of increase decrease or changes in deposit rates.

This however can apply to deposits with banks and need not be for instruments which are transferable i.e. bonds issued by banks. Banks should be free to issue bonds for any tenor from tradeable Bills of 91 days to 364 days and beyond those bonds of established tenor for any number of years by direct issue or by auction.

The reasons have been amplified in earlier compositions submitted to RBI. What is required to be established is that Banks should not do what is contrary to established banking practices – price deposits above the Bank rate.

Currently the Bank rate is 6 pc and the deposit rates are between 8 and 9.25 per cent. This implies that either RBIs determination of Bank rate is incorrect or the banking system is incorrect in arriving at Bank rates.

The Bank rate is one which Banks can have access RBI for refinance. This essentially implies that any deposit accepted from public should not exceed the Bank rate. Otherwise, transmission of the intentions will never take place as rivalry amongst banks will prevent deposits floating down. When costs do not float down, banks refuse to lend below cost. This has happened when inflation rate has come down below 5 that the interest charged by banks to individuals and small enterprises has not come down below 10.5 per cent.

Reserve Bank of India should take a stance by having Bank rate to be equal to or plus or minus the inflation rate. In the instant case Bank Rate ought to be 8.5 per cent. It should mandate that the deposit rates in the Banking system should not exceed the Bank rate.

When inflation drops, the Bank rate can be dropped which will persuade banks to reduce the deposit rates accordingly. In today's context, if RBI feels that the Bank rate of 6 per cent is the ideal rate deposit rates should not exceed 5.75per cent.

RBI must deliberate deeply on the interest rate management in the country. There should not be a situation where economic theory in respect of interest rates does not prevail in any segment of the economy.

Pricing of Loans and Advances

The pricing of loans and advances depends on pricing of deposits.

The RBI must go deep into practices of all banks, organizational behaviour, response to regulation and fairness to constituents. A pricing frame work needs to be put into place so that "freedom does not turn into license".

Regulation is essential with objectivity and reference points. The pricing of loans and advances is skewed in the Indian context. Recently there have been references that the Reserve Bank of India has not "understood" the reasoning behind the "teaser" loan rates for housing loans. At the same time, it has been announced that the bank has followed the rules and regulations 100 per cent.

The Reserve Bank needs to be a regulator for pricing of interest on loans. This complex area requires more examination and will be in the arena of operation only when interest rate management in the entire spectrum becomes visible.

Pricing of Export Finance

Rupee credit with subvention and the Foreign Currency Credit

The Committee was required to go into this area but it has refrained from any comment.

RBI must expand the scope of this issue into another Committee. The stakeholders need to be invited through their Apex associations as also the Ministry of Commerce.

The Questions are:

- Is rupee finance compatible with the monetary policy and its signals?
- Is foreign currency credit so called adequately meets the requirements of both banker as well as client?
- Is the mechanism conducive to save cost as well as be competitive for financial players?

The Gilt Yield Curve

The RBI needs to go into the issue of the Gilt Yield Curve which is imperfect in India. The activities in Bond markets are not similar to those of advanced economies and concern has been expressed from various quarters, including RBI and Government.

The basic aspects of bond market i.e. the Government securities markets have developed their own peculiarities which need to be addressed.

The Gilt Yield Curve and active trading for each tenor and appropriate pricing will be the result of an active Open Market Operations by Reserve Bank of India.

There must be a continuous improvement programme and issue of the right tenor in the next fifteen months as well as buy back and reissue of some securities in order to achieve active trading.

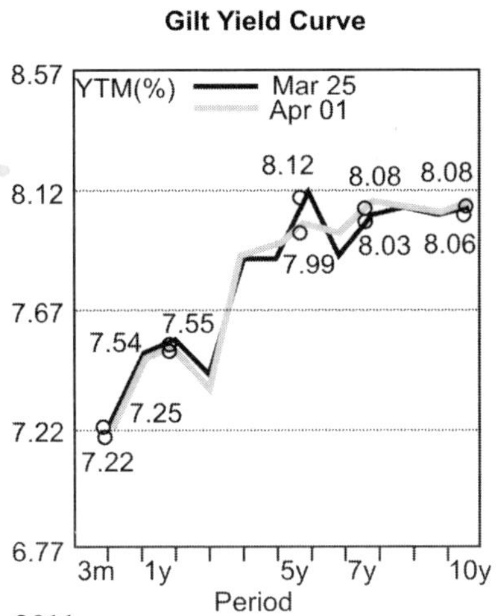

Source: *Business Line* 2011.

Government and RBI need to be responsive to the market operator's issues and concerns and make corrections accordingly in the short term and evolve sound policy for future actions. Enormous cost savings to Government and economic efficiency would be a natural result

Conclusion

The Reserve Bank of India and Government of India need to have a continuous programme on harmonising the interest rate structure in this nation. The rapid development of the economy, international developments, explosive growth in individual savings and dynamic entrepreneurial sectors will need different approaches. The nation has to leap clearly from its recent economic past.

This requires an objective, fair and judicious approach in the balancing act of the Reserve Bank of India in its major role of regulation of financial markets.

Government of India needs to sharply focus on abandoning the past and creating a vibrant future without disturbing the present.

NOTES

1. The evolution of the Bank rate in India and in other countries needs to be matter of study and research.
2. The Committee did a commendable job in finalizing the recommendations on Bank rate.
3. The RBI acted on the Committee recommendation and did a one time correction on the Bank Rate.
4. The comments made in the chapter are still worthy of consideration in making of policy and introducing good practices in implementation of policies on interest rates.
5. Currently, in global economies the rates of interest are near zero. The Gilt Yield Curve itself is now to be examined in the US | European and Indian context.

Twenty Two

Interest Rate Regulation of Bank Deposits and Loans

[2012]

The Reserve Bank of India has reached a new milestone in regulation when the Bank Rate has been revised objectively to 9.5 per cent and is in the process of developing its tools and deploying them effectively.

Reserve Bank of India ought to consider whether it has decontrolled interest rates or deregulated interest rates amongst the business organizations it regulates. This requires clarity on what constitutes control and regulation and the implication of decontrol and deregulation.

Decontrol and deregulation imply an absolute free market. What does RBI imply when it states that it has deregulated interest rates? What is the implication when it reports interest rates are decontrolled?

Reserve Bank needs to be a regulator and not a controller. Accustomed to a command and control structure prior to 1991 Government of India and RBI have embarked on a "phased" and "calibrated" decontrol and deregulation of interest rates.

The submission is that interest rates must be governed. It cannot have a status of being deregulated or unregulated in the current Indian context. This implies a regulation and not a control.

Regulation requires the governance on interest rates by all participants. This requires the three ingredients to make a well managed financial sector: education, organization and discipline.

Discipline implies self-discipline as well as actions from the regulator, Government, Competition Commission, Central vigilance and the like on different aspects that safeguard public interest.

The stakeholders need education and the guiding hand of academia as well as experienced practitioners to convey wisdom when cleverness prevails. Words of wisdom must also be heard, read, understood and respected. Action should emanate from understanding when demanded by situations.

While control is not said to be desirable in a free market economy, regulation is an accepted norm. Reserve Bank of India has to ask itself whether it ought to regulate interest rates of deposits and loans of all entities that borrow or lend to the public in the current context till the Indian financial marketplace is fit to be deregulated.

Deposit Rates

Deposit rates are determined by banks themselves and apparently concluded by Bank boards. Different banks adopt different approaches on deposit rates. The general conclusion can be that they resort to one-upmanship in different situations.

The Reserve Bank of India and the Banks themselves claim that they are deregulated and hence they have the option to adopt any deposit rate for any tenor as their "asset liability" matches permit.

A study of the behaviour of each bank and financial entity, including that of Government of India reveals different patterns of revision of deposit rates for different tenors. The following are features that follow interest rate revision and announcements.

- How is the pricing of deposit rates done? Is it objective or subjective?
- The rates are erratic and do not follow an objective pattern
- There is an attempt to increase deposits as an objective in itself and an aim for growth of deposits which are liabilities
- The pricing is used as an inducement for attraction of business to the bank in particular situations
- Differential rates are applied e.g. for senior citizens
- Huge advertisements and banners are erected for both deposits and advance rates as a measure to attract customers

- It is difficult to determine whether an action on interest rates is competition, rivalry or managerial ego.
- Sometimes housing loans of some banks have been lower than deposit rates of other banks.
- Urban Co-operative Banks and rural credit sometimes offer higher interest rates than State owned banks.
- The activities of individual banks have effects on others. There is also an effect when deposit rates influence the attraction of funds e.g. by companies and Government Savings Bank Rates.

The Necessities

- Timing of deposit or loan increase or decrease should not be in the middle of the month but at the beginning of each month.
- The Bank must notify to Reserve Bank of India that the Board intends to have a revision on interest rates.
- The notification must accompany a detailed objective note on reasoning for changes in interest rates given in confidence to Reserve Bank of India and the intention of the Board to vote on the changes.
- The decision of the Board must be submitted to Reserve Bank for Approval.
- The Reserve Bank must convey or reject the approval in three working days for the Bank. If accepted the Bank can proceed with the rate revision and if rejected the submitting bank must maintain status quo till the next opportunity for it to do so.
- The rejection or acceptance of Reserve Bank of India must be objective with pre determined parameters, limitations as well as guidance on the submission for a change in interest rates.
- When banks are following the indications and benchmarks provided by the monetary or credit policies, the action by Bank boards in response to that must also be measured and responsive and follow the above processes.
- All deposit takers must come within the regulation ambit.

Reserve Bank would be well within its regulatory framework if interest rates on deposits or loans exceed or fall below a well established reference. The RBI can monitor the effect of benchmarks and indications given from time to time.

The Bank Rate must be decided as the benchmark rate above which there should be no interest rate on Fixed Deposits by any entity to any class of customer.

This need not apply to Bonds. The writing of such a regulation or code itself may consume some time within RBI as and also come for critical review from academia, stakeholders, Government and important subjects of regulation the depositors and borrowers.

There is however, necessity for such a regulation. It is well within the powers and competency of Reserve Bank of India to form an internal committee or working group in this regard and arrive at a discussion paper. The practice of inviting the stakeholders for inputs and comments will give a stable policy.

The following may also be considered in addition on an immediate basis:

- The term of the fixed deposit accepted by banks can be a maximum of one year.

Any liability of the bank above that should be by issue of bonds across the counter or market related. These bonds—listed or unlisted for any period from one year to 10 years. These Bonds can be transferred by the investor through an established depository mechanism.

- The Reserve Bank can form a policy that will ensure uniformity in the acceptance of deposits e.g. the 90 days notice deposit where a customer can keep a deposit in perpetuity and is required to give a 90 days notice for withdrawal of the fixed deposit. The interest rate contract can be for one year.
- The Reserve Bank can also evolve a policy in consultancy with banks that customers can keep deposits for a term of one to five years on the understanding that the interest rate contract will be for one year only.
- Reserve Bank of India can ban all financial entities as well as manufacturing or like companies from accepting fixed deposits. They can be permitted to issue Commercial Paper for up to 364 days and bonds for any tenor above 1 year.

- Above practices will fit better in asset-liability matching, make the system respond to monetary policy and give borrowers and savers a balanced deal.

In the current context of a global situation where OECD countries and Switzerland have an annual interest rate of less than 1 per cent to the depositors, the inflation and interest rates in the Indian economy are at 6 to 10 per cent in the last two years.

Inflation is a monetary phenomenon and the responsibility lies with Parliament and Reserve Bank of India to attack the root cause of inflation in the Indian context. There is a need to arrest waste in public expenditure which is financed by the Indian public and the Reserve Bank of India.

If the much needed investment in India needs to be accelerated the financial situation needs to be fine-tuned to the advantage of the Indian saver and investor. This requires an immediate development of the Bond market and deepen, widen and broaden the debt market in Rupees for the Indian and global savers.

The organizational behaviour of Indian banks in terms of the structure and pricing of bank deposits are preventing the development of the debt market. This matter requires urgent attention and one-time measures as well as intense regulation. These are clearly mentioned above and there is sufficient and deep knowledge within Reserve Bank of India and Government of India to take decisive steps in this regard.

The propensity of Indian savers to adopt fixed deposits with banks is well known and banks are exhorted by Government and Reserve Bank of India to "mobilize" savings.

In the command and control era fixed deposits were following the control and command regime and there was hardly any difference between one bank and another and one tenor and another.

The deregulated regime has generated competition as desired but it must be critically examined whether interest rates offered on fixed deposits jeopardize the development of a bond market.

Bonds give options for lenders in terms of deploying savings as well as get higher interest without bank intermediation.

A study of portfolio of loans given by banks could reveal that there would be a potential of more than Rs. 2,50,000 crores as of now for borrowers to issue bonds instead of taking loans from

Banks. This also implies that Bankers can reduce liabilities by a like amount.

Savers could earn more than bank deposits and borrowers could pay less interest when a bond market develops.

Regulation of fixed deposits will automatically develop the bond markets. The corollary would be that Government and RBI should oversee the development of the Central and State Government bond market as well.

This requires a very well-defined policy on large and resourceful investment banks. Policy above is insufficient. RBI and Government must be proactive in hedging markets to higher levels of efficiency. This requires artful management of the transition.

The specialization will mean organised bond markets with commercial banks thriving in their own functions.

This will pave the way for self discipline, economic efficiency, income and employment generation and requisite goods and services for the Indian public.

Summary

- Banks have to be bound by regulation that Fixed Deposit interest rates shall not exceed 50 BPS below the Bank Rate to any class of customer.
- Have a distinct policy to regulate the policy on fixed deposits by all financial and other entities governed by RBI
- Encourage the development of the Bond market with issues by Government and Banks themselves which are investor friendly and pave the way for issuances by Corporates which will then minimize intermediation that is currently in vogue e.g. fixed deposits from customers and loans to borrowers. RBI can make a regulation that at least 15 per cent of Bank's liabilities should be in listed or unlisted bonds which are dematerialized and transferable.
- Interest rates by banks must follow the direction of the monetary and credit policies and stay within acceptable limits. Banks should not violate self-discipline and take the value of education in these matters. Reserve Bank must clearly define the procedure for determining interest rates by Banks for both borrowing and lending and seek the

prior permission of Reserve Bank of India in announcing their deposit rates and lending rates.

- Government of India and Reserve Bank of India must disseminate widely its policies that affect interest rates and issuance of internal debt so that the public is encouraged to invest directly in public debt than deposit the same with banks who then own Government paper. The goal of economic efficiency is to be constantly in sight.

Above steps will go a long way in developing Indian financial markets.

NOTES

1. The focus needs to be on regulation. How deposit rates can be regulated needs to have a discussion, debate and dialogue.
2. There needs to be a distinction between controlled, decontrolled, regulated and deregulated in the Indian context.

Twenty Three

Scope for Reduction in Interest Rates on Central Government Borrowings in the Near Term

[2012]

The global interest rates of all OECD countries are hovering around **.25 to .75 per cent** per annum as against India's rates of 8 to 9 per cent per annum paid by Government of India on majority of its holdings. (See Annex 6: Details of Current Rupee Loans of the Central Government Budget 2011-2012).

Observations

1. The Reserve Bank of India is currently engaged in the task of Open Market Operations to provide liquidity into the markets. This is normally done by purchase of designated securities. It has proclaimed that it has limitations to the extent which OMO can be made as also parameters it has prescribed for itself to operate OMO.
2. In USA, Open Market Operations are done on a daily basis by frontline troops of the Federal Reserve. Reserve Bank of India does OMO selectively on the basis of its own guidance from time to time.
3. Proposals have been made to Government of India and Reserve Bank of India by the undersigned that:
   a) Government of India and Reserve Bank of India should issue less of long term securities and more of Treasury Bills.
   b) The Outstanding Treasury Bills should be much higher than the current level of Rs. 2,88,000 crores as reflected

in the Annual statement against market loans of about Rs. 25,00,000 crores and total liabilities of Rs. 39,30,000 crores.

c) The outstanding bonds or loans available to the market should be of a tenor of three years to five years.

d) Longer tenor should be only as much as the market needs them.

e) The Gilt Yield curve in India has not been established as interest rates are skewed.

f) The Open Market Operations need to be done on a daily basis for treasury bills only to maintain equilibrium in market interest rates as well as to ensure liquidity absorption and infusion simultaneously.

4. This requires greater understanding within Government of India and interaction with the Reserve Bank of India. This gap in understanding can be easily filled by the Honourable Prime Minister ably aided by the Economic Advisory Council, Former Governors, the RBI Board, analysts and academia.

The proposals are as follows:

A. Issue of Short term Rupee Debt Papers only

Government of India and Reserve Bank of India come to an immediate understanding that the issue of Government debt shall be only in the form of Treasury Bills of 46, 91, 182 and 364 days to the extent of 90 per cent of the issues till March 2013. 7 per cent of the issues shall be in tenors up to ten years for establishing the current yield by auction and only 3 per cent can be regularly issued for tenors up to 30 years to establish availability to long term holders and establish the gilt yield curve.

The objective is to deepen, widen and broaden the Debt market beginning with Central Government securities and later extending it to State and local body's debts (Called the Municipal Bond Market in advanced countries).

This will automatically expand the Bond market of financial institutions, banks, financial and manufacturing companies eventually. This aspect will be dealt with separately.

B. One Time operation for correcting Government Debt Profile

There is a one-time opportunity of correcting the proportion of debt of various tenors of Government of India. This requires a studied and systematic view on how the profile of Government debt should be in the current context of a global change in how capital is moving in the world. India will be a destination for capital in debt markets once debt markets are broad, wide and deep.

1. This requires an active approach by Government of India as well as Reserve Bank of India.
    - Provide fiscal and financial stability to the users of capital
    - Ensure that Government of India borrowing does not crowd out private and public investment in essential capital goods—whether personal (like housing), private (like investment in agriculture, manufacturing, value addition and services) or public (like investments in railways, airports, roads, municipal services, health and social services).
    - Ensure that there is no imbalance in interest rates in relation to borrower, saver or investor in India.
    - Ensure that debt flows in and out do not destabilize Indian markets.
    - Government and RBI must challenge the long standing belief that GOI papers for rupee borrowings should be long term.
2. Currently Banks are holding a large proportion of Government debt. The rest is held by Insurers, pension and provident funds and mutual funds.
3. Banks today currently hold Government debt far in excess of the statutory requirement of 24 pc (around 29 pc). Bankers and RBI have publicly admitted that the long term debt of Government of India is ILLIQUID and is held for return purposes as well as SLR purposes.
4. On various occasions the Banks and RBI have expressed difficulties in introducing the practice of mark to market in Government Bonds, especially those of longer tenures. In some cases Banks are permitted to value the debt instruments on "Held to Maturity" basis.

5. The Reserve Bank, Planning Commission, Economic Advisory Council and the Government Economic Affairs Department and notables in the Nation's intellectual arena can focus on an "entrepreneurial" opportunity.
6. A one-time exercise over next five months can save the Government of India up to 3 per cent in interest savings on at least 50 per cent of its debt.
7. This requires RBI to increase the limit on FII investment in Rupee Debt and extend it to Treasury Bills. The virtuous cycle operates as follows:
   Government of India and Reserve Bank of India work on an Open Market Operations to buy back long term securities of certain coupon rate and tenor, let us say:

1.	10.18 Government Stock 2026	Rs. 15,000 crores
2.	8.30 Government Stock 2040	Rs. 32,000 crores
3.	8.33 Government Stock 2036	Rs. 59,000 crores
4.	8.32 Government Stock 2032	Rs. 15,000 crores
5.	8.24 Government Stock 2032	Rs. 53,000 crores
6.	8.26 Government Stock 2027	Rs. 51,000 crores
7.	8.24 Government Stock 2027	Rs. 53,000 crores
	Total:	**Rs. 2,78,000 crores**

8. The current market rates are hovering around these levels.
9. Banks and holders will be glad to unload long term securities which are always a mismatch in their Asset Liability configurations and will focus on short term paper up to five to ten years.
10. The approximate quantum of excess securities held by bankers would be in the region of Rs. 3,00,000 crores.
11. Government would be able to provide an exit policy for banks to get out of long term securities altogether.
12. Once liquidity returns to the market Government can issue as much Treasury Bills as much as the market needs and allow RBI to extinguish the long term loans held by it through mutual understanding. At the end of the exercise RBI holds only treasure bills.
13. This implies total Treasury Bills of Government of India will increase by Rs. 2,78,000 crores with a simultaneous reduction of Rs. 2,78,000 crores in Bonds.
14. Government of India and Reserve Bank of India can liberalize debt investment by foreign entities, foreign

friendly Governments like Malaysia, Japan, Russia, Iran, Mauritius, UAE and South Africa to hold Rupee balances and investments in Treasury Bills or Bonds as they have close economic and political relations.

15. In a global scenario of.25 per cent per annum a return of 5 to 6 per cent on short-term rupee securities would sound attractive even for foreign bankers. Reserve Bank can then issue treasury bills by auction and the entire Treasury Bill market rate will come down to 5 per cent on its own.
16. The annual savings for Government of India on a Treasury Bills portfolio of Rs. 7,00,000 crores would be not less than Rs. 28,000 crores in financial year 2012 - 2013 itself. This action reduces the interest outflow by interest reduction by market forces and not by policy fiat.
17. This will automatically reduce the deposit rates of Banks and create a virtuous cycle of lower interest rates for all sections.
18. When extended to another cycle of Rs. 300,000 crores Government of India will be able to reduce interest outgo to the extent of 2 per cent per annum on outstanding debt of Rs. 20,00,000 crores which would be an additional saving of Rs. 40,000 crores not only in a full year but year after year for a period of ten years.
19. This one-time change requires a major change in the approach of Government of India to its debt which is inherent from the period of 70s. The current global scenario of lower interest will operate to the full advantage of Government of India and pave the way to an active debt market.
20. Advantages are:
    - Banks will be able to operate comfortably at 24 per cent SLR
    - Public and international participation in Central Government Debt will reduce dependence on Banks in India
    - This will pave the way for reduction of SLR to 18 per cent which is the international norm (Singapore has 18 per cent SLR with permission to Banks to own foreign securities too in addition to domestic securities)

- Government and RBI in conjunction can mandate reduction in SLR to 18 per cent at the rate of 1 per cent per quarter over 6 quarters
- As a corollary, Government and RBI work together to have Indian banks to invest in permissible international foreign currency Government securities or bonds issued by Multilateral agencies to the extent of 4 per cent of SLR
- This will give clout to Indian banks to operate globally and leverage those securities for short term borrowings from time to time.

Savings in interest payouts reduces revenue deficits which itself provides fiscal advantages. There is scope for reduction in borrowings itself by monetizing the assets of Government of India and simultaneously reducing liabilities and a sharp reduction in revenue deficits over the next five years.

All proposals must be purposeful, actionable and result-oriented. Policy and action require concerted efforts by policy makers and executives within the current and potential frame work.

NOTES

1. The above proposals merit serious consideration.
2. In the current context various pronouncements have been made of receptivity to new proposals and scenarios for India to work on, in the near future.
3. Savings of interest by Government of India automatically implies economic efficiency.
4. There needs to be an interdisciplinary approach towards reduction of certain categories of liabilities and therefore corresponding reduction in outgo of Government of India on account of interested.
5. The reduction of SLR from the current level of 24 per cent to 18 per cent per annum will definitely release the banking sector from obligations to State Governments.

Twenty Four

Interest Rate Subsidies and Subvention

Interest rates subsidies in India are not new. In the command and control era, interest rates were subsidized by fiat and banks as well as financial institutions had to comply. The Differential Rate of Interest (DRI) scheme was announced for weaker sections. It was determined at 4 per cent. It did create the necessary economic, social and political impact. It was withdrawn after decisive steps in decontrol of interest rates. Till 1991, interest rates to "priority sector" were determined by Government and RBI. The interest rate to this sector was 12 per cent as against 16 to 22 per cent for "non-priority" sector. The interest rate on exports have been also subsidised. This has been called the "Packing Credit" and it has been in vogue since early 1980s.

Interest rate subsidies have a new name now, Subvention. New names do not take away the principle or character. There is need for a debate, discussion and dialogue whether interest rates subsidy or subvention need to be exercised at all by the Central and State Government. When any policy of subsidies or grants are initiated they do not have a time limit. The scheme perpetuates and expands. It can degenerate into an irreversible loss of capital. The Urea subsidy scheme which started with an initial outlay of Rs. 1000 crores has now ballooned to Rs. 75,000 crores. Any subsidy scheme creates special interests. The result is an anomaly, distortion or aberration. In 1970s and 80s Government of India used to lend to State government at concessional rates of interest. This practice was stopped after adopting the market economy model in the mid 1990s. Interest rate subsidies are extended to the export sectors, industry and to weaker sections. Appendix-reveals the outgo on interest subsidy by the Government of India.

Export Credit and Interest Rates: Packing Credit and Packing Credit and Foreign Currency

The Export Finance in rupees was devised in the 1980s as a special Government and Bank response for the Export sector to be competitive.

India's competitors in the world had access to finance at a lesser rate of interest. Exporters in India were at a disadvantage as their fixed and working capital investment in Indian rupees had higher interest outgo. Therefore, exporters were given an opportunity.

The Government and Reserve Bank of India resorted to directed finance to the export sectors. There came a stipulation that at least 10 per cent of the credit should be targeted for exports which continues to this date. The Reserve Bank provides refinance at varying amounts on actual finance at an announced lower interest rate from time to time. The RBI puts a conditionality that Interest rate should be lower on this finance to the exporter. The banks are required to charge rates specifically as against decontrol in charging rates in the domestic segment for other types of advances.

In the case of advance in rupees, the rate is determined by the Government of India and the Reserve Bank of India. Banks charge the interest on the announced rates. The borrower can claim the actual difference between the charged rate and the subvention date on the basis of actuals. Banks claim that amount from the Government of India. There is a budgetary provision for the payment of interest subsidy.

The effective rate on the Packing Credit (PC) today is 9 per cent. The subvention is at 2 per cent. There is a time limit on the subvention which is announced in the trade policy or from time to time. When exporters resort to PC their foreign currency gets exposed. They can get advantage of a depreciation on the rupee or take a hit if it appreciates. The exporter can also take advantage of a foreign currency hedge by selling potential realisation forward. In India forward premia is healthy and in tune with interest rate differentials.

It is required that both Packing Credit (PC) and particularly Packing Credit and Foreign Currency (PCFC) limits require prior sanction. The client has to take a specific permission for PCFC from within the Bank. The fund allocation is centralised as each bank requires the funding for PCFC on a specific basis. Therefore, the exchange rate also has to be fixed by the bank when the PCFC is granted. This will be within the overall limits of the clients eligibility for working capital. The client is then locked in on the exchange rate. The advance is denominated in foreign currency but the rupee amount is arrived at on the basis of an agreed rate on the future delivery in foreign currency.

An illustration would help: If the exporter has a position that he can export and have the export proceeds within the next six months or up to 360 days, the exporter will approach the bank and ask for a packing credit in foreign currency. The exporter requires to have the working capital limit within the sanction. If the agreed amount is US$ 100,000 then the branch will get the fund clearance. Once it gets a fund clearance the exporter has to act within the hour as the bank offers a specific exchange rate of the day say 62.13. The client agrees and this rate is locked in.

The bank then gets an agreement with the client that the future US$ proceeds will be converted at 62.13 and credited when the actual proceeds come in. It is obligatory for the client to bring in proceeds. If for any reason client fails, the bank could then reverse the transaction at the date of this effect. The client will have to bear the exchange rate cost as well as pay the differential interest rate. The advantage to the client is a lower effective interest rate. The rate is currently around 3. 75 to 4.25 per cent.

The outgo of interest will then be saved to the exporter. Most exporters prefer this transaction as they have a lock in on the exchange rate with a lower rate of interest. The exporter has a choice to take a pc or a PCFC. In the case of PC, the exporter has to satisfy the PC with the foreign currency proceeds.

The exporter has a choice because advantage can be taken of a depreciation of the rupee if it happens. The banking system is regulated to the extent that it is compulsory for all banks to lend up to 10 per cent of their advances to exporters. The Reserve Bank of India also provides a refinance for exporters currently up to 50 per cent of their export finance. Practitioners in exports and export finance and advisers on foreign exchange engage in a constant exercise of choices under Indian conditions. There are occasions when PC is advantageous when there is a premium in the forward markets for the foreign currency.

The major exercise going on now is to reduce revenue expenditure. The advocacy for a fine tuning of the system is of course biased towards saving the Government of India the outgo on subvention. This can be a conscious public choice. This sum is better spent on institution building and promotion of Indian products and services abroad and strengthening India's capabilities at WTO, UN and bilateral relations. Trade follows investment is an adage. Indian institutions need strategic investment especially in East Europe, Africa, Middle East and South America which will attract Indian merchandise and service imports or provide strategic materials to India's manufacture and re-export.

Exporters have enjoyed these "concessional" rates and this has not been proving detrimental to banks, borrowers or Governments as in the case of other special cases. Competitiveness in exports has made the export sector strong enough to contribute to growth and employment. It is worthwhile to document this contribution of public policy. It is also necessary to examine the intricacies of this scheme. The current scheme is published in the RBI website and the scheme is thoroughly explained.

It is debatable whether interest subvention of export credit on rupee credit can be done away or retained. Seemingly, in the current context finance in foreign currency for export is a sound option. If capital is considered scarce in India then exporters need not give credit to other commercial entities in OECD countries. Exporters can resort to factoring, but factoring also has costs. Interest rate subvention on Export packing credit is currently implemented as part of Foreign Trade Policy of Government of India. This implies a budgetary outflow as the Government reimburses the difference between the "commercial rate" and the rate at which banks are allowed to lend under the scheme.

Government support for capital of Exim Bank of India should be more aggressive and built up for the long run. This implies that banks can have access to funds in foreign currency as well as Indian. In the current context Reserve Bank can provide for 100 per cent refinance by Bill Discounting against export proceeds.

If Exim Bank were to be capitalised at Rs. 10,000 crores every year till the paid up capital is Rs. 90,000 crores (SDR 10 Billion) this will be enormous strength as a wholesale Bank. Over time, it can have the strength to borrow at LIBOR and then support commercial banks in India with requisite foreign currency financing at lower than what Banks are being charged today by overseas Banks. If this is possible then it can extend support Indian for banking facilities in India and anywhere in the world for exporters.

State Governments and Interest Rate Subvention

State Governments sometimes announce interest rate concessions to farmers and industries. This form of subvention is not regular but surfaces occasionally. Recently, a State Government announced an interest rate at 1 per cent to farmers. This is an implicit subsidy. If a farmer borrows a loan of a fixed amount, the interest payable is usually at monthly rests. The State Government either remits to the farmer or the financial agency the difference between the charged rate, which is the market rate or the decided rate and one per cent. The amount is then made available from the budget. This constitutes a revenue expenditure.

Similarly another State Government has announced "reimbursal" of interest rates above a certain rate to industries. In this case, the industry has to submit the relevant claim after the payment is effected to the financial agency. In the above cases conditions and limitations apply. The inducement in the case of farmer is to "save" him and in the case of industry is to "promote" industrial investment. Recently the Reserve Bank of India made an announcement about implementing a concessional rate of interest to a certain section of borrowers.

The implications are serious here as there is an interference in the factor market. If there needs to be a market rate of interest the State should not interfere with the rate of return of the factor. There are liberal and interventionist arguments for and against minimum wages, rent control and therefore interest cannot be excluded from the argument.

High interest rates are the result of very high inflation, reducing the interest rate for a particular class of borrower is an interference in the factor and not then truly a market rate. It is also specially mentionable in the Indian context the Central and State Governments are largely responsible for the inflationary pressures. This is not admitted and therefore hardly any mention. There are no steps taken to mitigate it. Containing deficits, refraining from finance from printed money and directly encouraging the increase in production and export of goods should be a live dynamic operating environment.

It would therefore be wiser that following steps are initiated:

A. An intelligent debate on the issue whether Central and State Governments should intervene in the interest rate segment for lowering interest rates or giving subsidies for specific sector.
B. Exercise restraint in public expenditure and deficit financing. This in itself can moderate inflation and reduce overall interest rates to all segments than specific interests.
C. Reserve Bank of India constitutes a Committee to examine interest rate subvention, subsidy and interventions in interest rate markets by Central and State Governments as well as on unusually high returns by any entity.
D. This committee can also examine whether special interest rates, especially lower, are appropriate. It could be an anomaly when offered by certain financial agencies. Certain automobile or housing finance companies induce customers to buy a specific model of a car or a particular home loan only for the customer of that particular asset. A recommendation should be available to the consumer that he has a choice not to take a loan but a corresponding value reduction needs to be given to the customer who pays upfront.
E. Central and State Governments should come to an understanding whether intervention can be done away with. They should agree in principle not to have an intervention in interest rate markets at all and instead work on a common purpose to reduce inflation over time with concrete steps: reduction of deficits, active promotion of elements of production, increase the productive capacity of the workforce and ensure the maximum return from resources leading to an entrepreneurial economy.

There is a contradiction in the real economy. The person with capital has a measure when he deploys capital; that is, return on capital. The person who borrows has also a measure; that is, the payment of interest. Therefore, both try to deploy capital for the best return. If the borrower is not able to earn the equivalent of twice the interest paid he would not be able to pay interest and return or provide for the return of the loan. Therefore, any borrower who earns less than the market rate of interest on borrowed capital risks the capital of society.

When subvention is provided by the State, it could dissuade the individuals or corporate not enjoying the facility to compete in the field or may result in deleterious undermining of each other in such economic conditions. Specific sectors do require support but need not distort the interest rate structure. It is better to provide support for the long term to develop knowledge and institution building. Effective functional organisations can encourage initiative and innovation amongst individuals.

This is not easy as yet but need not be difficult either. It is a challenge when words mean nothing nor useless activity. It needs praxeology, the science of action by a vast number of individuals with self motivation. The Nachiket Mor Committee Report has spelt out in great detail some of the aspects on subsidies of interest rate and impact of interest rates. This opens the subject to wider discussion. Harmony in interest rates can be achieved when there are no subsidies on interest.

Twenty Five

Management of Capital and Institution Building

Interest rate policy, the determination and movement of interest rates cannot be isolated from the management of capital. In the modern era capital flows are beyond the control of Governments and world institutions. This highlights the necessity of management of capital in the Indian context and the building of institutions.

The subject of interest rates is age old (140 *A money lender may use an interest rate to increase his capital as Vasishta decreed, and take one and a quarter per cent every month.* The Laws of Manu, Penguin Classics, page 167). The attempt in the previous chapters was addressed from a practical point of view. It is a vast attempt to generate a discourse on interest rates at a given moment considering the gigantic scale of capital today.

It would be pertinent to mention that Indians had complicity in the socialist and controlled system. Liberalisation was forced by the invisible hands of the market. Liberalism as a living political force requires far more focus and attention from a large cross section of Indian community.

Interest regulation is and never can be free. The recent allegations which turned into fact about the "fixing" of the London Inter Bank Offered Rate (LIBOR) by large banks is a case for academic and practical study. There needs to be a wider poll and consistent introspection in establishing benchmarks and reference points.

The interesting case of India is that it has vast resources. It has a Production Possibility Frontier which no OECD country has. It is mentioned as backward and is low in the benchmarks that developed nations or investors all over the world look for. India needs to establish its own benchmarks and terms of reference. It has the challenging task to lift itself by itself.

The attempt in this book from a succession of letters is just that. It is an input for debate, discussion and dialogue. It is also an attempt to give inputs to end anomalies, distortions and aberrations. It is a projection for individual efforts to be with the power of organisations.

India's development will happen at its own terms. It will be made possible by the efforts and aspirations of its own people. The ideas and capital from abroad will get assimilated at its own will, at the time when due and applied practically. This requires a rapid succession of ideas and opinions to arrive at early consensus to meet India's diverse as well as divisive minds. This book has material which has provided for that.

The aforesaid Chapters have covered the phenomena and movements in interest rates in India prior to the great divide of 1991 and later. The explanations provided are for various anomalies, distortions and aberrations. The focus of today needs to be moving towards harmony.

Global developments in finance and capital movements since 2008 provide rich material for academic discourse and practical applications. Indian interest rates are well governed now with a few exceptions and occasional erratic and errant behaviour.

We can go towards harmony taking advantage of the wisdom of the ancients and knowledge of the modern market economy. Interest rates are influenced and governed by Governments and regulators in these times. This Chapter gives some ideas on institution development and a method of getting away from the stupidities and mistakes of the past. These steps will result in harmonious development. It would be less painful and give more pleasant choices for the next phase of growth of the Indian economy. It will ensure the well-being of all its people. These proposals do not require a call for sacrifice nor make some citizens worse off at the cost of others.

1. Savings in Interest Payments of the Central Government

Interest rate savings if any, must first accrue to the Government of India. The tightening of interest rates in India to stave of inflation has an unnoticed victim beyond the citizen - it has weakened the

State as well. Interest payments of Government of India in 2013-14 are budgeted at Rs. 3,70,684 crores.

Interest Payments

(in crores of Rupees)

2011-2012 Actuals	2012-2013 Actuals	2013-2014 Budget Estimates	2013-2014 Revised Estimates	2014-2015 Budget Estimates
273150	313170	370684	380066	427011

The budgeted borrowing at the end of March 2014 could be Rs. 34,51,527 crores or more. The borrowings are short term and long term. Interest rates Short term securities and Long term securities have a difference of 1.5 per cent at present.

In the US, the short term rate is 0.25 per cent and the 2 year rate is.331 per cent, the 5 year rate is 1.52 per cent, 10 year rate is 2.67 per cent and 30 year rate is 3.62 per cent (all per annum). The difference between the 30 year and 2 year is as high as 3.3 per cent. (Source: Bloomberg, 30 January 2014)

In the current context, it is essential that Government of India should prefer short term rupee borrowings. The reason is that when inflation drops, Government of India has to reckon with higher payments till the perpetuity of the borrowing. In the case of the treasury bill, it can continue borrowing at lower rates without the borrower gaining on the holdings of the longer tenor. Inflation can be managed at a steady rate only when Government does not borrow to spend as it does now. It should borrow only to invest in assets. The entire macro-economic situation will change. When the Central Government runs a surplus budget on the revenue account for all time to come as well as a small surplus budget on the Capital account, a major transformation will happen. A new era in investment oriented growth will emerge

India has to consciously plan for a market driven lower cost of interest for itself. This requires careful, dramatic, definite and concrete policy, followed by action. "The State is an instrument of the citizen it serves" is an adage that has to be kept in mind.

The attainment of objectives requires steps that are not painful but pleasant. The State requires to be articulate and positive and should not resort to reactive announcements or remain silent. It must make clear statements what it means for the present and the future. It must demonstrate that it will deal firmly with the stupidities and mistakes of the past for a vibrant and sound, present and future.

A clear statement needs to be made that only treasury bills of 46 days, 91 days, 182 days and 364 days are to be auctioned on a weekly basis for the next 24 months up to 90 per cent of the total Issue of Government Paper. The balance of 10 per cent should be in bonds of 15 to 40 years maturity. This will enable long term investors to participate. A calibrated buyback of illiquid current long term outstanding loans can be swapped with short term loans up to 10 year maturity.

Reserve Bank of India needs to conduct Open Market Operations (OMO) in treasury bills only, on the lines conveyed in the earlier Chapter. These operations are refined by Central Banks the world over, at a single rate announced every quarter.

A well managed limited capital account convertibility is possible by issuing rupee denominated bonds that are acquired and redeemed in foreign exchange. This can be done on behalf of Government of India by the Reserve Bank of India. This requires conditions of a less volatile Rupee.

In the current context the convertible T. Bills could be priced as low as 4.5 per cent. The rupee T-bill can be priced at 7 per cent if an active OMO can be effected.

This may require unusual or out-of-the box or tried, tested and true steps other than the above. A well managed programme could save as much as Rs. 40,000 crores a year automatically reducing the revenue deficit and the fiscal deficit. A one per cent reduction in interest would imply a saving of Rs. 34,000 crores. A two per cent reduction would imply a saving of Rs. 68,000 crores, a three per cent reduction would imply a saving of Rs. 1,02,000 crores and a four per cent reduction would imply a saving of Rs. 1,36,000 crore.

It therefore is imperative of Government of India to target an inflation rate of 4 per cent and achieve it than resort to blame games.

2. Reduce the Interest Outgo of State Government

Savings for State Governments would occur if they exercise self-discipline in expenditure incurred out of servicing borrowing. Borrowings should be matched with investment. If Central Government and State Governments work together, they can facilitate and engineer a production increase that will outpace money supply. Therefore, reduction in wasteful expenditure, making state-owned enterprises productive and facilitating investment which provides decent returns should be conscious exercises by the State.

State Governments have strong hold over the Rule of Law and foster the judiciary; they must exercise prudence and foster the culture of keeping to contracts and performance. This will enable them to nurture the bond markets for themselves and expand financial markets. This will also help reduce their interest outgo for themselves and utilities managed by them in the long run.

State government should not impose high costs on stamp duties and registration in the creation of instruments. Interest rates would come down due to reduced inflation, influence of international markets, secure bond markets and a sound financial market. Savings on interest outgo by all State Governments, local bodies and State Owned Enterprises in a scenario of lowering of interest rates is a research topic in itself.

3. The Bond Market Development

Bond Market Development must require Fixed Deposits to be regulated and given a new direction. The Fixed Deposit is Fixed in the minds of Indian savers. The investors are not moving to bonds. This has been explained in the previous chapters. Banks and financial institutions should be given incentives to issue bonds. It also requires regulation and not decontrol.

The current situation requires Fixed Deposits by all entities to be regulated:

- By Tenor
- By Interest rates

This regulatory element has to be done very carefully, in a calibrated manner and taking in all the stakeholders and most of all orient the direction and purpose for bank managements. The context of higher inflation and complexity of lower global rates with relative play of money and exchange rates make it imperative that the approach to developing Bond markets need not be vexed or hexed.

Bond market development requires first, an active and dynamic market for Central Government securities across the financial market with participation from individuals, societies, trusts, companies and institutions amongst banks. Financial companies, Mutual Funds and Foreign Investors. Second, these participants must be facilitated and incentivised for active trading in bonds.

Government of India, State Governments and Reserve Bank of India should play a dynamic and proactive role to enthuse market participants and citizens. This requires rates of Fixed Deposits lower than the Bank rate and Government securities higher than the Fixed Deposit rate. These have been skewed even after liberalisation and hence requires regulation and not decontrol.

An active Bond market will reduce bank deposits and increase direct investment in securities. This will not remain long if the CRR is 3 per cent and SLR 18 per cent when a dynamic economy and population will have larger amounts of Current Accounts and Savings Accounts. With partial capital account convertibility, Indian Banks can attract global current accounts and wholesale banking which is remunerative for banks with capacity and capital.

4. Limited Capital Account Convertibility

The Tarapore Committee on Capital Account Convertibility meticulously went into all aspects on introducing Capital Account Convertibility in India.

Among the proposals that can be easily implemented are:

1. Opening Current Accounts and Savings Bank Accounts in Foreign Currency (FC) for Indian Nationals residing in India.
2. Opening FC accounts, Current and Saving, for all International entities and individuals living and working in India and institutions like Embassies, Consulates, International Banks and Institutions like World Bank, ADB, and FIIs.
3. Exporters are allowed EEFC Accounts. They can operate full-fledged Current Accounts and employees who travel frequently can also be allowed Current and Savings Accounts in FC.
4. Following persons and entities may be allowed to open foreign currency denominated Current Accounts and Savings in India:
   a) Non-Resident Indians and Indian companies and subsidiaries abroad and their employees

   b) Any foreign national with strict KYC norms
   c) Fortune 500 companies who intend to do business in India
   d) For students, professionals and Indians abroad
5. Commercial Banks in India should be allowed full convertibility up to 100 per cent of their Tier 1 Capital in APPROVED international securities.
6. Governments and Central Banks where Government has good political and trade relations and run a trade surplus in India should be allowed to invest in Convertible Rupee accounts or in FC accounts of their choice.
7. India can allow establishment of international banks who can open accounts of all currencies of all nations in the world.

5. Option to Prepay All Central Government Borrowings in Foreign Currency

India can reduce foreign debt and foreign exchange reserves the same time. The current situation in Indian economy should be looked in a clear perspective with a vision for the next thirty years. India resorted to foreign currency borrowings-Bilateral and Multilateral.

According to the Statement of Assets and Liabilities of the Budget Papers of the Government of India, External Debt was Rs. 32.03 crores in 1950-51. Currently the outstanding is Rs. 1,82,862.11 crores. In Dollar terms it is much higher as the declaration of liability is at "book" value. (Footnote: * Balances are according to book value.)

Therefore every time the rupee depreciates, Government of India is worse off. It is worthwhile to do a study on this aspect that how much Government of India had to pay out due to Rupee depreciation compared to the Interest rate savings? Again, multilateral project finance is also passed on to states with the currency risk borne by Government of India.

In the light of current global situation where short term rates are near zero, the reserves held by Reserve Bank of India do not yield any returns. These amounts are invested out of issued money, "neutralisation" of capital flows and as a safety device. It has been described as a "negative" carry. A scenario needs to be established whether Foreign exchange reserves and Indian Government's foreign currency debt can be drawn down together. It also means that India's foreign debt will be down by US Dollar 45 billion and reserves also come down to USD 220 billion. This will also imply RBI holding additional Rupee securities to the extent of Rs. 2,60,000 crores which is not new in its history or to Central Banks after the 2008 crisis.

In the case of international borrowings, outgo of interest as well as principal is in foreign currency. In the case of internal borrowings, outgo of interest will be rupees. If Reserve Bank of India holds Rs. 2,40,000 crores in Indian Government bonds then its rupee earnings would be Rs. 20,000 crores instead of Rs. 2,400 crores while it holds foreign currency in international bonds.

The Government and RBI can decide that commercial banks and RBI can deploy resources by buying securities of multilateral bodies. This is explained in the partial capital account convertibility scenario. To enable this, CRR can be comfortably reduced to 3 per cent. In the context of high inflation, a depreciating currency, high interest rates and foreign currency borrowing by Government of India and the private sector policy options need to be examined whether Government of India needs to borrow from foreign Governments and multilateral agencies.

This implies that the Government of India has a contingent liability that it requires higher outlay when it repays the loan borrowed in foreign currency. If inflation continues and currency depreciates Government of India will be worse off. This is obvious, as it has adopted the practice of buying foreign currency at the prevailing market rate at the time of repayment. How exactly should it be dealt with requires debate, dialogue and discussions. If India needs to stand tall in the comity of nations it should stand on equal terms. It should not be a borrower from other Governments, tied or otherwise. In the current situation as well as near future, India need not be a borrower from multilateral institutions as well. In fact, it can be a lender. It requires a one time, in-principle decision that Indian Government need not be a borrower in foreign currency for the next few decades. In fact it can allow other Central Banks and entities to invest in rupee securities.

This has to be done with humility and grace and with a grateful acknowledgement for aid in the past when India needs it most. The announcement requires to be in a decision in principle and conveyed through bilateral talks on India's position. It is a firm affirmation in Parliament and approved by it, that it will not seek any loans and also convey its readiness and intention to prepay earlier loans. This requires a budget exercise and it must be introduced in Parliament and endorsed by it. This would imply a drawdown of foreign currency reserves. The prepayment will induce a "crisis" like situation when Indian Government prepares to prepay something of the order of Rs. 2,40,000 crores.

This is enough to cause a "tightening" in bond markets. On the other hand, it would draw-down 40 billion USD in reserves which the RBI earns a paltry return and will not have difficulty in buying rupee securities to that extent. This can be done with a resolve to reduce the CRR by 1 per cent to 3 per cent and free the resource of the banking sector when Central Government chooses to increase the internal borrowings. This decision will induce Government to cut down unnecessary expenditure, expedite disinvestment and manage its internal debt more efficiently as it is freed from the management burden of external debt.

6. Instruments for Islamic Banking

India needs to develop instruments that conforms to Islamic Banking. India is regarded highly amongst all nations. It is the revenue deficit that makes the Indian paper poor in quality. That India has never defaulted in its external debt is an unparalleled phenomenon even by Western or New World standards. In the present economic condition, it needs to do more in order to have a consensus in parliament that Capital internal or external should not degenerate into expenditure.

This will enable inflation to be within reasonable limits and interest commitments will fall. This requires a near term commitment to stable exchange rates, limited capital account convertibility and make it attractive for Rupee instruments to be invested in.

A beginning can be made to have Rupee Bonds under the discounting method up to 3 years tenor. This can be designed in such a way that Central Banks or financial entities of friendly countries who have developed a methodology for investment called Shariat. They seek returns on assets like property which give them rent, equity investment, and returns where net revenue earned should not be in the form of interest. India should offer these instruments either by Central Government, State Government or financial companies.

This would enable cost of funds in its borrowing at around 4.5 per cent in relative terms. However, it requires foreign exchange management from free to a managed peg to allow depreciation of the rupee around 3 per cent per annum to account for inflation differentials till actual inflation settles down at 5 per cent in the medium term.

It is impossible to think in terms of inflation less than 9 per cent per annum for next three years when liberalisation sets in motion free pricing of products currently under control regulation or direction by Government of India. This can also mean deep discounted or profit generated option by Banks and can give Islamic banking products to nations who desire those options in India. These should be taxable too.

By offering Deep Discount Bonds, Government of India and financial institutions can comply with Shariat by issue of instruments which can be subscribed to by those entities who welcome such instruments.

The friendly countries like UAE and Brunei would then direct portfolio investment into India.

7. Capitalisation of Banks

Government can capitalise Exim Bank, NABARD, NHB and SIDBI up to Rs. 90,000 crores each over 5 years and develop them into wholesale banks. A similar capitalisation of a bank for large industry and a bank for reconstruction would help. These Banks should be permitted as commercial banks with a restriction that they can be wholesale bankers. They can operate current accounts of Central Governments, State Governments, International and National Bodies, in convertible currencies and for other national and international banks.

Capital for these Banks can be Authorised and Paid up at Rs. 90,000 crores, each subscribed in a period of 5 years from the Central Budget and proceeds from disinvestment and also converting the assets of Government of India. The shares of State Sector enterprises can be swapped for equity of Banks. Each of these entities are institutions and have performed reasonably well in their mandates. It is better to leverage the strengths of these institutions and make the financial system stronger. This will also give a stronger direction to intentions of the Government to finance and promote exports, rural development, housing and small enterprises. The step will provide Government respite in capitalising commercial banks. All Banks can be easily taken to the market on strong fundamentals for increasing capital.

Government control will be more basic and practical through these entities. State Owned Commercial Banks can be allowed to expand on their own strengths. The steps will give stability to the foreign currency flows and limited capital account convertibility granted to these entities will help them to do so. Existing Foreign exchange markets will have strong participants and counterparties. Central Government and State Governments and their entities and institutions can park their temporary surpluses safely. Capital can be leveraged for both short term and long term borrowings. Funds from these institutions will be channelled to Capital Assets while commercial banks will be having resources working capital.

8. Hindustan Zaveri Bank

Central government should promote the Hindustan Zaveri Bank (HZB) which will deal with bullion, be a large wholesale bank and leverage India's official gold and silver management. It will be a full fledged wholesale commercial bank and will act as banker to:

1. Central Government
2. All state Governments
3. International Bodies and International Banks and Entities
4. Investors and Funds—especially those specialised in precious metals and metals
5. It will be an All Authorised Bullion Dealer
6. It will be an authorised Foreign Exchange Dealer

The capital needs to be Rs. 1,00,000 crores solely owned by Government of India. A portion of the Gold Reserves bought by RBI need to be purchased by the Gold Bank and held as a reserve and shall constitute the national reserve in part. The Gold Imports can be channelled through this bank for 3 years to establish the flow on a regulated basis. Availability of Gold for export can be channelled through HZB and Exim Bank of India. This will enable Indian asset quality to be strengthened. Any issue of Rupee security by HZB can be convertible into any international currency.

HZB can also be given Capital Convertibility and therefore will invest in international securities and leverage them for

- creating an active and liquid market for Central and State Governments
- creating an atmosphere for Bond Trading as a custodial giant
- provide stability and equilibrium to domestic interest rates
- be an important player in the foreign transactions market and wholesale banking

India will have a well capitalised bullion backed world-class wholesale commercial bank. This will be an unique institution which will stabilise both Indian and world currencies in the near future. It will balance India's interest with world interest.

9. Central Government should Promote Bharath Investment and Guarantee Bank

Government of India needs to promote investment than indulge in current expenditure. The Government has exercised its prerogative to give a sovereign guarantee to loans given to State Governments and entities owned by it. The Budget papers specify in detail guarantees issued by it and commission earned.

Government should initiate a proposal to establish the Bharath Investment and Guarantee Bank. This can have an authorised capital of Rs. 1,20,000 crores and the initial Paid Up Capital can be Rs. 30,000 crores. It needs to get a full fledged licence as a commercial bank but confine itself to be a banker to Central Government State Governments Entities Banks and Financial Institutions investment companies and international institutions. It will take over the existing guarantees and free Government in future from issue of guarantees. Capitalised at Rs. 1,20,000 crores this will in future give guarantees on loans.

Parliament should approve this 100 per cent Central Government owned entity and commit Rs. 30,000 crores per year Equity for the next 4 years. This will create a financial institution in perpetuity for national interests. It can even guarantee Central and State Government bonds to third parties. This financial institution, with a large capital base and supported by Sovereign guarantee for any of its Bonds, its target should be able to get international finance at Libor rates. It should have full capital account convertibility with conditionalities and should hold foreign securities as well as regularly trade foreign currencies of all nations.

This will enable reduction in current account deficit and can act as a beacon for investment into India. This will be an ally of the Government in stabilising currency and interest rate markets. More important, it can focus on long term investment by Central and State Governments and public as well as private sectors.

10. Bond and Credit Insurance

Government can open up FDI for Bond and Credit Insurance companies. They will then charge the premium to international investors on rupee bonds that can be internationalised. Government must open for Foreign Direct Investment Insurance companies who will provide insurance on Bond issues from India to FIIs and for Investors in India. Bond insurance is paid for by borrowers on specific instruments by issuers. Mr. Warren Buffet, the worlds most acknowledged sound investor has interest in the Bond Insurance market in USA. It is worthwhile for Government of India to open up this sector.

The possibilities are:

a) There can be five licences for Bond Insurance companies for Indians and five licenses for international organisations.
b) Authorised Capital should be a minimum of Rs. 10,000 crores with no limit for maximum.
c) Promoters need to bring in Rs. 7,400 crores and begin operations. Rs. 2,400 crores need to be way of Issue to Indian citizens by IPO.
d) Bond insurance companies are given full capital account convertibility to the extent of Paid Up Capital under specific conditions.
e) Bond insurance companies can be authorised to charge premia on Bond Issues by any entity in India to any global or Indian investor.
f) Bond insurance premia can be charged to the lender or the borrower but currently in the Indian context it can be charged on the borrower as returns are attractive in India.

Regulation can be by Government, IRDA, MCA, RBI and any entity for any specific function of a Bond Insurance Company. An estimated publicly traded Bond issues can be as high as Rs. 30,00,000 crores by 2025 when a sound mechanism is in place. Bond markets need Bond insurance which is a specialised insurance market. This will have a higher confidence than rating and will provide the necessary fillip to bond issuances in India. This needs to be developed forthwith.

In a similar nature, reinsurance companies Indian Re and General Re must be promoted to expand rapidly. Government and its non insurance entities must open another re insurance corporation called India Re to expand the Indian re insurance market. General Re and India Re can have an IPO of 26 per cent for greater Indian public participation. This can also apply to General Insurance companies and encourage them to have an IPO of 26 per cent to give greater depth to equity and bond markets. Major Re insurance companies in the world like Munich Re and Swiss Re encouraged to start Indian operations with support of 26 per cent from Government and 48 per cent high net worth Individuals in expanding the Indian ReFunds with Insurance companies will expand when the breadth and depth of insurance and pension markets expand. This will automatically make the bond market active and bring harmony and equilibrium to interest rates in India. It will also generate equity to the extent of Rs. 1,00,000 crores that is needed for the infrastructure investment of Rs. 30,00,000 crores in major utilities projects.

11. Inflation and Interest Rates

Inflation is a chronic issue in India and now it is a wicked problem that refuses to go away. Inflation and Interest Rates need not be correlated now. The priority should be to generate investment or complete projects where substantial investments have been done. There is a correlation between inflation rates and interest rates wellknown to economists. It requires more elaboration in the Indian context. Apparently, citizens in India are to take the blame for inflation than the Government and the Reserve Bank of India. *(Please see a note on inflation in Appendix)*

The collective effort required is to manage inflation and reduce the overall impact of undeservedly higher interest rates. Therefore, it is an appeal to the polity in India to understand the effects of reduced interest rates overall on Central and State Governments, home owners and businesses. This is addressed in the last Chapter and it is hoped that it gets urgent attention. The Indian collective effort needs to be on managing inflation as it would seem impossible to control it in the near term. There are deeper economic factors beyond the control of Government and individuals that are driving prices high.

One cannot enjoy inflation but its effects need not be construed as only damaging. Inflation in India can get reduced by decreasing money supply and reducing Government expenditure both of which are addressed seriously. Increasing production rapidly cannot be done merely by reducing interest rates. There needs to be a combined effort with elements of production and productivity increases to have a rapid expansion in availability of goods within India at the same costs.

The simplest approach one can now have is to have monetary and fiscal management, without ignoring the need to moderate price increases, a concerted effort to increase the Gross Domestic Product which will outpace money supply. This requires a sound explanation of price theory and choices for every citizen in India in the context of a functioning and vibrant market economy. Today we have the legacies of a feudal, monarchical, colonial, communist and socialist administrations and polity in a functioning democracy. Let us assume that going to a market economy is evolutionary rather than revolutionary.

In a distorted and contorted state of affairs today the direction of resources, state, public or private should be:

- Availability of electricity without interruption or disruptions
- Existing roads free of potholes and upcoming and new roads coming up
- A massive investment in Railways that will stimulate the economy and good for the next 70 years
- Taking water to the next six steps of efficient handling and availability for all beneficial purposes
- Eliminating public sector wastage and converting waste into wealth

The priority should be to generate investment or complete projects where substantial investments have been done. A lower interest rate regime specifically for long term investments will increase production, productivity, creation of assets, entrepreneurial activity and lower long term costs.

12. Interest Rate Regulation

Interest Rates in the world are clearly "market" driven as well as a consequence of decisions of Governments and Central Banks, independently or in tandem. A casual study will determine the interest rate movements driven by regulators, i.e. Central Banks of OECD countries. Interest rate movements in China are influenced by its Government and managed by the Central Bank.

In USA and Europe, interest rates have been deliberately lowered for the short term as a stimulus for coming out of recession. OECD countries have followed suit. Interest rates are low in neutral countries like Hong Kong, Taiwan, South Korea, Singapore and Switzerland. In Singapore and South East Asian Nations, it is due to abundance of savings. In Switzerland, it is done deliberately to prevent currency appreciation and inflow of capital as a match to prevent funds seeking arbitrage or as a safe haven.

In the Indian context interest rates have had aberrations, anomalies and distortions after 1991. Till then, interest rates were directed and controlled. In 24 years of management of economic affairs since 1991, interest rates have been decontrolled. The Government and RBI have consciously nurtured a market oriented interest rate policy with adequate responses to external situations and internal developments.

The questions are:

- Is decontrol appropriate in the current context?
- Is the extent of Regulation required determinable and can it be practiced?
- Interest rates need to be governed?
- Is regulation required? If so, in what manner and how policy and administration is done and required to be done?
- Do market participants have the required self-discipline?
- Is education and organisation sufficiently available and developed for an orderly market economy and capable of responses to situations and developments?

These questions have been raised and attempted to be answered in the previous chapters. A holistic view needs to be taken now by Government of India and Reserve Bank of India as to how a policy will evolve for interest rate management. The Policy needs to be commensurate with the size and stature as a nation in the world economy and in the interest of economic justice to all citizens within the nations.

13. Statutory Liquidity Ratio (SLR) to be Reduced to 18 Per cent in Six Quarters

The current SLR (Statutory Liquidity Ratio) is 24 per cent. The evolution of SLR is known to the senior bankers, the RBI, the Ministry, economists and academic faculty as well as students of banking and public finance. It is a declared short term objective that the SLR in our nation should come lower and be at par with "advanced" economies or economically stronger nations. The nearest benchmark is Singapore who has prescribed an SLR of 18 per cent and allowed 4 per cent of it in foreign currency.

It can be then assumed that Indian commercial banks should be comfortable with this arrangements and State owned Banks, Commercial Banks Grameen Banks and co-operative banks urban or rural need to adhere to this regulation. Earlier, there is a mention about the Statutory part and liquidity part of the permitted instruments. The Regulator prescribes the instruments but it also admits that the Government securities are illiquid; especially the longer maturity securities. A peculiarity exists that Commercial Banks have short term borrowings from the public and end up subscribing to long term securities. The Regulator and the Banks have an arrangement on valuation of these securities on mark to market (which has scarce dealings) and YTM method or the book value method.

There needs to be a regulation that a minimum compulsory investment to be made by banks to the extent of 4 per cent of Liabilities in approved bonds denominated in international currency. The following proposals should address all the issues:

A Reserve Bank of India announces the decision that the SLR will be 18 per cent with a phased reduction of 1 per cent per quarter from April 1 2014.

B The permitted securities shall be less than 5 years only to the extent of 70 per cent of the requirement and the balance 30 per cent will not exceed 10 years. This will be for a period of 3 years and later all SLR securities will be less than 5 years including treasury Bills

C The accommodation for this will be that Government of India will issue only Treasury Bills and Bonds less than 5 years in the next 18 months as there are more than sufficient long term securities in the market.

D Reserve Bank of India needs to conduct a one time continuous open market operation with a window to absorb all long dated securities which are held by all commercial banks and hold them till other entities buy them in the open market over time. This implies that it will have arrangements in active OMO in Treasury Bills at the same time.

E On active Open Market Operation, all Standing facilities as well as LAF will cease on a daily basis and work only in a crisis, or when a particular bank invokes a predetermined emergency requirement clause citing exceptional circumstances or a sign of weakness when a stress test is conducted.

F The Commercial Banks shall be permitted to have foreign currency investments in permitted international currencies Long term Bonds issued by World Bank and Similar organisations

- US Dollar
- Yen
- Euro (permitted countries only)
- Swiss Franc
- Rouble
- Ringgit
- Real
- Rand
- UAE Dirham
- Singapore Dollar
- Australian Dollar
- Canadian Dollar

All securities other than issued by Multilateral agencies must be short term medium term or long term that are tradable i.e. that they can be sold in a day. The motive is to internationalise the rupee with Commercial Banks as the vehicles.

G Commercial Banks can then also be offered Limited Capital account convertibility in all above currencies.

H In the current scenario banks have Excess SLR securities. With private investment in bonds going up, Banks will be comfortable with the 14 per cent rupee and 4 per cent foreign currency SLR

I This will relieve RBI to carry on the function of foreign exchange reserves as commercial banks will be active in the forex market while RBI acts as the bastion.

J In the scenario where inflation will be lower in three years, Government of India will not have a large outstanding of long dated securities and hence benefit from the generation of peoples savings, world capital and reducing its own dissaving.

The above steps will integrate the international finance with Indian finance and will contribute to economic stability even under volatile conditions. The measure will integrate India with the world economy, help generate savings, direct resources to productive long term investments and reduce interest rates to Government as well as eligible mortgage and bond markets.

14. Increasing Capital in Commercial Banks

There must be a serious look at options for increasing Tier 1 capital of all banks and financial institutions. In the Indian context it will be rewarding in the long term. It will also increase the Return on Capital for all as Indian nominal rates are high. The key aspects governing interest rates of a nation in its currency are safety of principal and the macroeconomic features of a nation. Within a nation, interest rates range from zero to the maximum commercially declared rate from a particular lender to a particular borrower. Informal rates, street rates, rates between friends and relatives, usury all are reported but do not fall within official reviews. What is socially desirable may not be economically feasible.

There needs to be a discussion and debate on the rates accessible by Indian commercial banks or institutions. As of now the rates range from 275 to 425 "basis points" over Libor say of 0.25 per cent. Indian Banks should be strong enough to command Libor rates. However the "country risk" weighs down and premium on Libor goes up. Even Libor has come under a cloud on allegations about manipulations and fixing. As a measured response Indian commercial banks need to be strengthened to the point they can access at Libor plus.25 pts for the short term. This can be enabled with a pledge of assets they own which can be convertible at an instant.

15. Housing Finance Rates

Housing finance can get refinanced at special rates so that the mortgage market will open up. If this is internationalised, the mortgage discount and rediscount will get opened up. Housing Finance Rates in India are reasonable but proportionately higher than global standards. Housing finance is secured finance and hence must command the best pricing in interest lower than all other forms of finance. The interest of Central and State Government lies in making a safe and secure environment for mortgage lending,

There is an immediate need for at least 2 crores reasonably priced dwelling for the lower middle class and the rural working class. The aspiring middle class and upper middle class also needs affordable finance for affordable housing.

The dissaving in Government sectors (which use Capital savings, expenditure out of issue of currency,) is something that needs to be addressed so that savings within the country are deployed by intermediaries into this segment of finance.

1 crore people building their homes at a cost of around Rs. 1,50,000 in villages and small towns would generate a development of Rs. 1,50,000 crores. Their own labour and savings will contribute to 25 per cent margin and land; and balance will be construction material and labour.

Finance should be available at 7 to 8 per cent in the Indian context on mortgage loans.

High inflation for which the root cause is printed money, financing Government expenditure over years and also investment in unproductive areas is preventing the orderly development of rural mass housing. Other complementary factors are land titles, self discipline and organisation.

There are multitude Government schemes (Indira Awas Yojana) but the voluntary, constructive self driven housing development will far outpace such schemes.

The following steps needs to be taken:

RBI can make a deeper study on housing finance, its structure and source of funds with a mandate to develop a long term bond market to finance housing loans. It can create a window of Rs. 70,000 crores in 90 days and refinance to enable National Housing bank to re-discount short term bills of any housing entity who banks with it.

Essentially this should be financing the cash flow of repayments coming in from borrowers which can be directed into an escrow account to meet the specific liability. To avoid this as a permanent source of finance as well as for market discipline, each entity can be mandated to will to repay the borrowed amount within 90 days and will be eligible to secure it again in 7 working days when it requires the same.

RBI can open the window at 6.5 per cent and NHB can lend at 7 per cent. This will mean an effective beginning for a future Bond market. Government of India can expand the Capital of NHB to Rs. 90,000 crores with Rs. 10,000 crores infused each year for 9 years on a committed basis.

NHB can also be a banker to other banks, as well as Housing Finance companies and State Governments. This will enable it to have CASA accounts as well. However, it will act as a lender to lenders and not direct financing. This will clear the way for a term Bond market for issues from Housing finance company and also enable commercial banks to issue Bonds backed by their lending to mortgage based housing finance.

16. Case for Investment Banks in India

India does not have Investment Banks. In fact, it does not have a concept for definition, establishment, development, regulation and effectiveness of Investment Banks. This discussion requires now to be put in public domain. The usefulness of Investment Banks in India also needs to be expedited.

In the current context, India has a definite need of physical assets of the order of Rs. 30,00,000 crores in following key areas:

1. Electricity generation, transmission and distribution
2. Air and Sea Port Border Assets
3. Railways
4. Roads
5. Public transportation in Cities and major towns

6. Irrigation Dams—Major, Medium, Small and Micro
7. Metals
8. Petroleum Exploration, Extraction, Refining, Storage and Distribution
9. Enterprise Parks, Industrial land for expansion and export undertakings
10. Overseas Indian investment: strategic and commercial

This requires high focus and attention and acquiring of skills and expertise in issue of instruments in finance e.g. bonds, than borrowings, deposits and loans. Asset backed finance is not new in India and the world. Sufficient risk capital also known as equity needs to be there to leverage the global availability of capital. The Government and RBI need to work forthwith on this. This will help equilibrium in interest rate and channel global capital into much needed fixed capital assets.

Economic Literacy, Market Economy and Development Economics

The greatest development yet to happen is to spread economic and accounting literacy to citizens of India. Savers are enticed to the slightest higher rate of interest. When abnormal or paranormal rates are offered, it is the beginning of a Ponzi scheme or default. Interest rates can be afforded to be paid only when the borrower has higher than normal returns on investment or sales. This can happen only if there is entrepreneurial activity or higher productivity.

There is an institutional need for making this happen. The possibility is the development of true return on factor that is financial capital. Citizens need to learn than be taught. This will end the activity by a few people to take advantage of the gullibility amongst the citizens. In India the rates for microfinance were managed institutionally while the unorganised markets have interest rates (also called usury).

The following events have been significant world events over the last 25 years:

- The Junk Bond market created by New York investment bankers
- The recent phenomena where the single European currency had different interest rates for the bonds of different countries e.g. Germany at the lowest and Greek, Spain, Italy and Portugal at different higher rates

- The lowest rates ever in the world has been for the Japanese yen at 0.25 per cent for more than ten years while the Swiss, Franc, Euro and Dollar had short term rates at 0.25 per cent from 2008.

These phenomena have to be studied and the entire world economy is poised for harmonious development. Economic history is in the making. This will be India's Century and India must lead the world into prosperity and peace.

In a market economy "no one is worse off without anyone else being better off". When we have options for economic efficiency policy, regulation or lack of it should not make the whole nation worse off.

Preamble of the Indian Constitution mentions boldly and wisely, justice, economic and the dignity of the individual. Regulation of interest rates falls in the realm of ensuring economic justice and this cannot be done in isolation. Integration is the key and therefore there can be a clear vision for the economy only when we strive for harmony.

There are situations abroad that are beyond the control of Governments. What needs to be done is an Indian response to an Indian situation. The thoughts and ideas mentioned before can induce debate, dialogue and discussion towards a common purpose: equilibrium and harmony in interest rates in a market economy. This is possible and can be achieved in a short time. This is the confidence that we need to affirm in ourselves.

The objective of Government and of course of Reserve Bank of India needs to be economic efficiency. The distortions, anomalies and aberrations should be taken as events in the past. They might have resulted from many factors beyond the control of citizens or Government or the Reserve Bank of India. What needs to be done now is to establish harmony and equilibrium by taking measures within the control of respective organisations.

The subject of interest should generate passion and the vast amount of data and information should be distilled. Sound policy and more important good practices will emanate from new knowledge.

The study of interest rates should be carried on by the reader. Whatever aforesaid is only a stimulus for thought and then should go into the realm of praxeology - the science of action.

Epilogue

Interest is just one form of return in the complex factor called Capital. This book would be an opening for the earnest in authority to strike a balance amongst opposites. It started with anomalies, aberrations and distortions. These have been largely addressed. Harmony would arise when an equanimous view is projected in conflict resolution. Citizens would appreciate and applaud when the effects of a right decision is taken in public interest.

Interest rates are governed and also operate in free market or regulated conditions. The fundamentals in the world financial markets and in the Indian nation keep changing by the minute. One of the reasons in decline in the Euro is a perception that US Dollar interest rates may rise and that of Euro may not.

The shift of capital to commodities caused an increase in price and exported inflation to emerging countries. This was not sustainable and capital has been withdrawn and the search is on for new investment avenues. It is fortuitous for India that a rapid decline in global crude oil prices has taken effect and that too within a fortnight. This brings forth an economic fact that nothing can remain "artificially" high for too long.

The Taming of Inflation in India drama has yet to come to a curtain call. The presence of black to grey incomes, unearned money in the form of bribes or illegal rents and rents in cash, flooding of unchecked counterfeits and unabated Government wasteful expenditure are the true causes of inflation abetted by the relentless printing of money even after the liberalisation process in 1991. The coddling of the villains is still on and inflation has to come down "logically" and hence we have to "live" with the current interest rates and inflation.

In Japan, the interest rates are zero because inflation rates are zero. This is a remarkable phenomenon of public savings, production and productivity. In Europe, interest rates are zero because US interest rates are near Zero. In Switzerland and Frankfurt, the rates of interest are—.01 per cent for banks, in order to encourage banks to lend to commercial sectors. Public expenditure in Japan has not induced inflation or growth to the degree imagined. In India, black money and Government expenditure are contributing to inflation.

The lesson for India is that prices can come down with increased production and productivity in articles of mass consumption. What is not generally liked is its coming down by the drop in aggregate demand. The taming of inflation requires classic and modern steps. India is an exception where probably inflation can be considered to have desirable and undesirable side effects. The prescription is to address the absence of education, organisation and self discipline. This requires regulation which has not merely salutary, but deep effects to end this wicked problem.

This also requires decisions on an everyday basis and those which undo the idiocies, mistakes and follies of the past. The only certainty is that the future is uncertain. Hence, action to be taken has to be both necessary and with the wisdom of anticipation. The day to day lives of citizens are affected by the benign guidance of the wise at the helm of affairs. The contrary is also true when citizens suffer from the inaction of those hands and brains that control and regulate.

The weighted average interest rate on term deposits declined to 8.63 per cent in 2013 from 9.19 per cent as at end-March 2012. The weighted average interest rate in respect of all loans and advances with credit limit of over 0.2 million declined to 12.05 per cent as at the end of March 2013 from 12.57 per cent a year ago.

The latest news report reveals that Rs. 34,000 crores have been written off as bad loans by banks in 2013-14. Naturally, these are from gross profits and no bank yet has reported a net loss. Imagination runs wild, that if this was not written off, Government of India would have earned Rs. 11,000 crores in Corporate Taxes. Aggressive credit marketing creates waste. The finance minister exhorts banks to lend in 2011 but in 2013 laments that NPAs have increased and wants banks to rein in NPAs.

The money comes from charging a higher interest to borrowers of integrity. This anomaly can arise with a normal banking behaviour of risk taking. There is a risk in lending but not as much as in taking deposits. The loans which are defaulted on by borrowers come from various factors to borrowers across all segments. Today, "non-performing" loans are said to be Rs. 2,10,000 crores. This implies banks are losing approximately Rs. 20,000 crores as legitimate interest earning a year.

Stated clearly, borrowers cannot repay those amounts and have stopped paying interest on them. The banking industry continues to pay interest at Rs. 17,000 crores a year on the deposits raised to lend those amounts. In India, the difficulty to realise the assets lent speedily raises the costs for all borrowers.

We now hear of terms, defaulters and "willful" defaulters, automatically making other defaulters "non-willful" defaulters, a new definition in the Indian bankers dictionary. When a contract is not performed he is called a defaulter. Default is when a person does not pay even when he has the money. An insolvent is a person who cannot pay because he does not have liquid assets and he would have to realise those assets into cash in order to repay the loan and an assumption that the assets he has exceeds the loan and he requires time to sell his assets and satisfy the loan. A bankrupt is a person who has assets less than his loan and he and his creditors know approximately the net value and therefore he has to exit with loss to his creditors. There is still scope for old fashioned credit, character and capability.

This process of bad loan recovery is excruciatingly slow and bankers as well as borrowers go through agonising processes. It is the prime responsibility of State Government to ensure a sound judicial administration. There is no problem that Indians cannot solve. It is conflict resolution and settling of disputes and issues that drags. This results in economic inefficiency and can be described as Government failure as defined by Nobel Prize Winning Economist Samuelson.

The commercial banking sector needs close monitoring and attention in today's context. They should have sustained profitability. That is why there is an imperative to allow Indian banks partial capital account convertibility and introduce "carry trade". This is taking benefit of borrowing in one currency and lending in another, which banks alone can do. It should be obvious that investments for the long range requires equity which is determined by the cost of capital and borrowings which interest cannot be paid immediately but amortised over time. This adds to the costs of electricity, water and other utilities which Indians pay disproportionately more and with poorer quality amongst peers.

The frequency of announcements in wrong doing in the Indian nation is never ending in the political arena, in Government, in Institutions or amongst the public at large. This is dealt with in the Indian way. The Indian public is more forgiving than any other nation in the world. The Dalai Lama said, "Forgiveness does not mean condoning wrong".

Government of India spends this year Rs. 4,27,011 crores in interest payments. This amounts to Rs. 1,170 crores every single day whether it is a working day, Saturday and Sunday or a Government holiday. Addressing quality in Government revenue expenditure automatically saves capital for investment, especially, investment partly in the form of equity for the long term that India needs.

In its free history, India has never been a defaulter in its obligations abroad though the same cannot be said within. The new Indian Government need not owe any other Government or agency in the world. It can make the rupee convertible and have sovereign borrowings in rupees free of conditionality. The Indian citizen has always been short-changed by inflation, by dysfunctional or lethargic parts of Government and muddled policies.

If India is to be declared a market economy, then the functions of State, a judicial administration that settles disputes and a State that delivers the actions on property rights must be at maximum efficiency. Harmony is some distance away and now citizens live on hope.

Financial markets seems complicated to the people at large. We try to simplify the complex. The person in authority needs to see the complexities in the simple. Any breakdown is a corruption and need not be symbolic as a sign for bribery or obstruction.

Action on breakdown needs to be as swift as a series of actions, training and coaching on preventing breakdowns and failure. The emergency response created years ago to deal with natural disasters is a good example—when Cyclone Phalin hit the Eastern Coast.

Sound institutions need not have just brains and intelligence but large hearts and compassion, with a reassurance for all and a stern eye for the wrongdoing. Institutions have been created brilliantly and have built and sustained. There are instances of redundancy and failure. In today's financial world, institutions are cowed by the enormous growth of citizen power which directs resources into areas which they have no control and influence.

In India, we have the need for more institutions. These are not required to substitute poor performance of Government authority or mediocrity in public, political and academic life. They need to support, augment and give the much needed excellence and specialisation in respective spheres that takes Government from perceived weaknesses to strength.

Intellectual dishonesty cannot be converted to honesty from public or academic opinion but its recognition from within. The misallocation or wrong allocations of capital made from Governments cannot be righted by the actions of the private sector or citizens whether regulated or unregulated.

This book is a motley collection of writings. Shorn of verbiage, it is a search for harmony. In an interconnected world, the Indian financial system looks like a collection of islands. We need ferries or connected cables. This book addresses intellectual dishonesty. The honest person does not declare himself honest while the dishonest seeks cover under a host of ideas and statements.

Steps which are whimsical take away from one citizen and give it away to some other "beneficiary". The requirements of social justice need not destroy economic efficiency.

Hypocrisy prevails. Mahatma Gandhi said that happiness is in a person when thought, word and deeds are the same. How can we have a happy financial system when thoughts are not converted to deeds, deeds are those which oppose economic theory and practice and written words are different from oral orders? Hypocrisy is a declared evil which is a characteristic of a demoniac person. It requires thirty six good qualities in a person for confronting a hypocrite in power or authority.

It was French economist J B Say who said, "an entrepreneur is one who shifts resources from a lower yield to a higher yield". It is obvious that Central Government and State Government shifts resources from a higher cost to lower yield if not waste. An entrepreneurial approach within Government should focus on functions of State, economic efficiency and redistribution of income for social justice.

In the aftermath of the financial meltdown in 2008, Indian and foreign owned commercial banks in India enjoyed enormous profits. In the developed world markets, commercial banking is not as lucrative as in India as other forms of financial intermediation have reduced the opportunities of profitability. In a shocking series of development, Governments went bankrupt and commercial banks had to be taken over by Governments.

Commercial Banks in India and other forms of Investment banks and specialised banks will continue to be profitable in India in the years to come, even as new intermediation and new instruments come into public lives.

Policy and action need to be credible. Harmony as in a symphony conducted by the renowned conductor Zubin Mehta is a pleasure to watch with dedicated practiced members who are playing to notes. The market is cacophony and appears chaotic as it is meant to be; a place for competition and rivalry. So discordant notes are obvious.

Control, regulation and authority need to be in harmony with the application of knowledge. Responses and reactions are two different modes to phenomena as they arise. There is tremendous scope for application of data, information, practices and knowledge in the immediate future.

ANNEXURES

Notes to Annexures

1. (Annexure 1: Research Topics) Study and research in economics and interest rates would be a never ending topic. The research papers of Reserve Bank of India, speeches of the Governor, Deputy Governors and commentaries in the media are rich in inputs. Studies in classical, neo-classical and modern theories in economics need to show a direction for application. Authority and administration demand that adequate study and research is needed to back their decision making process. The list is therefore partial and there is scope for faculty and economists to engage in constructive study and research. The scope also extends to organisational behaviour, consumer action and policy action and atrophy.

One must appreciate the meticulous and precise guidelines and instruction to banks by RBI at all times. RBI speeches constitute intent and a detailed precise view on developments in India and globally and in constant public domain. The public must get involved in these processes. RBI constantly invites public comments and discussion. Stakeholders like borrowers and depositors and users of banking services need to understand the workings or RBI and Banks better than now. Informed debate, discussion and dialogue needs to be done at Trade Associations, Universities, dedicated public institutions, academic circles and all kinds of media.

Atrophy in policy or action needs intervention by way of all possible democratic, human and organisational means. Institutions that make human change possible will give the "maximum happiness to the maximum people for the maximum time" (Motto of Chinmaya Mission).

Policy steps are slow and incremental. There is need for measured, structural and long term changes in the direction of the banking system.

2. (Annexure 2: On Inflation By Late Professor B R Shenoy)

The responses of interest rate action against inflation and the responses of interest rates to zero and lack of inflation in OECD countries needs to be studied. The responses to inflation need to be more than increasing interest rates - production and productivity of articles of mass consumption. High interest rates deter investment in the Indian economy while low interest rates are not stimulating investment in OECD countries. The world divided by society, nations, institutions, subjects and disciplines is full of contradictions and paradoxes. There is lament that there is no inflation in Europe (in fact lurking dangers of deflation) and there is talk on inflation being high in India and refusing to come down. Can we not export inflation to Japan and Europe and reduce it in India?

The notes are picked from the treatise on inflation written by Late Professor B R Shenoy, the liberal economist, whose views on Inflation in the Indian context are both classic and contemporary. These can be applied to the current context with an analysis of the impact of black incomes.

Public clamor on price increases must vociferously demand reduction in indirect taxes and Government expenditure. Investments directed to growth in production and productivity alone will contain inflation in the medium term.

What is happening to vegetables, onions and spices today is what happened to other produce decades ago. When reading inflation there would be a gross error on the part of media to call it "food inflation" "metal inflation" and the like. What is required to be attacked is wasteful public expenditure by printed money which financed Government directly in the past and does indirectly now.

Inflation is also caused by generation of black incomes and then wealth which is used for conspicuous and wasteful consumption by the privileged few to the detriment of other citizens.

3. (Annexure 3: Open Market Operations) The Open Market Operations in the world and subjects like the massive action of the advanced countries on creation of money are beyond the comprehension of the author. Nevertheless, as there is an impact on Indian public, discussion on all these topics must necessarily go to increased penetration amongst citizenry. The extracts are from the web and should act as a stimulant. One has to appreciate the

Wikipedia and other non-profit organisations for the data and knowledge. It is worthwhile to pursue it.

4. (Annexure 4: Budget at a Glance 2014 -15) Budget papers require serious attention on the massive outgo of interest payments. This is an outcome of the creation of inflation by Government expenditure and printing of money. The latent forces that fuel inflation from budgetary deficits over years have not been addressed nor the measurement and impact of corruption, bribery and the parallel moneys in the Indian market place.

5. (Annexure 5: Budget at a Glance - Receipts 2014 -15) The most significant gap as a contingency and outgo is the effect of rupee depreciation on the foreign currency loans taken by the Government of India. This gap requires to be addressed factually as well as action to be taken. Researchers on public finance need to connect the rupee liability as show in the liabilities of India and actual liabilities shown in Annexure.

6. (Annexure 6: Receipts - Details of Current Rupee Loans of the Central Government 2014 -15) The Budget at a glance reveals an alarming increase in absolute interest payouts; thanks to the high inflation and high interest rates. A Vicious cycle needs to be turned Virtuous.

The rupee loans of Government of India outstanding as at the end of the year are presented with the budget papers. Research would be useful in interest rates on Government papers in the short tenors and the long tenors. Government of India tends to pay enormous amounts in interest every year for the next thirty years.

7. (Annexure 9: Deposit Rates of Commercial Banks) Deposit rates in India and interest rates in the world give a pointer on differences prevailing within the Indian system. The possible impact of world interest rates in the Indian context will provide corrective actions. The anomalies are seen with a wide difference in the deposit rates which are not similar in mature economies. This requires study and research to match Central Banking regulation and state policy.

The annexure on deposit rates are a matter for study and research to arrive at regulatory decisions. Deposit rates by banks will be sensitive to public opinion, competition commission, regulatory practice and self-discipline of bankers. This requires holistic study on policy influences as described in the book. The choice of instruments for savers will be a continuous study and part of conscious, unconscious and random choices of savers based on information and habits.

8. (Annexure 10: World Interest Rates) The deposit rates on interest rates in India and the world and corresponding correlation with exchange rate is continuously a research in policy as well as day to day practical area.

9. (Annexure 11: External Debt) External debt as shown in budget and the current figures in foreign currency shows the lack of provision for currency depreciation in the Statement of Assets. The burden of annual outgos in interest rates and repayments is bound to increase.

10. (Annexure 12: Acknowledgments on Interest Rate papers) Acknowledgements have encouraged the author to develop the ideas for innovation and entrepreneurship in the Indian financial sector. The book would have served its purpose if policy changes goad action and activity towards economic efficiency, encourage production and productivity in India and generate investment which in turn would enable employment, meet necessities, utilities and requirements of every Indian citizen and quality commensuration with the resource availability in India.

I
Research Topics

I. Government, Monetary Policy and Financial Sector

1. The CRR needs to be reduced to 3 per cent overnight.
2. Indian banks to be allowed to trade and deposit gold in RBI approved banks and leverage the same for external Borrowings. Banks will be permitted to borrow against these gold deposits from correspondents on hypothecation as a source of low cost borrowing for the near term.
3. Indian Government to allow commercial banks a nominal amount of Gold, say 45 to 50 metric tonnes in proportion to their assets.
4. Reserve Bank and Government of India to allow a calibrated amount of 250 metric tonnes per annum duty free, with an agreement that profits will accrue for debt redemption in foreign currency.
5. Reserve Bank and Government will begin a calibrated approach in furthering Capital Account convertibility.
6. SLR to be reduced to 18 per cent in next 5 quarters beginning January.
7. Government of India and Reserve Bank jointly announce convertible rupee treasury bills. Purchase and sale will be settled in four foreign currencies GBP, Yen, Euro and US dollar at the time of purchase and redemption.
8. Commercial Banks to have SLR only in Government securities of less than 10 years and in two areas only in less than 5 years.
9. Bank rate to be reduced to 8.5 per cent.
10. Commercial Banks are prohibited from raising deposit rates beyond.25 basis points for any tenure.
11. As a temporary measure, Commercial Banks are restricted from raising Fixed Deposits beyond 1 year.
12. Banks permitted to issue transferable and tradable bonds from 2 to 5 years at a rate regulated by RBI for next two years.

13. Differential rate of interest on any category of deposits e.g., senior citizens withdrawn.
14. RBI to begin exercises to mortgage finance as a specialty and have block rediscounting on receivable from mortgage as a secure finance.
15. Commercial Banks are required to have compulsory foreign securities as part of statutory liquidity ratio to the extent of 4 per cent of the SLR. These securities need to be in bonds of multilateral institutions.
16. Banks allowed to take current and deposit accounts up to 1 year from their correspondent banks and permitted entities in four foreign currencies and up to 25 currencies in the next one year.
17. Banks need to be allowed fungibility in the investment of Government securities and permitted carry trade.
18. ECB s in current form to be banned for next three years.
19. Indian Companies can float Dollar denominated bonds in the Indian exchanges and FIIs can be allowed to invest in Foreign Currency Bonds and Indian currency bonds.
20. Government of India and Reserve Bank can calibrate buyback of long dated bonds and extinguish them. The focus needs to be on short term bonds with an intention to reduce the interest payouts of Government of India and decrease the revenue deficit on an immediate and long term basis.
21. Sufficient liquidity to support Government disinvestment programme and enable Government to float publicly owned investment banks.
22. Long term finance and equity to focus an investment plan of Rs. 35 lakh crores in 10 years for basic needs of a growing young population.

II. Research Areas for Faculty and Students of Economics

1. Interest Rate Structure in OECD Countries and India - a Comparison and Evaluation
2. Interest Rate structure in Group of 20 - Other than OECD
3. Interest Rate structure with India's Partner countries in External Trade and Investment
4. Inflation rate and interest rate differentials—Comparison between USA and India

5. Historical Interest Rate structure in India
6. Pre-Independence, Post-Independence – Decadal
7. Pre 1991 and Post 1991 Interest rates in India
8. Interest rates and Forex Premia – Deviations
9. Research on Return on Asset and Interest rate in respect to Commercial and Household rentals in India
10. Euro Interest Rates behaviour in Europe on account of Greek Fiscal Problems
11. Interest Rates and Returns on Capital
12. Interest Outgo of Government of India and State Government - An evaluation of Revenue Expenditure
13. Interest Rate Structure in Developing Countries and India
14. India's Competitiveness and Trading Centres: Hong Kong, Singapore and Dubai Access to Capital and Cost
15. Interest Rates at Near Zero - How is Return on Capital Measured Vs Return on Capital in India
16. A Study on Interest Rate Payments by Corporates in India
17. Erosion of Citizen's Capital by the States and Centre In India
18. Inflation and Interest Rates in Developing Nations
19. A Detailed Study of Borrowings by Government: Central and State and Options for Reduction in Revenue Deficits
20. Interventions by Government in Interest Rate subsidy or provision of Capital
21. A study of Issue of Bonds: Petroleum and Fertiliser Subsidies: impact on revenue deficit due to Interest Payments
22. Are Derivatives on Interest Rates premature in Indian context?
23. A study on Causes and Cure for Inflation in India: Thinking Beyond Conventional
24. A study on The Bank Rate as a Signal for Deposit Rates
25. Study of forward Premia and Interest Rates
26. Correlation of Profit, Returns and Interest - Can innovation profits be distinguished from Return on Capital Employed?
27. Mortgage Rates in India - Case for Lower Rates of Interest

II
On Inflation

By Late Professor B.R. Shenoy

Economic development even like the growth of an infant into manhood, is not a disease to cause any inflationary upset

...

There is but one major answer to our query regarding the cause of the current phase of the price rise, as also of the worsening of the price situation.

Like the debasement of the coinage by medieval kings both are direct outcomes of reckless expenditure by the State.

...

There is little difference between debasement of the coinage and printing money.

In both cases the monetary circulation would increase

...

Prices generally rise by the extent of the increase in money supply over the national product

...

Once inflation has taken place as a result of the attempt to "invest" from non-existent resources, prices will rise. The correctives to boiling water - rising prices - is to remove from underneath it the fire of budget deficit. It is little use getting angry when prices rise or blame 'those who hoard, speculate and profiteer'. It is equally wrong to say 'raising prices for private profit in this national emergency was a treachery to the country.

...

Despicable though profiteering is, the real act of treachery lies in printing money to meet Government outlays and in misdirecting the resources of the nation in spectacular than useful channels of investment. It is this policy that has involved the double crime of retarding economic development and denying the common man the elementary needs of living.

...

We like to shout from the house tops we are a progressive people, abreast of the thinking of the enlightened part of the world in this nuclear era; yet in the field of economic and monetary policies, we often speak the language of medieval monarchs.

...

We are, instead, seeking to make the traders scapegoat. Monopolies and semi-monopolies apart, contrary to popular belief and the emphatic assertions of administrators, traders have no more control on the prices than the thermometer has on temperature.

...

Like the rest of the community traders are but creatures of prices which are determined for all by the forces of supply and demand over which individual traders have no control.

...

Inflation cannot be controlled by tampering with its consequences; nor by replacing the normal channels of trade.

...

We have undermined the currency standard by inflating the money supply, which has led to price rise.

...

A general price rise is a monetary phenomenon - the result of an expansion of money at a rate faster than the expansion of the national product

...

In 1955-56 when the current phase of inflation began, inflation was wholly due to budget deficits and the attendant secondary expansion of money by commercial banks

...

The analogy if the experience of King Canute with the rising tide will apply. To achieve price stabilization, it is imperative to pursue a policy of monetary equilibrium through correct monetary and fiscal measures.

...

Inflation is all pervasive it affects all commodities sooner or later

...

It is not practical or indeed possible to hold down prices in general when inflation drives them up.

...

Under inflation, both wholesale and retail prices move up

...

A policy of waste of public funds cannot cease to be such, or get transformed into a virtue, because it is pursued in the wake of another policy error, inflation in the name of a programme of price stabilization.

...

It is not practical to hold down individual prices in general under inflation. Any attempt to hold down individual prices would alter the price pattern and the production pattern. This will undermine price control

...

Price inflation may ensue from two factors, monetary and non-monetary. A distinction must be made between the two, if we must avoid serious policy errors

...

Non monetary factors causing price inflation

Non monetary factors include crop failure, inadequate imports, price rigging by traders who have monopoly control over stocks, global short supply of commodities, e.g. petroleum, commodity taxations, labour unrest and seasonal and other temporary shortages. These factors may drive up the prices of the individual commodities affected, of their substitutes, and, in less measure, of the manufactures based on these commodities. But as a rule – extreme cases of famine conditions in a dominantly agricultural economies apart – a general rise in commodity prices cannot arise from non – monetary factors.

...

The second factor responsible for inflation is monetary- an overall expansion of money, i.e. an expansion of money which outpaces the expansion of the national product

...

Money, like water, is all pervasive. When the expansion of money outpaces the expansion of national product, the prices of commodities in general would go up, even as the water in a tank would rise when rain in the catchment area exceeds the absorptive capacity of the soil.

...

But the price inflation problem caused by the monetary factor a never ending general rise in prices has been with us for over two decades in its current phase.

...

Importance of identifying cause of inflation

It is important to identify, as a first step, the factors responsible for the price rise which we may wish to bring under control. This identification is essential for three reasons:

(i) Though both factors – monetary and non-monetary – may operate simultaneously, they are not functionally inter-related, i.e., the operation of either factor does not involve the emergence of the other factor too.

(ii) Non Monetary factors impinge on the prices of the individual commodities affected, while the monetary factor impinges on the prices of all commodities, though the non-monetary factors may accentuate, or more than negate, the price inflation ensuing from the monetary factor.

(iii) Naturally, therefore, the remedy for price inflation would depend on the factors causing it, that is price inflation ensuing from the monetary factor cannot be corrected by non- monetary measures; and price inflation ensuing from non-monetary factors cannot be corrected by monetary measures.

Thus the Corrective to the price inflation of pulses and edible oils – which represent the working of non- monetary factors – lies in remedying the shortages through liberalizing imports or through increasing domestic production. Edible oils illustrate the efficacy of this remedy: liberalized imports of edible oils reduced the extent of the price inflation from 81 per cent in June 1977 to 28 per cent in September 1977, relative to the price position a years ago. In the case of pulses, on the other hand, price inflation deteriorated during the same period, as outside sources of supply did not exist and shortages could be corrected by increased domestic production alone. To the extent that the price rise may be attributed to the monetary factor, some price relief may, however, result from a control of money supply.

Policy Conclusions

The policy conclusions emerging from the foregoing discussion may be briefly recalled:

(i) Price inflation is of two categories, (a) that caused by monetary factors, that is by an overexpansion of money; and (b) that caused by monetary factors, for example crop failures or inadequate imports. Inflation (a) impinges on commodities in general and its extent is indicated by a rise in the General Price Index and an expansion in money supply per physical unit of the national product; and inflation (b) impinges only on the individual commodities affected. It is most important, as a first step, to identify the factors causing price inflation, as inflation (a) cannot be corrected by measures applicable to inflation (b); and inflation (b) cannot be corrected by measures applicable to inflation (a).

(ii) We have inflation of both categories in India. Price inflation of pulses, of edible oils and petroleum are examples of inflation (b); and a doubling of the General Price Index since 1968 – 69, in response to a corresponding increase in money supply per physical unit of the national product, is a case of inflation (a), which has been with us since 1954-

55, zero year of the current phase of inflation. This category of inflation has been the source many of our major ailments, among them perverse income shifts, social tensions and political unrest and instabilities.

(iii) The remedy for inflation (b) is non-monetary: increased imports and expanded domestic production.

(iv) The remedy for inflation (a) is to adjust the expansion of money to the expansion of the national product. This calls for elimination of inflationary deficit financing. This can be done in two ways: by reducing government outlays, and by increasing revenues are already excessive, and have been causing great national damage, elimination of inflationary deficit financing must be achieved through drastic cuts in expenditure and outlays.

(v) The anti-inflationary policy measures of the Congress regime date back to May 1956 and assumed blitz dimensions in 1974. Yet, they failed to make any visible dent of price inflation. The explanation lies in the efficacious measures of inflation control, more particularly, the attempts to curb money-caused inflation by non-monetary measures. If the Janata government must achieve inflation control, these fallacies of the Congress regime must be discarded.

...

It would be futile to attempt to regulate prices by issuing price control orders so long as surplus purchasing power remained in circulation and was being continually added to

.... They can amount to no more than a farce!

In the long run created money which is only meant to increase the productive capacity of the nation would not be self- liquidating character as it is sometimes believed

This line of argument is based on misconceptions about the real character of the processes through which inflationary finance operates otherwise there is no limit to prosperity to which the printing press may not take us.

...

Nor is there any device by which the evils of inflation may be securely bottled up so that the creation of capital initiated by it might continue unhampered.

...

In other words, the only, method of preventing the evils of inflation is not to indulge in it

...

As a result of the tug-of-war between the consumption and the instrumental entrepreneurs which must ensure as a result of inflationary finance, orderly progress of the economy would be impossible in a regime of created money.

...

The price level of consumption goods would consequently jump up for two reasons: short supply and higher expenditure.

The rise in the price level of consumer goods would be the beginning of the end of the projects financed by inflation

...

For a solution of the problem, we must tackle it at its roots. The futile and self-damaging effort to "invest" non-existent resources must be abandoned.

This would necessitate drastic cuts in the public sector plan outlay. This latter requirement will demand a drastic cut in the civilian expenditure charged to Revenues, for which vast scope exists.

Prof. B.R. Shenoy s statements as an erudite economist make it clear that the so le responsibility for inflation in India lies in the sphere of Government.

Source: *Theoretical Vision*, B.R. Shenoy, Edited by R.K. Amin and Parth J. Shah, Page nos: 83, 84, 85, 88, 89, 91, 92, 93, 96, 97, 99 101, 103, 105, 118, 119, 121, 126, 127.

III
Open Market Operation

An **open market operation** (also known as **OMO**) is an activity by a central bank to buy or sell government bonds on the open market. A central bank uses them as the primary means of implementing monetary policy. The usual aim of open market operations is to manipulate the short term interest rate and the supply of base money in an economy, and thus indirectly control the total money supply, in effect expanding money or contracting the money supply. This involves meeting the demand of base money at the target interest rate by buying and selling government securities, or other financial instruments. Monetary targets, such as inflation, interest rates, or exchange rates, are used to guide this implementation.

Contents

Process of Open Market

Since most money now exists in the form of electronic records rather than in the form of paper, open market operations are conducted simply by electronically increasing or decreasing (*crediting* or *debiting*) the amount of base money that a bank has in its reserve account at the central bank. Thus, the process does not literally require new currency. However, this will increase the central bank's requirement to print currency when the member bank demands banknotes, in exchange for a decrease in its electronic balance.

When there is an increased demand for base money, the central bank must act if it wishes to maintain the short-term interest rate. It does this by increasing the supply of base money. The central bank goes to the open market to buy a financial asset, such as government bonds. To pay for these assets, bank reserves in the form of new base money (for example newly printed cash) are transferred to the seller's bank and the seller's account is credited. Thus, the total amount of base money in the economy is increased. Conversely, if the central bank sells these assets in the open market, the amount of base money held by the buyer's bank is decreased, effectively reducing base money.

The process works because the central bank has the authority to bring money in and out of existence. They are the only point in the whole system with the unlimited ability to produce money. Another organization may be able to influence the open market for a period time, but the central bank will always be able to overpower their influence with an infinite supply of money.

Possible Targets

(ii) Under inflation targeting, open market operations target a specific short term interest rate in the debt markets. This target is changed periodically to achieve and maintain an inflation rate within a target range. However, other variants of monetary policy also often target interest rates: the US Federal Reserve, the Bank of England and the European Central Bank use variations on interest rate targets to guide open market operations.

(iii) Besides interest rate targeting there are other possible targets of open markets operations. A second possible target is the contraction of the money supply, as was the case in the U.S. in the late 1970s through the early 1980s under Fed Chairman Paul Volcker.

(iv) Under a currency board open market operations would be used to achieve and maintain a fixed exchange rate with relation to some foreign currency.

(v) Under a gold standard, notes would be convertible to gold, so there would be no open market operations. However, open market operations could be used to keep the value of a fiat currency constant relative to gold.

(vi) A central bank can also use a mixture of policy settings that change depending on circumstances. A central bank may peg its exchange rate (like a currency board) with different levels or forms of commitment. The looser the exchange rate peg, the more latitude the central bank has to target other variables (such as interest rates). It may instead target a basket of foreign currencies rather than a single currency. In some instances it is empowered to use additional means other than open market operations, such as hanges in reserve requirements or capital controls, to achieve monetary outcomes.

How Open Market Operations are Conducted

United States

In the United States, as of 2006, the Federal Reserve sets an interest rate target for the Federal funds (overnight bank reserves) market. When the actual Federal funds rate is higher than the target, the New York Reserve Bank will usually increase the money supply via a repo (effectively borrowing from the dealers' perspective; lending for the Reserve Bank). When the actual Federal funds rate is less than the target, the Bank will usually decrease the money supply via a reverse repo (effectively lending from the dealers' perspective; borrowing for the Reserve Bank).

In the U.S., the Federal Reserve most commonly uses overnight repurchase agreements (repos) to temporarily create money, or reverse repos to temporarily destroy money, which offset temporary changes in the level of bank reserves. The Federal Reserve also makes outright purchases and sales of securities through the System Open Market Account (SOMA) with its manager over the Trading Desk at the New York Reserve Bank. The trade of securities in the SOMA changes the balance of bank reserves, which also affects short term interest rates. The SOMA manager is responsible for trades that result in a short term interest rate near the target rate set by the Federal Open Market Committee (FOMC), or create money by the outright purchase of securities. More rarely will it permanently destroy money by the outright sale of securities. These trades are made with a group of about 22 (currently 18 as an immediate aftermath of 08/09 credit crisis) banks or bond dealers that are called primary dealers.

Money is created or destroyed by changing the reserve account of the bank with the Federal Reserve. The Federal Reserve has conducted open market operations in this manner since the 1920s, through the Open Market Desk at the Federal Reserve Bank of New York, under the direction of the Federal Open Market Committee. The open market operation is also a means through which inflation can be controlled because when treasury bills are sold to commercial banks these banks can no longer give out loans to the public for the period and therefore money is being reduced from circulation.

Eurozone

The European Central Bank has similar mechanisms for their operations; it describes its methods as a four-tiered approach with different goals: beside its main goal of steering and smoothing Eurozone interest rates while managing the liquidity situation in the market the ECB also has the aim of signaling the stance of monetary policy with its operations.

Broadly speaking, the ECB controls liquidity in the banking system via Refinancing Operations, which are basically repurchase agreements, i.e. banks put up acceptable collateral with the ECB and receive a cash loan in return. These are the following main categories of refinancing operations that can be employed depending on the desired outcome:

- The regular weekly main refinancing operations (MRO) with maturity of one week and,
- The monthly longer-term refinancing operations (LTRO) provide liquidity to the financial sector, while ad-hoc
- "Fine-tuning operations" (in the form of reverse or outright transactions, foreign exchange swaps and the collection of fixed-term deposits) aim to smooth interest rates caused by liquidity fluctuations in the market and
- "Structural operations" are used to adjust the central banks' longer-term structural positions vis-a-vis the financial sector.

Refinancing operations are conducted via an auction mechanism. The ECB specifies the amount of liquidity it wishes to auction (called the allotted amount) and asks banks for expressions of interest. In a fixed rate tender the ECB also specifies the interest rate at which it is willing to lend money; alternatively, in a variable rate tender the interest rate is not specified and banks bid against each other (subject to a minimum bid rate specified by the ECB) to access the available liquidity.

MRO auctions are held on Mondays, with settlement (i.e. disbursal of the funds) occurring the following Wednesday. For example at its auction on 2008 October 6, the ECB made available 250 million in EUR on October 8 at a minimum rate of 4.25 per cent. It received 271 million in bids, and the allotted amount (250) was awarded at an average weighted rate of 4.99 per cent.

Since mid-October 2008, however, the ECB has been following a different procedure on a temporary basis, the fixed rate MRO with full allotment. In this case the ECB specifies the rate but not the amount of credit made available, and banks can request as much as they wish (subject as always to being able to provide sufficient collateral). This procedure was made necessary by the financial crisis of 2008 and is expected to end at some time in the future.

Though the ECB's main refinancing operations (MRO) are from repo auctions with a (bi)weekly maturity and monthly maturation, Long Term Refinancing Operations (LTROs) are also issued, which traditionally mature after three months; since 2008, tenders are now offered for six months, 12 months and 36 months.

Switzerland

The Swiss National Bank currently targets the 3 month Swiss franc LIBOR rate. The primary way the SNB influences the 3 month Swiss franc LIBOR rate is through open market operations, with the most important monetary policy instrument being repo transactions.

India

India's Open Market Operation is much influenced by the fact that it is a developing country and that the capital flows are much different than those in the other developed countries. Thus Reserve Bank Of India, being the Central Bank of the country, has to make policies and use instruments accordingly. Prior to the 1991 financial reforms, RBI's major source of funding and control over credit and interest rates was the CRR (Cash reserve ratio) and the SLR (Statutory Liquidity Ratio). But after the reforms, the use of CRR as an effective tool was de-emphasized and the use of open market operations increased. OMO's are more effective in adjusting market liquidity.

The two traditional type of OMO's used by RBI:

1. Outright purchase (PEMO): Is outright buying or selling of government securities. (Permanent).
2. Repurchase agreement (REPO): Is short term, and are subject to repurchase.

However, even after sidelining CRR as an instrument, there was still less liquidity and skewedness in the market. And thus, on the recommendations of the Narsimham Committee Report (1998), The RBI brought together a Liquidity Adjustment Facility (LAF). It commenced in June, 2000, and it was set up to oversee liquidity on a daily basis and to monitor market interest rates. For the LAF, two rates are set by the RBI: repo rate and reverse repo rate. The repo rate is applicable while selling securities to RBI (daily injection of liquidity), while the reverse repo rate is applicable when banks buy back those securities (daily absorption of liquidity). Also, these interest rates fixed by the RBI also help in determining other market interest rates.

India experiences large capital inflows every day, and even though the OMO and the LAF policies were able to withhold the inflows, another instrument was needed to keep the liquidity intact. Thus, on the recommendations of the Working Group of RBI on instruments of Sterilization (December, 2003), a new scheme known as the Market stabilization scheme (MSS) was set up. The LAF and the OMO's were dealing with day to day liquidity management, whereas the MSS was set up to sterilize the liquidity absorption and make it more enduring.

According to this scheme, the RBI issues additional T-bills and securities to absorb the liquidity. And the money goes into the Market Stabilization scheme Account (MSSA). The RBI cannot use this account for paying any interest or discounts and cannot credit any premiums to this account. The Government, in collaboration with the RBI, fixes a ceiling amount on the issue of these instruments.

But for an open market operation instrument to be effective, there has to be an active securities market for RBI to make any kind of effect on the liquidity and rates of interest.

IV
Budget at a Glance

(In crore of Rupees)

	2012-2013 Actuals	2013-2014 Budget Estimates	2013-2014 Revised Estimates	2014-2015 Budget Estimates
1. Revenue Receipts	**879232**	**1056331**	**1029252**	**1189763**
2. Tax Revenue (net to centre)	741877	884078	836026	977258
3. Non-Tax Revenue	137355	172252	193226	212505
4. Capital Receipts (5+6+7)	**531140**	**608967**	**561182**	**605129**
5. Recoveries of Loans	15060	10654	10802	10527
6. Other Receipts	25890	55814	25841	63425
7. Borrowings and other liabilities *	490190	542499	524539	531177
8. Total Receipts (1+4)	**1410372**	**1665297**	**1590434**	**1794892**
9. Non-Plan Expenditure	**996747**	**1109975**	**1114902**	**1219892**
10. On Revenue Account of which,	914306	992908	1027689	1114609
11. Interest Payments	313170	370684	380066	427011
12. On Capital Account	82441	117067	87214	105283
13. Plan Expenditure	**413625**	**555322**	**475532**	**575000**
14. On Revenue Account	329208	443260	371851	453503
15. On Capital Account	84417	112062	103681	121497
16. Total Expenditure (9+13)	**1410372**	**1665297**	**1590434**	**1794892**
17. Revenue Expenditure (10+14)	1243514	1436169	1399540	1568111
18. Of Which, Grants for creation of Capital Assets	115710	174633	138228	168104
19. Capital Expenditure (12+15)	166858	229129	190894	226781
20. Revenue Deficit (17-1)	**364282 (3.6)**	**379838 (3.3)**	**370288 (3.3)**	**378348 (2.9)**
21. Effective Revenue Deficit (20-18)	**248572 (2.5)**	**205205 (1.8)**	**232060 (2.0)**	**210244 (1.6)**
22. Fiscal Deficit {16-(1+5+6)}	**490190 (4.8)**	**542499 (4.8)**	**524539 (4.6)**	**531177 (4.1)**

(Contd.)

	2012-2013 Actuals	2013-2014 Budget Estimates	2013-2014 Revised Estimates	2014-2015 Budget Estimates
23. Primary Deficit (22-11)	**177020 (1.8)**	**171814 (1.5)**	**144473 (1.3)**	**104166 (0.8)**

cé* Actuals for 2012-13 in this document are provisional.

Excluding receipts under Market Stabilisation Scheme. Includes draw-down of Cash Balance.

Notes

1. GDP for BE 2014-2015 has been projected at ₹ 12876653 crore assuming 13.4 per cent growth over the Advance Estimates of 2013-2014 (₹ 11355073 crore) released by CSO.
2. Individual items in this document may not sum up to the totals due to rounding off.

V
Receipts

(In crore of Rupees)

	2012-2013 Actuals	2013-2014 Budget Estimates	2013-2014 Revised Estimates	2014-2015 Budget Estimates
REVENUE RECEIPTS				
1. Tax Revenue				
Gross Tax Revenue	**1036235**	**1235870**	**1158906**	**1364524**
Corporation Tax	356326	419520	393677	451005
Taxes on Income	201487	247639	241691	284266
Wealth Tax	846	950	950	950
Customs	165346	187308	175056	201819
Union Excise Duties	176535	197554	179538	207110
Service Tax	132601	180141	164927	215973
Taxes of Union Territories	3094	2758	3067	3401
Less - NCCD transferred to the National Calamity Contingency Fund/National Disaster Response Fund	*2810*	*4800*	*4650*	*5050*
Less - States' share	**291547**	**346992**	**318230**	**382216**
1(a) Centre's Net Tax Revenue	**741877**	**884078**	**836026**	**977258**
2. Non-Tax Revenue				
Interest receipts	20761	17764	21018	19751
Dividend and Profits	53761	73866	88188	90229
External Grants	2311	1456	3135	2405
Other Non Tax Revenue	59405	78000	79788	99009
Receipts of Union Territories	1117	1166	1097	1111
Total Non Tax Revenue	**137355**	**172252**	**193226**	**212505**
Total Revenue Receipts (1a+2)	***879232***	***1056331***	***1029252***	***1189763***
3. Capital Receipts				
A. Non-debt Receipts				
Recoveries of loans and advances[@]	15060	10654	10802	10527

	2012-2013 Actuals	2013-2014 Budget Estimates	2013-2014 Revised Estimates	2014-2015 Budget Estimates
Miscellaneous Capital Receipts	25890	55814	25841	63425
Total	**40950**	**66468**	**36643**	**73952**
B. Debt Receipts*				
Market Loans	467356	484000	453902	461205
Short term borrowings	53350	19844	22678	34553
External Assistance (Net)	7201	10560	5440	5734
Securities issued against Small Savings	8626	5798	11605	8229
State Provident Fund (Net)	10920	10000	10000	12000
Other Receipts (Net)	-6252	12297	5914	-7704
Total	***541202***	***542499***	***509539***	***514017***
Total Capital Receipts (A+B)	**582152**	**608967**	**546182**	**587969**
4. DRAW-DOWN OF CASH BALANCE	**-51012**	**...**	**15000**	**17160**
Total Receipts (1a+2+3+4)	***1410372***	***1665297***	***1590434***	***1794892***
Financing of Fiscal Deficit (3B+4)	**490190**	**542499**	**524539**	**531177**
Receipts under MSS (Net)	**...**	**20000**	**...**	**20000**

@ excludes recoveries of short-term loans and advances from States, loans to Government servants, etc.	11564	11400	13505	12290

* The receipts are net of repayments.

VI

Receipts Budget, 2014-2015

Details of Current Rupee Loans of the Central Government

(In crores of Rupees)

Name of Loan	Earliest date of maturity	As at the end of 1950-1951	As at the end of 2009-2010	As at the end of 2010-2011	As at the end of 2011-2012	As at the end of 2012-2013	Revised 2013-2014	Budget 2014-2015
(1)	(2)	(3)	(4)	(5)	(6)	(7)	(8)	(9)
Market Loans								
3.00% Loan, 1951-54	15.09.1951	86.73	...	...	...	...	...	...
3.00% Loan, 1953-55	15.07.1953	114.60	...	...	...	...	...	...
2.25% Loan, 1954	15.11.1954	35.06	...	...	...	...	...	...
3.50% Loan, 1954-59	15.12.1954	12.87	...	...	...	...	...	...
4.50% Loan, 1955-60	15.09.1955	9.06	...	...	...	...	...	...
2.50% Loan, 1955	01.10.1955	60.45	...	...	...	...	...	...
3.00% Victory Loan, 1957	01.09.1957	114.07	...	...	...	...	...	...
4.50% Loan, 1958-68	01.06.1958	5.85	...	...	...	...	...	...
3.00% Second Victory Loan, 1959-61.	15.08.1959	113.66	...	...	...	...	...	...
2.75% Loan, 1960	15.07.1960	45.63	...	...	...	...	...	...
4.00% Loan, 1960-70	15.09.1960	63.30	...	...	...	...	...	...

(1)	(2)	(3)	(4)	(5)	(6)	(7)	(8)	(9)
2.50% Loan, 1961	01.08.1961	57.01	...	...	...	...	...	...
2.75% Loan, 1962	15.11.1962	75.87	...	...	...	...	...	...
3.00% Loan, 1963-65.	01.06.1963	116.17	...	...	...	...	...	...
3.00% Loan, 1964	15.06.1964	30.33	...	...	...	...	...	...
3.00% Funding Loan, 1966-68	01.10.1966	110.12	...	...	...	...	...	...
3.00% First Development Loan, 1970-75	15.10.1970	115.06	...	...	...	...	...	...
2.75% Loan, 1976	16.09.1976	14.77	...	...	...	...	...	...
7.50% Loan, 2010	12.05.2010	...	1456.22	...	...	...	...	...
7.55% Government Stock, 2010	14.05.2010	...	23000.00	...	...	...	...	...
11.50% Loan, 2010	11.06.2010	...	7152.81	...	...	...	...	...
12.25% Government Stock, 2010	02.07.2010	...	15515.00	...	...	...	...	...
11.30% Government Stock, 2010	28.07.2010	...	33683.00	...	...	...	...	...
8.75% Loan, 2010	13.12.2010	...	500.22	...	...	...	...	...
12.32% Government Stock, 2011	29.01.2011	...	9462.00	...	...	...	...	...
6.57% Government Stock, 2011(PP)	24.02.2011	...	20817.00	...	...	...	...	...
8.00% Loan, 2011	27.04.2011	...	1472.92	1472.92	...	...	...	...
10.95% Government Stock, 2011	30.05.2011	...	12000.00	12000.00	...	...	...	...
9.39% Government Stock, 2011	02.07.2011	...	37000.00	37000.00	...	...	...	...
11.50% Loan, 2011	05.08.2011	...	2861.36	2861.36	...	...	...	...
Govt. of India Floating Rate Bonds, 2011	08.08.2011	...	6000.00	6000.00	...	...	...	...
12.00% Loan, 2011	21.10.2011	...	3246.91	3246.91	...	...	...	...
11.50% Government Stock, 2011	24.11.2011	...	11000.00	11000.00	...	...	...	...
6.85% Government Stock, 2012	05.04.2012	...	15000.00	26000.00	26000.00	...	...	...

(1)	(2)	(3)	(4)	(5)	(6)	(7)	(8)	(9)
7.40% Government Stock, 2012	03.05.2012	...	33000.00	33000.00	33000.00	...	...	
10.25% Loan, 2012	01.06.2012	...	1574.13	1574.13	1574.13	...	...	...
6.72% Government Stock, 2007/12	18.07.2012	...	546.81	546.81	541.81	...	...	...
11.03% Government Stock, 2012	18.07.2012	...	13500.00	13500.00	13500.00	...	...	...
9.40% Government Stock, 2012	11.09.2012	...	11000.00	11000.00	11000.00	...	...	...
Govt. of India Floating Rate Bonds, 2012	10.11.2012	...	5000.00	5000.00	5000.00	...	...	...
9.00% Loan, 2013	24.05.2013	...	1751.33	1751.33	1751.33	1751.33	...	...
9.81% Government Stock, 2013	30.05.2013	...	11000.00	11000.00	11000.00	11000.00	...	...
12.40% Government Stock, 2013	20.08.2013	...	11983.91	11983.91	11983.91	11983.91	...	...
7.27% Government Stock, 2013	03.09.2013	...	42000.00	42000.00	42000.00	42000.00	...	...
Govt. of India Floating Rate Bonds, 2013	10.09.2013	...	4000.00	4000.00	4000.00	4000.00	...	...
5.32% Government Stock, 2014	16.02.2014	...	5000.00	5000.00	5000.00	5000.00	...	...
6.72% Government Stock, 2014	24.02.2014	...	15273.60	15273.60	15273.60	15273.60	...	...
7.37% Government Stock, 2014	16.04.2014	...	37000.00	37000.00	37000.00	37000.00	35778.63	...
6.07% Government Stock, 2014	15.05.2014	...	40000.00	40000.00	40000.00	40000.00	38548.20	...
Govt. of India Floating Rate Bonds, 2014	20.05.2014	...	5000.00	5000.00	5000.00	5000.00	5000.00	...
10.00% Loan, 2014	30.05.2014	...	2333.26	2333.26	2333.26	2333.26	1552.08	...
7.32% Government Stock 2014	20.10.2014	...	18000.00	18000.00	18000.00	18000.00	18000.00	...
10.50% Loan, 2014	29.10.2014	...	1755.10	1755.10	1755.10	1755.10	1303.83	...
7.56% Government Stock 2014	03.11.2014	...	41000.00	41000.00	41000.00	41000.00	40845.08	...
11.83% Government Stock, 2014	12.11.2014	...	11500.00	11500.00	11500.00	11500.00	6259.76	...
10.47% Government Stock, 2015	12.02.2015	...	6430.00	6430.00	6430.00	6430.00	4390.98	...
10.79% Government Stock, 2015	19.05.2015	...	2683.45	2683.45	2683.45	2683.45	1052.06	999.37

(1)	(2)	(3)	(4)	(5)	(6)	(7)	(8)	(9)
11.50% Loan, 2015	21.05.2015	...	3560.50	3560.50	3560.50	3560.50	2387.91	1899.16
6.49% Government Stock, 2015	08.06.2015	...	40000.00	40000.00	40000.00	40000.00	39500.66	39500.14
7.17% Government Stock, 2015	14.06.2015	...	...	56000.00	56000.00	56000.00	55450.00	55449.93
Govt. of India Floating Rate Bonds, 2015	02.07.2015	...	6000.00	6000.00	6000.00	6000.00	6000.00	6000.00
11.43% Government Stock, 2015	07.08.2015	...	12000.00	12000.00	12000.00	12000.00	8192.87	7204.30
Govt. of India Floating Rate Bonds, 2015 II	10.08.2015	...	6000.00	6000.00	6000.00	6000.00	6000.00	6000.00
7.38% Government Stock, 2015	03.09.2015	...	39000.00	58000.00	58000.00	58000.00	54744.92	54386.74
9.85% Government Stock, 2015	16.10.2015	...	10000.00	10000.00	10000.00	10000.00	7654.00	7437.78
7.59% Government Stock, 2016	12.04.2016	...	50000.00	50000.00	68000.00	68000.00	68000.00	68000.00
10.71% Government Stock, 2016	19.04.2016	...	9000.00	9000.00	9000.00	9000.00	9000.00	9000.00
Govt. of India Floating Rate Bonds, 2016	07.05.2016	...	6000.00	6000.00	6000.00	6000.00	6000.00	6000.00
5.59% Government Stock, 2016	04.06.2016	...	6000.00	6000.00	6000.00	6000.00	6000.00	6000.00
12.30% Government Stock, 2016	02.07.2016	...	13129.84	13129.84	13129.84	13129.84	13129.84	13129.84
7.02% Government Stock, 2016	17.08.2016	...	39000.00	60000.00	60000.00	60000.00	60000.00	60000.00
8.07% Government Stock, 2017	15.01.2017	...	49000.00	49000.00	69000.00	69000.00	69000.00	69000.00
7.49% Government Stock, 2017	16.04.2017	...	43000.00	53000.00	53000.00	53000.00	53000.00	53000.00
Govt. of India Floating Rate Bonds, 2017	02.07.2017	...	3000.00	3000.00	3000.00	3000.00	3000.00	3000.00
8.07% Government Stock, 2017	03.07.2017	...	...	...	...	50000.00	50000.00	50000.00
7.99% Government Stock, 2017	09.07.2017	...	34000.00	59000.00	71000.00	71000.00	71000.00	71000.00
7.46% Government Stock, 2017	28.08.2017	...	36886.80	57886.80	57886.80	57886.80	57886.80	57886.80
6.25% Government Stock, 2018	02.01.2018	...	10886.80	10886.80	10886.80	10886.80	10886.80	10886.80
7.83% Government Stock, 2018	11.04.2018	...	...	...	64000.00	64000.00	73000.00	73000.00
8.24% Government Stock, 2018	22.04.2018	...	50000.00	50000.00	56000.00	75000.00	75000.00	75000.00

(1)	(2)	(3)	(4)	(5)	(6)	(7)	(8)	(9)
10.45% Government Stock, 2018	30.04.2018	...	3716.00	3716.00	3716.00	3716.00	3716.00	3716.00
5.69% Government Stock, 2013	25.09.2018	...	10000.00	10000.00	10000.00	10000.00	10000.00	10000.00
12.60% Government Stock, 2018	23.11.2018	...	12631.88	12631.88	12631.88	12631.88	12631.88	12631.88
5.64% Government Stock, 2019	02.01.2019	...	10000.00	10000.00	10000.00	10000.00	10000.00	10000.00
6.05% Government Stock 2019	02.02.2019	...	53000.00	53000.00	53000.00	53000.00	53000.00	53000.00
7.28% Government Stock 2019	03.06.2019	...	...	...	...	...	53000.00	53000.00
6.05% Government Stock, 2019	12.06.2019	...	4000.00	4000.00	4000.00	4000.00	4000.00	4000.00
6.90% Government Stock, 2019	13.07.2019	...	45000.00	45000.00	45000.00	45000.00	45000.00	45000.00
10.03% Government Stock, 2019	09.08.2019	...	6000.00	6000.00	6000.00	6000.00	6000.00	6000.00
6.35% Government Stock, 2020	02.01.2020	...	51000.00	56000.00	56000.00	56000.00	56000.00	56000.00
8.19% Government Stock, 2020	16.01.2020	...	...	...	14000.00	74000.00	74000.00	74000.00
10.70% Government Stock, 2020	22.04.2020	...	6000.00	6000.00	6000.00	6000.00	6000.00	6000.00
7.80% Government Stock, 2020	03.05.2020	...	...	60000.00	60000.00	60000.00	60000.00	60000.00
Govt. of India Floating Rate Bonds, 2020	21.12.2020	...	5000.00	8000.00	13000.00	13000.00	13000.00	13000.00
8.12% Government Stock, 2020	10.12.2020	...	...	...	...	13000.00	76000.00	76000.00
11.60% Government Stock, 2020	27.12.2020	...	5000.00	5000.00	5000.00	5000.00	5000.00	5000.00
7.80% Government Stock, 2021	11.04.2021	...	...	...	68000.00	68000.00	68000.00	68000.00
7.94% Government Stock, 2021	24.05.2021	...	49000.00	49000.00	49000.00	49000.00	49000.00	49000.00
10.25% Government Stock, 2021	30.05.2021	...	26213.32	26213.32	26213.32	26213.32	26213.32	26213.32

(1)	(2)	(3)	(4)	(5)	(6)	(7)	(8)	(9)
8.79% Government Stock, 2021	08.11.2021	...	...	...	56000.00	83000.00	83000.00	83000.00
8.20% Government Stock, 2022	15.02.2022	...	23000.00	56000.00	56000.00	56000.00	56000.00	56000.00
8.35% Government Stock, 2022	14.05.2022	...	44000.00	44000.00	44000.00	44000.00	44000.00	44000.00
8.15% Government Stock, 2022	11.06.2022	...	...	...	...	70000.00	83000.00	83000.00
8.08% Government Stock, 2022	02.08.2022	...	...	28000.00	59000.00	59000.00	59000.00	59000.00
8.13% Government Stock, 2022	21.09.2022	...	...	35000.00	68000.00	68000.00	68000.00	68000.00
6.30% Government Stock, 2023	09.04.2023	...	13000.00	13000.00	13000.00	13000.00	13000.00	13000.00
7.16% Government Stock, 2023	20.05.2023	...	...	...	...	...	77000.00	77000.00
6.17% Government Stock, 2023	12.06.2023	...	6000.00	6000.00	6000.00	6000.00	6000.00	6000.00
8.83% Government Stock, 2023	25.11.2023	...	...	...	...	...	33000.00	33000.00
7.35% Government Stock, 2024	22.06.2024	...	10000.00	10000.00	10000.00	10000.00	10000.00	10000.00
9.15% Government Stock, 2024	14.11.2024	...	...	...	48000.00	92000.00	92000.00	92000.00
8.20% Government Stock, 2025	24.09.2025	...	...	...	...	59000.00	90000.00	90000.00
8.33% Government Stock, 2026	09.07.2026	...	...	...	...	60000.00	90000.00	90000.00
10.18% Government Stock, 2026	11.09.2026	...	15000.00	15000.00	15000.00	15000.00	15000.00	15000.00
8.24% Government Stock, 2027	15.02.2027	...	50000.00	53000.00	53000.00	53000.00	72000.00	72000.00
8.26% Government Stock, 2027	02.08.2027	...	...	51000.00	72000.00	72000.00	72000.00	72000.00
8.28% Government Stock 2027	21.09.2027	...	...	...	25000.00	35000.00	74000.00	74000.00
6.01% Government Stock, 2028	25.03.2028	...	15000.00	15000.00	15000.00	15000.00	15000.00	15000.00
6.13% Government Stock, 2028	04.06.2028	...	11000.00	11000.00	11000.00	11000.00	11000.00	11000.00
9.20% Government Stock, 2030	30.09.2030	...	...	...	...	...	17000.00	17000.00
8.97% Government Stock, 2030	05.12.2030	...	...	...	19000.00	73000.00	90000.00	90000.00
8.28% Government Stock, 2032	15.02.2032	...	39000.00	50000.00	62000.00	76000.00	88000.00	88000.00

(1)	(2)	(3)	(4)	(5)	(6)	(7)	(8)	(9)
8.32% Government Stock, 2032	02.08.2032	...	...	13000.00	13000.00	13000.00	60000.00	60000.00
7.95% Government Stock, 2032	28.08.2032	...	59000.00	59000.00	59000.00	59000.00	59000.00	59000.00
7.50% Government Stock, 2034	10.08.2034	...	60000.00	60000.00	60000.00	60000.00	60000.00	60000.00
Govt. of India Floating Rate Bonds, 2035	25.01.2035	...	350.00	350.00	350.00	350.00	350.00	350.00
7.40% Government Stock, 2035	09.09.2035	...	42000.00	42000.00	42000.00	42000.00	52000.00	52000.00
8.33% Government Stock, 2036	07.06.2036	...	59000.00	59000.00	59000.00	86000.00	86000.00	86000.00
6.83% Government Stock, 2039	19.01.2039	...	13000.00	13000.00	13000.00	13000.00	13000.00	13000.00
8.30% Government Stock, 2040	02.07.2040	...	...	32000.00	72000.00	72000.00	72000.00	72000.00
8.83% Government Stock, 2041	12.12.2041	...	...	...	18000.00	60000.00	90000.00	90000.00
8.30% Government Stock, 2042	31.12.2042	...	...	...	...	9000.00	56000.00	56000.00
9.23% Government Stock, 2043	23.12.2043	...	...	...	...	...	35011.92	39472.28
3.00% Loan, 1896-97		8.93	...	...	...	...	...	...
3.00% Conversion Loan, 1946		248.92	...	...	...	...	...	...
Loans matured but not collected by the holders till the end of the year		6.49	618.83	654.02	439.00	413.09	413.19	413.10
Difference under Investigation/ Reconciliation			24.97	-9.51	3.06	0.92	0.94	0.92
Adjustment on account of buyback and switching of securities in the intervening period of RE and Regular Budget		...	...	...	...	...	...	527.98
Buy Back of Securities in 2013-14		...	...	...	...	...	-15000.00	...
Switching of Securities in 2013-14								

(1)	(2)	(3)	(4)	(5)	(6)	(7)	(8)	(9)
(Rs. 2000 crore each from O/s of 2014-15 and 2015-16)			...	...	...	...	-4000.00	...
Issue of Securities in lieu of Switching		...	...	...	...	...	4000.00	50000.00
Estimated Borrowings in 2014-15		...	...	...	...	...	...	600000.00
Buy Back/Switching of Securities in 2014-15		...	...	...	...	...	...	-50000.00
Loans floated under Market Stabilisation Scheme		...	2737.00	2737.00	...	...	...	20000.00
7.55% Government Stock 2010(RI)	14.05.2010	...	2420.00	2420.00	...	...	...	...
11.30% Government Stock 2010(RI)	28.07.2010	...	317.00	317.00	...	...	...	...
Estimated Borrowings in 2013-14		...	...	...	...	...	...	20000.00
TOTAL-CURRENT LOANS								
(Excluding loans under MSS)		**1444.95**	**1734517.97**	**2059932.43**	**2496143.79**	**2963499.80**	**3414901.67**	**3881106.34**

VII

Receipts Budget, 2014-2015

STATEMENT OF ASSETS
(Capital Investments and Loans by the Central Government)

(In crores of Rupees)

At the end of:

		Accounts				(provisional)	Revised	Budget
		1950-1951	2009-2010	2010-2011	2011-2012	2012-2013	2013-2014	2014-2015
(1)	**(2)**	**(3)**	**(4)**	**(5)**	**(6)**	**(7)**	**(8)**	**(9)**
A.	**Capital Outlay**							
1.	**General Services**	**496.74**	**421898.65**	**492831.88**	**569010.36**	**648488.91**	**736569.70**	**844213.06**
	(i) Defence Services	260.93	383669.14	445725.14	513627.52	584126.64	662998.87	757586.82
	(ii) Other General Services	235.81	38229.51	47106.74	55382.84	64362.27	73570.83	86626.24
2.	**Social Services**	**26.25**	**20436.86**	**24533.02**	**29115.93**	**34226.12**	**38203.37**	**44933.75**
3.	**Economic Services**	**965.02**	**458542.83**	**520919.95**	**579805.35**	**642947.52**	**683228.85**	**726786.19**
	(i) Agriculture and Allied Activities	7.78	9351.95	9675.72	11253.92	12927.30	13767.21	14196.07
	(ii) Rural Development	...	67.58	69.66	70.84	72.36	72.36	72.36
	(iii) Special Areas Programme	...	3580.37	3725.37	3894.02	4438.40	8366.46	13077.52

(1)	(2)	(3)	(4)	(5)	(6)	(7)	(8)	(9)
	(iv) Water and Power Development	5.59	61693.74	59869.56	62804.02	63856.08	64337.17	65097.76
	(a) Irrigation & Flood Control	5.59	406.43	433.07	468.86	497.56	515.26	593.79
	(b) Energy	...	61287.31	59436.49	62335.16	63358.52	63821.91	64503.97
	(v) Industry and Minerals	34.34	53011.75	54252.30	56777.72	56898.22	59951.85	64968.21
	(vi) Transport	830.40	179410.59	208788.12	239584.02	275945.11	322613.78	374466.52
	(a) Railways	817.93	67419.52	130375.86	150389.30	174521.19	201521.19	231621.19
	(b) Other Transport Services	12.47	111991.07	78412.26	89194.72	101423.92	121092.59	142845.33
	(vii) Communication	49.98	9433.14	10383.11	10844.39	13380.02	14853.49	19413.18
	(a) Postal Services	49.98	2240.38	2514.11	2724.34	2870.61	3132.55	3604.09
	(b) Telecommunications Services	...	4718.39	4718.39	4742.39	4742.39	5628.96	6825.11
	(c) Other Communications Services	...	2474.37	3150.61	3377.66	5767.02	6091.98	8983.98
	(viii) Science & Technology and Environment	...	14082.49	16495.98	18656.14	21094.05	24307.74	28953.11
	(ix) General Economic Services	36.93	127911.22	157660.13	175920.28	194335.98	174958.79	146541.46
Disbursement of UT's		...	...	...	...	...	1253.39	2887.89
Grand Total		***1488.01***	***900878.34***	***1038284.85***	***1177931.64***	***1325662.55***	***1459255.31***	***1618820.89***
B. Loans advanced by the Central Government								
State Governments		195.58	143152.16	144169.86	143547.65	144812.42	147384.23	150709.60
Union Territory Governments		...	895.12	848.69	804.21	4087.53	4015.14	3960.83
Foreign Governments		0.01	4037.40	4232.19	4977.77	6538.77	7781.48	10568.29
Investment in Special Securities of States under NSSF		...	482762.05	526062.56	517276.72	517221.27	517752.10	512954.12

(1)	(2)	(3)	(4)	(5)	(6)	(7)	(8)	(9)
Investment of NSSF in other Instruments		...	1500.00	1500.00	1500.00	1500.00	1500.00	1500.00
Public Sector Enterprises, Railway								
Reserve Fund, Port Trusts, Municipalities and Statutory Bodies Co-operative & Educational Inst., Displaced Persons and Private Inst. etc.		24.58	70304.07	78324.99	80210.26	80096.39	86210.32	93352.41
Government Servants		0.51	1277.68	1080.71	895.10	729.86	554.86	379.86
TOTAL		**220.68**	**703928.48**	**756219.00**	**749211.71**	**754986.24**	**765198.13**	**773425.11**
Total-Capital Outlay and Loans								
Advanced by the Cen. Govt.		**1708.69**	**1604806.82**	**1794503.85**	**1927143.35**	**2080648.79**	**2224453.44**	**2392246.00**
Cash balance under MSS		**...**	**2737.00**	**...**	**...**	**...**	**...**	**20000.00**
Grand Total		***1708.69***	***1607543.82***	***1794503.85***	***1927143.35***	***2080648.79***	***2224453.44***	***2412246.00***
Excess of Liabilities over Capital Outlay								
and Loans Advanced		856.71	1922116.08	2143970.06	2589808.62	2989642.93	3362695.89	3810111.55
Total		**2565.40**	**3529659.90**	**3938473.91**	**4516951.97**	**5070291.72**	**5587149.33**	**6222357.55**

* Balances are according to book value.

VIII

Receipts Budget 2014 -2015

Statement of Liabilities of the Central Government

As at the end of .... (in crores of rupees)

	Accounts				(provisional)	Revised	Budget
	1950-1951	**2009-2010**	**2010-2011**	**2011-2012**	**2012-2013**	**2013-2014**	**2014-2015**
(1)	**(2)**	**(3)**	**(4)**	**(5)**	**(6)**	**(7)**	**(8)**
A. Public Debt	**2054.33**	**2462422.05**	**2824753.92**	**3400709.83**	**3941854.81**	**4433025.81**	**4960065.15**
1. Internal Debt	**2022.30**	**2328338.90**	**2667114.82**	**3230622.22**	**3764566.00**	**4250296.51**	**4771602.07**
(i) of which under MSS	...	2737.00	...	...	...	...	20000.00
(a) Dated securities under MSS	...	2737.00	...	...	...	...	20000.00
(b) 91 days Treasury Bills under MSS	...	...	...	...	...	...	...
(c) 182 days Treasury Bills under MSS	...	...	...	...	...	...	...
(d) 364 days Treasury Bills under MSS	...	...	...	...	...	...	...
(ii) Market Loans (Annex. 6+6A+6B)	1444.95	1746618.73	2072033.19	2516952.54	2984308.55	3442210.42	3908415.09
(iii) Spl. Securities converted into Marketable Securities (Annex. 6 C)	358.02	76817.95	76817.95	76817.95	76817.95	72817.95	67817.95
(iv) Other special Securities issued to Reserve Bank	...	1489.27	1489.28	1489.28	1489.28	1489.28	1489.28

(1)	(2)	(3)	(4)	(5)	(6)	(7)	(8)
(v) Compensation and other bonds	6.73	38731.52	31005.37	18719.06	13836.92	13520.85	12629.30
(vi) 14 days Treasury Bills	...	95667.77	103100.18	97800.22	118380.19	97704.44	97704.44
(vii) 91 days Treasury Bills	...	71548.76	70390.51	124655.78	105142.03	136266.71	150720.58
(viii) 182 days Treasury Bills	...	21500.00	22000.55	52001.25	64196.08	69984.73	69984.73
(ix) 364 days Treasury Bills	...	41493.23	42477.69	90377.74	130466.89	136907.60	157006.60
(x) Ways & Means Advances	...	...	...	...	...	...	...
(xi) Cash Management Bills	...	...	...	...	...	...	...
(xii) Securities issued to International Financial Institutions	212.60	24482.60	29314.81	29625.59	32226.11	30088.01	28299.06
(xiii) Securities against small savings	...	207252.07	218485.29	208182.81	216808.32	228412.84	236641.36
(xiv) Spl. Sec. issued agt. Securitisaion of Bal. under POLIF (Annex. 6 D)	...	...	...	14000.00	20893.68	20893.68	20893.68
2. External Debt*	**32.03**	**134083.15**	**157639.10**	**170087.61**	**177288.81**	**182729.30**	**188463.08**
B. Other Liabilities	**811.07**	**1067537.85**	**1114019.99**	**1116542.14**	**1128736.91**	**1154423.52**	**1262592.40**
1. National Small Savings Fund	336.87	521194.40	568614.40	582010.82	597737.05	622134.90	647020.66
2. State Provident Funds	95.05	99433.07	111946.78	122751.22	133671.94	143671.94	155671.94
3. Other Accounts	16.10	327457.39	304697.07	277903.57	257423.95	234992.18	296999.26
(i) Spl Sec in lieu of Subsidies (OMCs, Fertiliser Cos, FCI)	...	187886.02	182123.04	172090.74	166329.17	166329.17	162829.17
(ii) Other items	16.10	139571.37	122574.03	105812.83	91094.78	68663.01	134170.09
4. Reserve Funds and Deposits	363.05	119452.99	128761.74	133876.53	139903.97	153624.50	162900.54
(i) Bearing interest	260.85	72874.68	70421.33	74412.89	83871.32	96132.76	106542.75
(ii) Not bearing interest	102.20	46578.31	58340.41	59463.64	56032.65	57491.74	56357.79
Total - Liabilities	**2865.40**	**3529959.90**	**3938773.91**	**4517251.97**	**5070591.72**	**5587449.33**	**6222657.55**

(1)	(2)	(3)	(4)	(5)	(6)	(7)	(8)
Amount due from Pakistan on account of share of pre-partition debt (approx).	-300.00	-300.00	-300.00	-300.00	-300.00	-300.00	-300.00
Net Liabilities of the Central Government	2565.40	3529659.90	3938473.91	4516951.97	5070291.72	5587149.33	6222357.55
Excess of Capital Outlay and Loans over Liabilities							
Total (Net)	**2565.40**	**3529659.90**	**3938473.91**	**4516951.97**	**5070291.72**	**5587149.33**	**6222357.55**

* Balances are according to book value.

IX
Deposit Rates of Commercial Banks

Name	Interest	Deposit period
(1)	(2)	(3)
Karur Vysya Bank	10.00%	271 days to 1 years
Lakshmi Vilas Bank	10.00%	1 year
Tamilnad Mercantile Bank Ltd	10.00%	1 year to 2 years
DCB Bank	9.75%	2 years to 3 years
Andhra Bank	9.50%	1 year to 2 years
Catholic Syrian Bank	9.50%	1 year to 2 years
Karur Vysya Bank	9.50%	Above 1 year and Upto 2 years
Lakshmi Vilas Bank	9.50%	Above 1 year to less than 2 years
Tamilnad Mercantile Bank Ltd	9.50%	Above 2 years - 5 years
Andhra Bank	9.25%	9 months to less than 1 year
Bank of Maharashtra	9.25%	444 Days
City Union Bank	9.25%	Above 1 year to 2 years
Dhanalakshmi Bank	9.25%	240 days and 375 days
IndusInd Bank	9.25%	1 year and 2 years 6 months
ING Vysya Bank	9.25%	1 year
Karnataka Bank	9.25%	1 year to 2 years
Karur Vysya Bank	9.25%	Above 2 years to 3 years
Kotak Mahindra Bank	9.25%	270 days
Lakshmi Vilas Bank	9.25%	2 years to 5 years
Punjab & Sind Bank	9.25%	500 days
South Indian Bank	9.25%	2 years
Union Bank of India	9.25%	7 year 7 months
Bank of Maharashtra	9.15%	3 Years
Bank of Maharashtra	9.10%	1 year to 3 years
Yes Bank	9.10%	15 Months 15 days to 16 months
Axis Bank	9.00%	12 months to less than 13 months
Bank Of India	9.00%	1 year to 8 years
Canara Bank	9.00%	1 year
HDFC	9.00%	1 year 1 day to 1 year 16 days
ICICI Bank	9.00%	390 days to 2 years
IDBI Bank	9.00%	Above 1 year to 5 years
Punjab National Bank	9.00%	1 year, 2 years

(1)	(2)	(3)
Royal Bank of Scotland	9.00%	6 months
South Indian Bank	9.00%	Above 2 years to less than 3 years
State Bank of India	9.00%	1 year to 10 years
Tamilnad Mercantile Bank Ltd	9.00%	Above 5 years - 10 years
Union Bank of India	9.00%	1 year to less than 7 year 7 months
Vijaya Bank	9.00%	More than 1 year
Yes Bank	9.00%	1 Year to 15 months 14 days
Bank Of Baroda	8.90%	1111 days
Royal Bank of Scotland	8.75%	1 year to less than 2 years
City Bank	8.50%	365 days to 400 days

http://www.coziie.com/fixed-deposits/banks-paying-high-interest-rates-india#sthash.Mzw1c3lt.dpuf

X

World Interest Rates

http://www.worldinterestrates.info/

Country	Current Rate	Previous Rate	Change	Last Change
Australia	**2.5%**	0%	2.5%	Nov 06 2013
Brazil	**7.25%**	7.5%	-0.25%	Oct 10 2012
Canada	**1%**	0.75%	0.25%	Sep 08 2010
Chile	**4%**	4.25%	-0.25%	Mar 13 2014
China	**6%**	6.31%	-0.31%	Jul 05 2012
Colombia	**3.25%**	3.75%	-0.5%	Mar 25 2013
Czech Republic	**0.75%**	1%	-0.25%	May 06 2010
Denmark	**1.25%**	0.75%	0.5%	Jul 08 2011
Egypt	**9.25%**	8.25%	1%	Nov 24 2011
European Monetary Union	**0.75%**	1%	-0.25%	Jul 05 2012
Hong Kong SAR	**0.5%**	1.5%	-1%	Dec 17 2008
Hungary	**6%**	6.25%	-0.25%	Nov 27 2012
Iceland	**6%**	5.75%	0.25%	Nov 14 2012
India	**8%**	8.5%	-0.5%	Apr 17 2012
Indonesia	**7.5%**	7.25%	0.25%	Nov 12 2013
Israel	**0.75%**	1%	-0.25%	Feb 24 2014
Japan	**0.1%**	0.3%	-0.2%	Dec 19 2008
Korea, Republic of	**2.75%**	3.25%	-0.5%	Oct 11 2012
Malaysia	**3%**	2.75%	0.25%	Jul 08 2010
Mexico	**3.5%**	3.75%	-0.25%	Oct 25 2013
New Zealand	**2.5%**	3%	-0.5%	Mar 09 2011
Norway	**1.5%**	1.75%	-0.25%	Mar 14 2012
Philippines	**3.5%**	3.75%	-0.25%	Oct 25 2012
Poland	**4.5%**	4.75%	-0.25%	Nov 07 2012
South Africa	**5%**	5.5%	-0.5%	Jul 19 2012
Sweden	**1.25%**	1.5%	-0.25%	Sep 06 2012
Switzerland	**0%**	0.25%	-0.25%	Aug 03 2011
Taiwan	**1.875%**	1.75%	0.125%	Jul 01 2011
Thailand	**2%**	2.25%	-0.25%	Mar 12 2014
Turkey	**5.75%**	6.25%	-0.5%	Aug 05 2011
United Kingdom	**0.5%**	1%	-0.5%	Mar 05 2009
United States	**0.25%**	1%	-0.75%	Dec 16 2008

XI
India's External Debt

Table 1: External Debt - Outstanding and Variation

(US$ billions)

Memo Items	Outstanding at the end of			Absolute variation		Percentage variation	
	Jun-13	Mar-14	Jun-14	Jun-14	Jun-14	Jun-14	Jun-14
	PR	PR	P	over	over	over	over
				Jun-13	Mar-14	Jun-13	Mar-14
1. Multilateral	51.7	53.4	53.7	2.0	0.4	3.9	0.7
2. Bilateral	24.8	24.7	24.7	-0.1	0.0	-0.4	0.1
3. IMF	6.0	6.1	6.1	0.2	0.0	2.8	0.0
4. Export Credit	17.5	15.9	16.0	-1.5	0.1	-8.5	0.8
5. Commercial Borrowings	135.8	147.6	153.8	18.0	6.3	13.3	4.3
6. NRI Deposits	71.1	103.8	106.3	35.1	2.4	49.4	2.3
7. Rupee Debt	1.2	1.5	1.5	0.2	0.0	19.8	1.9
8. Short term Debt	96.8	89.2	87.9	-8.9	-1.3	-9.2	-1.5
Of which							
Short term trade credit	89.2	81.7	82.0	-7.3	0.2	-8.2	0.3
Total Debt	405.0	442.2	450.1	45.1	7.9	11.1	1.8
Memo Items							
A. Long-Term Debt	308.2	353.0	362.2	54.0	9.3	17.5	2.6
B. Short-Term Debt	96.8	89.2	87.9	-8.9	-1.3	-9.2	-1.5

P: Provisional. PR: Partially Revised.

Source: Ministry of Finance, Government of India and Reserve Bank of India

Table 2: Residual Maturity of External Debt Outstanding as at End-JUNE 2014

(US$ billions)

Components	Short-term up to one year	Long-term 1 to 2 years	2 to 3 years	More than3 years	Total (2 to 5)
1. Sovereign Debt (long-term) $	7.4	7.8	8.2	61.1	84.5
2. External Commercial Borrowings (including trade credit) #	24.6	25.2	24.0	97.7	171.5
3. NRI deposits {(i)+(ii)+(iii)}	55.0	9.6	26.7	14.9	106.3
(i) FCNR(B)	11.7	3.2	20.7	6.9	42.6
(ii) NR(E)RA	36.1	5.4	5.5	7.6	54.7
(iii) NRO	7.2	1.0	0.4	0.4	9.0
4. Short-term Debt* (Original maturity)	87.9				
Total (1 to 4)	**174.9**	**42.7**	**58.8**	**173.7**	**450.1**
Memo Items					
Short-term debt (Residual maturity as per cent of total external debt)	**38.9**				
Short-term debt (Residual maturity as per cent of Reserves)	**55.3**				

$: Inclusive of FII Investments in Govt. Securities

* Also includes FII investment in sovereign debt and commercial paper.

\# External Commercial Borrowings are inclusive of trade credit, FII investment in corporate debt instruments and a portion of non-Govt. multilateral and bilateral borrowing and therefore may not tally with the ECB provided in other Tables under original maturity

Note: Residual Maturity of NRI Deposits is estimated on the basis of returns submitted by authorised dealer

Source: Ministry of Finance, Government of India and Reserve Bank of India

Table 3: Government and Non-Government External Debt

(US$ billion)

Sr. No.	Components	End-March			End-June
		2012	2013 PR	2014 PR	2014 P
	Sovereign Debt (I+II)	**81.9**	**81.6**	**81.5**	**85.4**
A.	*(As a percentage of GDP)*	4.7	4.4	4.3	4.4
I.	External Debt on Government Account under External Assistance	63.4	61.3	62.2	62.4
II.	Other Government External Debt @	18.5	20.3	19.3	23.0
	Non-Government Debt #	**278.9**	**327.8**	**360.7**	**364.8**
B.	*(As a percentage of GDP)*	15.8	17.6	19.1	18.8
	Total External Debt (A+B)	**360.8**	**409.4**	**442.2**	**450.1**
C.	*(As a percentage of GDP)*	20.5	22.0	23.4	23.2

@: Other Government external debt includes Defence Debt, Investment in Treasury Bills/ Government Securities by FIIs, Foreign Central Banks and International Institutions and IMF.

#: Includes external debt of Monetary Authority.

Source: Ministry of Finance, Government of India and Reserve Bank of India

Table 4: India's Key External Debt Indicators

End-March	External Debt	Ratio of External Debt to GDP	Debt Service Ratio	Ratio of Foreign Exchange Reserves to Total Debt	Ratio of Concessional Debt to Total Debt	Ratio of Short-Term Debt to Foreign Exchange Reserves	Ratio of Short-Term Debt to Total Debt
	(US$ billion)	(per cent)	(per cent)	(per cent)	(per cent)	(per cent)	(per cent)
1	2	3	4	5	6	7	8
1991	83.8	28.7	35.3	7.0	45.9	146.5	10.2
1996	93.7	27.0	26.2	23.1	44.7	23.2	5.4
2001	101.3	22.5	16.6	41.7	35.4	8.6	3.6
2002	98.8	21.1	13.7	54.7	35.9	5.1	2.8
2003	104.9	20.3	16.0*	72.5	36.8	6.1	4.5

1	2	3	4	5	6	7	8
2004	112.6	18.0	16.1**	100.3	35.8	3.9	3.9
2005	134.0	18.1	5.9^	105.6	30.7	12.5	13.2
2006	139.1	16.8	10.1#	109.0	28.4	12.9	14.0
2007	172.4	17.5	4.7	115.6	23.0	14.1	16.3
2008	224.4	18.0	4.8	138.0	19.7	14.8	20.4
2009	224.5	20.3	4.4	112.2	18.7	17.2	19.3
2010	260.9	18.2	5.8	106.9	16.8	18.8	20.1
2011R	317.9	18.2	4.4	95.9	14.9	21.3	20.4
2012 PR	360.8	20.5	6.0	81.6	13.3	26.6	21.7
2013 PR	409.4	22.0	5.9	71.3	11.1	33.1	23.6
2014 PR	442.2	23.4	5.9	68.8	10.5	29.3	20.2
End-June 2014 P	450.1	23.2	8.1	70.2	10.3	27.8	19.5

P: Provisional. PR: Partially Revised. R: Revised

*: Works out to 12.4 per cent, with the exclusion of pre payment of external debt of US$ 3, 430 million.

**: Works out to 8.2 per cent with the exclusion of pre payment of external debt of US$ 3, 797 million and redemption of Resurgent India Bonds (RIBs) of US$ 5, 549 million.

^: Works out to 5.7 per cent with the exclusion of pre payment of external debt of US$ 381 million.

#: Works out to 6.3 per cent with the exclusion of India Millennium Deposits (IMDs) repayments of US$ 7.1 billion and pre payment of external debt of US$ 23.5 million.

Source: Ministry of Finance, Government of India and Reserve Bank of India

XII
Acknowledgements

These writings came about after an inspiring lecture by Dr A. Vasudevan, Executive Director, Reserve Bank of India in Mangalore. I kept sending each copy of my paper to him. I received from him an email after a considerable time that he had retired from the RBI but acknowledged that what I wrote made a contribution to policy making at India's Central Bank. It was a moment of joy.

****

Deputy Governor

Reserve Bank of India

Central Office

Shaheed Bhagat Singh Road
Mumbai 400 001

June 9, 1998

Dear Shri Giridhar Prabhu,

Thank you very much for your paper entitled "Interest Rate Policy – Distortion in Call Money Rates".

I enjoyed reading it, which is very incisive, purposive and pragmatic.

I am examining the suggestions internally,
With Regards,

Yours sincerely,
Y.V. Reddy

****

Kalpana Morparia
Senior General Manager
The Industrial Credit and Investment Corporation of India Limited
163, Backbay Reclamation
Mumbai – 400 020

June 11, 1998

Dear Shri Prabhu,
I thank you for your letter dated May 27, 1998 enclosing the analyses in Distortion in Call Money rates. Your suggestions are extremely valuable and we are sure that they would be helpful in the formulation of policy and procedures in interest rate management.

With best regards,

Yours sincerely
Kalpana Morparia

****

Adviser-in- Charge
Reserve Bank of India
Central Office
Monetary Policy Department
Central Office Building
Mumbai – 400 001

D.O.NO.MPD.1576/01.03.003/98-99

Dear Shri Giridhar Prabhu,

Interest Rate Policy

We acknowledge, with thanks, the receipt of your letter to Executive Director dated November 26, 1998 enclosing two analytical papers on the above subject. The suggestions on effecting saving on Interest payments of Government of India and for bringing out a calendar of primary issues of government securities are Indeed very thoughtful. These will be given their due consideration in our working.

With regards,

Yours sincerely,
K. Kanagasabapathy

****

Bibek Debroy
Rajiv Gandhi Foundation
Director, Research
Jawahar Bhawan
Dr. Rajendra Prasad Road
New Delhi – 110 001

15 January 1999

Dear Mr. Prabhu,
Thank you for your letter of 26 December and for sending the articles on interest rate policy. I enjoyed reading them immensely and agree with almost all that you say.

With best wishes and regards,

Yours sincerely
B. Debroy

****

A M A Batcha Director
Reserve Bank of India Central Office
Monetary Policy Department shahid Bhagat Singh Road Mumbai – 400 001

April 13, 1999

Dear Sir,
Interest Rate Policy – VII- Evolution of an Interest Rate Structure for India-A discussion paper

We acknowledge with thanks receipt of your letter dated March 6, 1999 addressed to our Dy. Governor, Shri Jagdish Capoor on the captioned subject.

Yours faithfully,
A M A Batcha
Director

****

S. Divakara
Secretary
Forum of Free Enterprise
Mr. S.S. Bhandare
Economic Advisor
Tata Services Ltd
"Bombay House"
Homi Mody Street
Mumbai – 400 001

Dear Mr. Bhandare,

The enclosed note on Interest Rate Policy – VIII has been prepared and sent to us by our friend Mr. G Giridhar Prabhu from Mangalore. We hope you will find the contents of interest to you.

With kind regards,

Yours sincerely,
S Divakara
Secretary

****

C Rangarajan
Raj Bhavan
Hyderabad

July 26, 1999

Dear Mr. Prabhu

Many thanks for sending me copies of your various papers on Interest Rate Policy. I shall be happy to go through them. Even a cursory glance indicates how deeply you have gone into these issues.

With regards,

Yours sincerely,
C Rangarajan

****

N K Singh
Secretary to Prime Minister
Prime Minister's Office
South Block
New Delhi – 110 011

August 16, 1999

Dear Shri Prabhu,

I acknowledge the receipt of the letter dated 28th July, 1999 and I have gone through your paper with great interest.

With Best Wishes,

Yours sincerely,
N K Singh

****

Principal
Dr. Nitte Shankara Adyanthaya Memorial
First Grade College
Nitte, Karkala Taluk, Udupi Dist – 574 110
Karnataka

27.09.09

Dear Mr. Prabhu,

Seasons Greetings,

Thank you for sending me a copy of your paper on Interest Rate Policy – VIII – Interest Rates and Exchange Rate Premia". I have gone through the paper with great interest and have felt that you need send it for publication in academic journals for wider readership. That your "words" in the article are your, experience is quite evident in the paper. I am looking forward to inviting you to our Institute to address MBA students on this subject.

Since the students are out for implant training, this session can be arranged somewhere in November.

While hoping that you would accept our invitation to be with us in the near future. I wish more such research papers would be published in the days to come.

Thank you,

Sincerely,
Principal

****

E.A.S. Sarma
Secretary, Government of India, Ministry of Finance,
Department of Economic Affairs, New Delhi

3rd November, 1999

Dear Shri Prabhu

Thank you for sending me your Paper on "Interest Rate Policy – X – Interest Rates charged to State Governments on Central Government Loan – Opportunity for Markets". I am forwarding your Paper to Dr. Shankar N Acharya, Chief Economic Adviser, Department of Economic Affairs for his perusal and necessary action.

Let me take this opportunity to thank you for continuing your interest in important areas of economic policy and sending us your suggestions.

With regards,

Yours sincerely
E.A.S. Sarma

****

Seema G. Jere
Officer on Special Duty

To
Minister of State for Finance (Revenue)
Government of India
Ministry of Finance
Dept of Revenue
North Block
New Delhi – 110 001

10 Nov. 1999

Dear Shri Prabhu,

Thank you for your letter dated 26th October, 1999 conveying felicitations to Shri V Dhananjaya Kumar, Hon'ble Minister of State for Finance (revenue), along with suggestions on Interest Rate Policy of the Government. Your suggestions are appreciated, and will be taken into consideration at the appropriate time.

With regards,

Yours sincerely
Seema G Jere

****

M Damodaran, IAS
Joint Secretary
Ministry of Finance
Department of Economic Affairs
(Banking Division)
"Jeevan Deep"
Parliament Streeet
New Delhi – 110 001

18.04.2000

Dear Mr. Prabhu,
Thank you for your letter of 8th April, 2000 enclosing the paper on Interest Rate Policy – XI – Immediate Positions April, 2000

With regards,

Yours sincerely
M Damodaran

****

J R Prabhu
Banking Ombudsmah
(Maharashtra & Goa) Garment House, Worli
Mumbai

April 20, 2000

Dear Shri Prabhu,
I acknowledge with thanks copies of papers made available by you to Government of India and RBI. Your suggestions would require in-depth examination by the regulators. I appreciate your useful role in formulation of policy measures.

In case I come to Mangalore, It will be great pleasure to have discussions with you on these issues.

With regards,

Yours sincerely,
J R Prabhu

****

P Mukherjee
Vice President
Treasury
UTI Bank Ltd
Central Office, Market Towers P
13th Floor, Cuffe Parade
Colaba
Mumbai
UTIB/CO/TR/1080/00-01

9th May 2000

Dear Sir,

Interest Rate Policy

We acknowledge receipt of your letter dated 29th April 2000, on the captioned subject, addressed to our Chairman and Managing Director, Dr. P J Nayak.

We are examining the suggestions made in the policy paper, which we find to be of considerable interest to us.

Yours faithfully,
P Mukherjee
Vice President (Treasury)

****

Rajneesh Goel, IAS Private Secretary to
Minister of State for Finance (Revenue)
New Delhi – 110 001

21 Aug 2000

Dear Shri Prabhu,

I am in receipt of your letter dated 1st August, 2000 enclosing therewith a paper on „Interest

Rate Policy-XII-Action from Reserve Bank of India.

Since the matter pertains to Banking Division, I am sending your letter to the office of Hon'ble Minister of State for Finance (Expenditure, Banking & Insurance) (Shri Balasahen Vikhe Patil) for information and necessary action.

With regards,

Yours sincerely
Rajneesh Goel

****

Jaya Mohanty
Director
Reserve Bank of India
Central Office
Monetary Policy Department
Shahid Bhagat Singh Road
Mumbai – 400 001

MPD No. 660/10.03.01/2000-01 August 26, 2000

Dear Sir,

Interest Rate Policy

We appreciate the keen interest shown by you in your paper on the captioned subject. We have noted the concerns expressed therein.

Yours faithfully,
Jaya Mohanty

****

MPD.No.1814/10.03.01/2000-2001 30.12.2000

Leela Vasudevan
Assistant Manager
Reserve Bank of India
Central Office
Monetary Policy Department
Shahid Bhagat Singh Road
Mumbai – 400 001

Dear Sir,
Interest Rate Policy – XI
Immediate Positions April, 2000
We appreciate the keen interest shown by you in your paper on the captioned subject. We have noted the concern expressed therein.

Yours faithfully
Leela Vasudevan
Assistant Manager

****

No.RS/LOP/328/2001 21st March, 2001
Manmohan Singh
Leader of Opposition
(Rajya Sabha)
43, Parliament House
New Delhi – 110 001

Dear Shri Prabhu,

Kindly refer to your letter of 15th March, 2001 to which you have enclosed papers of Interest rate policy. I shall study your papers with interest.

With kind regards,

Yours faithfully,
Manmohan Singh

****

P S Shenoy
Chairman & Managing Director
Bank of Baroda

March 28, 2001

Dear Shri Prabhu,

Many thanks for your kind letter of March 15, 2001 enclosing 3 papers on Interest Rate Policy. I shall go through them and will communicate with you soon.

It would be nice to hear from you on Economic Fiscal, Monetary and banking matters as I consider that your views are very educative and knowledgeable.

With kind regards

Yours sincerely
P S Shenoy

****

Dr. C Rangarajan Governor Andhra Pradesh Raj Bhavan
Hyberabad 500 041

March 30, 2001

Dear Shri Prabhu,

Many thanks for your letter of March 19, 2001. I have quickly gone through the various papers that you have sent. I am indeed very happy that you are showing great interest in areas such as interest rate policy, which do not normally attract any attention.

Wish you all the best,

Yours sincerely
C Rangarajan

****

P J Nayak
Chairman & Managing Director
UTI Bnak Ltd
Central Office
Maker Towers "F" 13th Floor
Cuffe Parade, Colaba
Mumbai – 400 005

Dear Shri Prabhu,

Thank you for your letter dated 31st March, 2001 enclosing four papers about Interest Rate Policy. I look forward to reading them.

Many thanks once again for the useful information.

Yours sincerely,
P J Nayak

****

B K Bhol
Director
Reserve Bank of India
Central Office
Monetary Policy Department
Central Office Building
Mumbai – 400 001

DO.MPD/3364/10.03.08/2000-01 May 26, 2001

Dear Shri Prabhu,
Re: Expert Committee to the Review the System of Administered

Interest Rates and Other Related Issues

We acknowledge the receipt of your letter dated May 18, 2001, addressed to Dr. Y V Reddy, Deputy Governor and Shri K Kanagasabapaty, Adviser in Charge, Monetary Policy Department, Reserve Bank of India. I Take this opportunity to draw your kind attention to the following.

The Honourable Finance Minister in his budget speech had announced the constitution of an Expert Committee to review the Administered Interest Rates in India. Subsequently, Ministry of Finance has set up the above-mentioned Committee with Dr. Y V Reddy, Deputy Governor, Reserve Bank of India as the Chairman. The office order to this effect is enclosed for your ready reference.

The committee in its first meeting held on May 04, 2001 had suggested that we obtain views of some experts. In this light, I have pleasure in soliciting your valuable views on various terms of reference. For your convenience, a list of issues before the Committee is also enclosed.

With regards,

Yours sincerely,
(B K Bhol)
Secretary

****

A.M. Ameer Batcha
Dy. General Manager & Member of Faculty
Bankers Training College
Reserve Bank Of India
Mumbai – 400 028

Date: 6.6.01

Dear Shri Prabhu,

Thank you for your letter dated May 18, 2001 in regard to current issues in Interest Rate Management – May 2001.

I request you to address all your future correspondence to the Adviser-in-Charge, MPD, RBI, Mumbai.

Now I am working as a faculty in BTC. It would be a pleasure if you send me a copy of the same for my information.

I wish you continue with your pre-occupation about the interest rate prevailing in India which in a way holds the key for future development in a deregulated environment.

With regards,

Yours sincerely
A M Ameer Batcha

****

Leela Vasudevan
Assistant Manager
Reserve Bank of India
Central Office
Monetary Policy Department
Shahid Bhagat Singh Road
Mumbai – 400 001

MPD.No.752/10.03.01/2001-02 September 3, 2001

Dear Sir,

Current Issues in Interest Rate Management – May 2001
We acknowledge receipt of your letter dated May 18, 2001 on the captioned subject and have noted the suggestions.

Yours faithfully
(Leela Vasudevan)
Assistant Manager

****

Dr. B K Bhol
Secretary
Reserve Bank Of India
Central Office
Monetary Policy Department
Central Office Building
Mumbai – 400 001

D.O.MPD.No.1184/10.03.08/2001-02 October 11, 2001

Dear Shri Prabhu,

Expert Committee to Review the System Administered Interest Rates and Other Related Issues

As you are aware, the Government of India had constituted the above mentioned Committee in April 2001 under the chairmanship of Dr. Y V Reddy, Deputy Governor, RBI. The Committee has a submitted its Report to the Ministry of Finance recently. The Government has placed the Report in the public domain vide their website www.finmin.nic.in.

The Committee has been immensely benefited by your contributions in the preparation of the Report.

I have the pleasure of forwarding a copy of the Report Including Technical Papers for your ready reference.

With kind regards,

Yours sincerely
B K Bhol

****

P J Nayak
Chairman and Managing Director
UTI Bank Ltd
Central Office
Maker Towers "F" 13th Floor
Cuffe Parade, Colaba
Mumbai 400 005

31st December, 2001

Dear Shri Prabhu,

Thank you for your letter dated 26th December 2001 enclosing the paper about Interest Rate Policy. I look forward to reading it.

Yours sincerely
P J Nayak

****

Rakesh Mohan
Deputy Governor
Reserve Bank of India
Central Office
Shahid Bhagat Sing Road
Mumbai – 400 001

October 14, 2002

Dear Shri Prabhu,

I thank you for sending me a copy of the paper on interest Rate Policy and related papers. I am requesting the concerned department to examine your suggestions.

With regards,

Yours sincerely,
Rakesh Mohan

****

Index